Sustainable Finance: Challenges, Opportunities and Future Prospects

Çiydem Çatak / Mehtap Öner (eds.)

Sustainable Finance: Challenges, Opportunities and Future Prospects

PETER LANG

Lausanne - Berlin - Bruxelles - Chennai - New York - Oxford

Library of Congress Cataloging-in-Publication Data
A CIP catalog record for this book has been applied for at the Library of Congress.

Bibliographic information published by the Deutsche Nationalbibliothek. The German National Library lists this publication in the German National Bibliography; detailed bibliographic data is available on the Internet at http://dnb.d-nb.de.

ISSN 1867-500X
ISBN 978-3-631-90581-4
E-PUB 978-3-631-91231-7
E-BOOK 978-3-631-90582-1
DOI 10.3726/b21415

Published by Peter Lang GmbH, Berlin, Deutschland

info@peterlang.com - www.peterlang.com

Preface

In recent years, the issues of global warming, climate change, sustainable energy and social responsibility have become increasingly important. Every year, numerous studies are conducted and international conferences held on these issues. Climate change as a result of global warming, on the one hand puts the search for new resources to the agenda, and on the other hand it forces individuals and institutions to act more responsibly. The importance of renewable energy is increasing day by day. These developments have led to the emergence of the concept of "sustainability" in finance, as in many other fields, and also the inclusion of environmental, social and corporate governance issues and perspectives in investment decisions.

Sustainability is a long-term perspective and stands for shared values. It is about meeting the needs of the present without jeopardizing the potential to meet the needs of future generations.

A sustainable financial system emerges as a system that creates financial assets and enables them to be valued and traded in a way that shapes real wealth to meet the long-term needs of an inclusive and environmentally sustainable economy[1]. Sustainable finance encompasses not only climate change but also environmental issues, the protection of nature, i.e. biological wealth, the prevention of air and environmental pollution, the circular economy including waste recycling, social issues including human rights and corporate governance in working life. With this broad spectrum, sustainable finance addresses investments in sustainable projects and activities over the long term and introduces new financial instruments to the global financial system. As a result of these developments, sustainable finance has emerged as a new field of finance that is fed from many disciplines. Sustainable finance has given rise to definitions such as green bonds and green banking, as well as sustainability indices in the stock markets. Like many stock exchanges, Borsa Istanbul has created sustainability indices that include the shares of companies with high corporate sustainability performance in order to improve the understanding, knowledge and practices on sustainability among traded companies.

Companies aim to make a difference by constantly "creating value", or in other words, by making creation "continuous". Ensuring continuity in value creation is

---

1 UNEP Inquiry into the Design of a Sustainable Financial System, 2015. The Financial System We Need, United Nations Environment Program, s. 13.

possible through strategy, management quality and institutionalization. Strategy is the structuring that ensures continuity in doing the right job, management quality is doing the job right, and institutionalization is the structure that will ensure continuity

"Sustainability" adds value to companies and helps to establish this awareness. As a result of some evaluations in Borsa Istanbul, companies that are included in the "BIST Sustainability Index" by scoring above a certain level gain an advantage or privilege through these features.

"Sustainable Finance: Challenges, Opportunities and Future Prospects" edited by Dr. Çatak and Assoc. Prof. Dr. Öner, consists of various articles aiming to draw readers' attention to these developments. As one of the few books written in a field that is considered quite new in Turkey, this book has fulfilled an important mission and is a pioneer in the field. In addition to the topic of sustainable finance, the book contains several articles on social responsibility and corporate governance. I would like to congratulate the editors of the book, my colleague from the Turkish-German University, Dr. Çiydem Çatak, and the authors of the articles, my students from the Faculty of Business Administration, Istanbul University, Dr. Ahmet Kerem Özdemir and Dr. Semra Taşpunar Altuntaş, as well as all the authors who contributed to this book with their articles, for their contributions to this field. I hope that this book, which is a pioneer in this field, will be followed by further studies.

Bodrum, 16.08.2023

Prof. Dr. Mehmet Şükrü Tekbaş

Table of Contents

List of Contributors

Assoc. Prof. Dr. Çağrı Aksoy Hazır
Faculty of Business Administration
Department of Accounting and Finance
Marmara University, Istanbul, Turkey
cagri.aksoy@marmara.edu.tr

Asst. Prof. Dr. Semra Taşpunar Altuntaş
School of Business, Department of Finance
Istanbul University, Istanbul, Turkey
staspunar@istanbul.edu.tr

Prof. Dr. Aslı Aybars
Faculty of Business Administration
Department of Accounting and Finance
Marmara University, Istanbul, Turkey
asli.aybars@marmara.edu.tr

Asst. Prof. Dr. Çiydem Çatak
Faculty of Economics and Administrative Sciences
Department of Business Administration
Turkish German University, Istanbul, Turkey
catak@tau.edu.tr

Svenja Sabine Keitel
Master FACT-Finance, Auditing, Controlling, Taxation
Friedrich-Alexander-Universität
Erlangen-Nürnberg, Germany
svenja1998@gmx.net

Prof. Dr. Kersten Kellermann
Konjunkturforschungsstelle Vierländereck (KOVL)
Tübingen, Germany
kersten.kellermann@kovl.li

Asst. Prof. Dr. Sezer Külah
Faculty of Business Administration
Department of Accounting and Finance
Marmara University, Istanbul, Türkiye
sezer.kulah@marmara.edu.tr

Prof. Dr. Elif Nuroğlu
Faculty of Economics and Administrative Sciences
Department of Economics
Turkish German University, Istanbul, Turkey
nuroglu@tau.edu.tr

Assoc. Prof. Dr. Mehtap Öner
Faculty of Business Administration
Department of Accounting and Finance
Marmara University, Istanbul, Turkey
mehtap.oner@marmara.edu.tr

Asst. Prof. Dr. Ahmet Kerem Özdemir
School of Business, Department of Finance
Istanbul University, Istanbul, Turkey
keremozd@istanbul.edu.tr

Dr. Carsten-Henning Schlag
Konjunkturforschungsstelle Vierländereck (KOVL)
Tübingen, Germany
carsten.schlag@kovl.li

Asst. Prof. Dr. Ömer Faruk Tan
Faculty of Business Administration
Department of Accounting and Finance
Marmara University, Istanbul, Türkiye
omer.tan@marmara.edu.tr

Onursal Yazar
PhD- Faculty of Business Administration
Department of Accounting and Finance
Marmara University, Istanbul, Turkey
onursalyazar@yahoo.com

Res. Asst. Sena Yılmaz Arslan
Faculty of Economics and Administrative Sciences
Department of Business Administration
Turkish German University, Istanbul, Turkey
sena.yilmaz@tau.edu.tr

Emre Zehir
Economist, JCR Eurasia Rating
Istanbul, Turkey
emre.zehir@jcrer.com.tr

Ahmet Kerem ÖZDEMİR and Semra TAŞPUNAR ALTUNTAŞ

Sustainable Financial Instruments: Integrating ESG Factors into Financial Decision-Making

Abstract: In today's world, the urgent need for sustainable practices and responsible stewardship of our planet has become increasingly evident. Sustainable financial instruments offer a comprehensive exploration of the evolving landscape of finance and investments, concentrating on the instrumental function that financial mechanisms can play in creating a sustainable and resilient future. Drawing upon real-world examples and cutting-edge research, sustainable financial instruments involve the development, implementation, and impact of various financial tools designed to foster sustainable development. It explores the crucial linkages between finance and sustainability, illustrating how financial instruments can be aligned with environmental, social, and governance (ESG) principles to drive positive change. From green bonds and impact investing to carbon pricing and sustainable indices, the chapter offers a comprehensive analysis of these innovative mechanisms, highlighting their potential to redirect capital towards environmentally and socially responsible projects.

For this purpose, this section includes understanding sustainable financial instruments, benefits and drivers of sustainable financial instruments, key considerations in designing sustainable financial instruments, challenges and limitations and such topics. Beyond the financial realm, sustainable financial instruments explore the broader implications and transformative potential of sustainable finance. It examines the purpose of financial institutions, corporations, governments, and individuals in driving the adoption of sustainable practices and fostering a conversion to a low-carbon, resource-efficient economy. Ultimately, sustainable financial instruments serve as a roadmap for policymakers, investors, financial professionals, and individuals who are seeking to navigate the complex landscape of sustainable finance.

Keywords: Sutainable Financial Instruments, ESG, Financial Decision-Making

1. Introduction

Sustainable finance mentions to the integration of ESG factors into financial decision-making processes and investment strategies. It aims to promote long-term sustainable development by thinking about not only financial returns but also the impact of investments on society and the environment. Sustainable finance encompasses various practices, such as responsible investing, green finance, impact investing, and socially responsible investing. The importance of sustainable finance lies in its ability to address serious global challenges, including climate change, resource depletion, socio-economic inequality, and corporate governance issues. Here are some key reasons why sustainable finance is significant:

- Environmental impact,
- Social development,
- Long-term value creation,
- Risk management,
- Reputation and stakeholder expectations
- Regulatory environment.

Sustainable finance encourages investments in environmentally amicably projects and companies, such as renewable energy, clean technology, and sustainable agriculture. By allocating capital to these areas, it supports the transition to a low-carbon and resource-efficient economy, helping to mitigate climate change and protect natural resources. It also focuses on social factors, including human rights, labor standards, community development, and diversity and inclusion. It promotes investments that contribute positively to society, such as affordable housing, education, healthcare, and fair labor practices. This supports social progress and reduces inequalities. Integrating ESG considerations into financial decision-making recognizes that sustainable practices can lead to long-term value creation. By assessing the risks and opportunities associated with ESG factors, investors can make more intelligent judgments that consider the sustainability and resilience of investments over time.

Sustainable finance helps identify and manage risks associated with ESG issues. For example, climate change can pose physical and transitional risks to businesses and investments. By incorporating climate-related considerations into investment strategies, investors can better assess and manage these risks, reducing the potential for financial losses. With growing awareness and demand for sustainable practices, companies and financial institutions that prioritize sustainability are likely to enhance their reputation and attract stakeholders who value responsible and ethical business practices. Sustainable finance helps satisfy the prospects of various stakeholders, covering investors, consumers, employees, and regulators.

Governments and regulatory bodies are progressively acquainting approaches and regulations that encourage or necessitate sustainable finance practices. By aligning with these frameworks, financial institutions can ensure compliance, access new opportunities, and avoid potential legal and reputational risks. Overall, sustainable finance plays a crucial role in aligning financial flows with sustainable development goals, fostering a more inclusive, resilient, and environmentally conscious economy. It enables investors and institutions to make choices that balance financial returns with positive social and environmental impacts.

There has been a significant raise in interest and order for sustainable financial instruments in latest years. These instruments are designed to support sustainable investments and allocate capital towards projects and companies that have positive environmental, social, and governance (ESG) impacts. If we take an overview of the main factors that increase the interest in sustainable financial instruments; in particular, investor demand is noteworthy. Investors, ranging from individual retail investors to institutional asset managers, are increasingly seeking investment opportunities that align with their values and contribute to sustainable development. They recognize that sustainable investments can offer attractive financial returns while also addressing global challenges. As a result, there is increasing demand for financial instruments that enable investors to combine ESG considerations into their investment portfolios.

The other main factor is risk and return considerations: The awareness of ESG risks and chances has heightened. Investors are recognizing that ESG factors can have a substance impact on financial performance and long-term value creation. Sustainable financial instruments provide a framework for assessing and managing these risks while seeking competitive returns. By integrating ESG factors into investment deciding, investors can enhance risk management and potentially generate superior risk-adjusted returns. The financial industry has responded to the growing demand for sustainable investments by developing a wide range of financial instruments tailored to the different preferences and objectives of investors. These instruments include green bonds, social bonds, sustainability-linked bonds, green loans, green and sustainable equity funds, and ESG-themed exchange-traded funds (ETFs), among others. The development of standardized models, such as the Green Bond Principles and Sustainability-Linked Bond Principles, has provided guidelines and transparency to issuers and investors, fostering market growth.

Various stakeholders, including customers, employees, and civil society organizations, are exerting pressure on companies and financial institutions to adopt sustainable practices. They are becoming more informed of the environmental and social impacts of their investments and demanding greater accountability. To meet these expectations, financial institutions are integrating sustainability considerations into their product offerings and investment strategies.

In the following sections, sustainable financial instruments will be briefly explained. Thereafter, each instrument will be detailed by the help of examples and main issues in the relevant literature are summarized. After introducing all instruments, the benefits and drivers of sustainable financial instruments will be discussed. In this respect, firstly, the advantages of sustainable financial instruments for issuers and investors, and then benefits and drivers from regulation and policy perspectives are clarified.

2. Types of Sustainable Financial Instruments

According to Lindenberg (2014) "green finance" comprises three segments: (i) funding of private and public green investments aimed at preventing or minimizing environmental damage; (ii) funding public policies for promoting the development and enhancement of environmental protection measures and/or adaption of projects and enterprises, and (iii) parts of the financial scheme association to green or sustainable financial instruments. Sustainable finance instruments are financial products or services that aim to support sustainable development by aligning ESG considerations with financial decision-making. Here are some examples:

(a) *Green Bonds:* These are debt (fixed income) securities issued to fund environmentally kindly projects in areas such as renewable energy, energy-efficiency and emission reduction.
(b) *Social Bonds:* Social bonds are a kind of financial tool or investment that is published to increase funds for projects or initiatives that have a direct social impact. The proceeds from social bond issues are dedicated to financing projects that address various social problems and promote positive social outcomes. These projects typically focus on areas such as affordable housing, healthcare, education, employment generation, community development, or social welfare programs. The purpose of social bonds is to provide capital to support initiatives that can make a tangible difference in society. They provide an avenue for investors to align their financial objectives with their social and environmental values, while also supporting projects that can create a meaningful social impact.
(c) *Sustainability and Sustainability-Linked Bonds (SLB):* Sustainability Linked Bonds (SLBs) are a kind of financial instrument that are linked to the issuer's sustainability performance or achievement of predefined sustainability targets. SLBs are a subset of sustainable finance instruments and are designed to incentivize and finance issuers' sustainability goals. Unlike green bonds or social bonds, where the use of proceeds is earmarked for specific environmentally or socially beneficial projects, SLBs are not project-specific. Instead, the financial characteristics of SLBs are linked to the

issuer's sustainability performance metrics or key performance indicators (KPIs). Typically, the interest rate on an SLB is tied to the issuer's predefined key performance indicator(s) and if the issuer meets certain sustainability targets, the interest rate on the bond is reduced.

(d) *Green Loans:* Green loans are financial instruments specifically designed to fund projects or initiatives that have a positive environmental influence. They are a type of loan product that encourages and supports sustainable and eco-friendly projects. Green loans can be provided by banks, financial institutions, or other lending entities. The distinguishing feature of green loans is that the funds borrowed must be used exclusively for environmentally beneficial purposes. Green loans offer benefits to both borrowers and lenders. For borrowers, they provide access to capital for environmentally focused projects and initiatives, often at favorable interest rates. For lenders, green loans offer opportunities to support sustainable initiatives and align their lending activities with their environmental objectives.

(e) *ESG Funds:* ESG funds are investment vehicles that incorporate environmental, social, and governance factors into their investment policies. ESG stands for Environmental, Social, and Governance, representing the three pillars of consideration for these funds. ESG funds aim to produce both financial returns and positive societal or environmental impact by investing in companies that demonstrate strong ESG practices. These funds consider a broad range of factors when evaluating potential investments, including environmental, social and governance factor. The goal of ESG funds is to align investors' financial goals with their values and contribute to sustainable development.

(f) *Impact Investing:* Impact investing refers to making investments with the purpose of producing both financial returns and measurable positive social or environmental impact. It goes beyond the traditional approach of considering only financial returns and takes into account the broader results of investments on association and the ecosystem. The primary objective of impact investing is to create positive and sustainable change in areas such as social equality, environmental sustainability, healthcare, education, clean energy, poverty alleviation, and more. Impact investors actively seek chances that align with their values and support projects or businesses that address social and environmental challenges.

(g) *Carbon Offsetting:* This is a way to offset carbon emissions by investing in carbon reduction projects, such as renewable energy or reforestation. These sustainable finance instruments provide investors with the opportunity to back up sustainable development while also producing financial returns. They also provide companies with access to funding for their sustainable projects and initiatives. Let's examine these instruments in more detail.

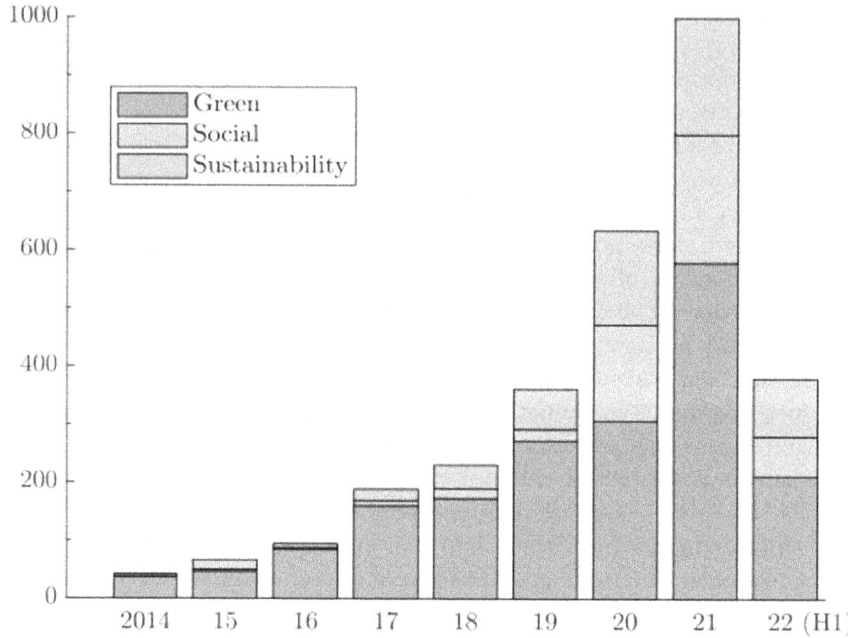

Figure 1: Issuance of green social and sustainability securities (in $bn)
Source: Climatebonds, 2022

According to Gutterman (2021) as a distinct class of assets sustainable bonds comprise green bonds, social and social-impact bonds, sustainability bonds and sustainability-linked bonds. Jones and Comfort (2020) emphasize the role of these debt instruments distinguished by their main use of gains. Based on Gutterman's classification (see also Mocanu et al., 2021) we will discuss the most popular ones. According to Figure 1 (CBI, 2022), the cumulative total GSS+ issuance stands at $3.3 tn at the end of June 2022. About $3 tn comes from GSS assets. We have the following breakdown: 62.3 % for green bonds, 17 % for social bonds and 20.7 % for sustainability bonds. The market is dominated by DM issuers (approximatively 63 %), while the remaining part is half of EM issuers and half of supranational issuers.

Green Bonds are debt securities issued to fund environmentally sustainable or climate-friendly investment plans in areas such as renewable energy, sustainable water management, clean transport. After the European Investment Bank's (EIB) green bond issue (in fact it was an equity-linked bond) for the first time in 2007 and the World Bank's first green bond labeled issue in 2008, the market for green bonds has become one of the fastest-growing sections of global financial markets. The publication of the Green Bond Principles by ICMA in January 2014, accelerated the growth of the market even further.

Monk and Perkins (2020) identify three sets of factors that have been influential on the appearance and spreading of these debt instruments: (a) the strategic, goal-oriented actions of entrepreneurs and financial intermediaries who helped the evolution of the market for green bonds; (b) a set of mainly self-reinforcing processes (e.g., positive outwardness, increased awareness, legalization etc.) that resulted in an increased interest for this innovative instrument; and (c) general conditions favoring the development of financial instruments which positively address various sustainability goals especially related with climate change and environmental concerns. According to Climate Bonds Initiative data, green bonds' share was slightly above 2.5 % of the global bond market in 2022.[1] Insufficient liquidity, lack of clearly defined standards and the absence of a widely accepted set of related definitions,[2] transparency and information related issues, lack of specification and quantification of their benefits and short-termism of financial markets are among the most important factors inhibiting the market's further development (Mihálovits and Tapaszti, 2018; Pham and Huynh, 2020; Lebelle et al., 2022). But then, government policies encouraging the issuance of green bonds (through awareness programs, market-making arrangements, public-private partnerships, subsidies, tax benefits etc.) may alleviate these restraints and support the market's expansion (Barua and Chiesa, 2019; Ning et al., 2023).

Two competing views draw the framework of sustainable finance and investment research and address the impact of green bond funding on key financial performance indicators (mostly cost of funding and market price/value). According to the mainstream shareholder value maximization

---

1 https://www.climatebonds.net/resources/press-releases/2023/01/green-and-other-labelled-bonds-held-market-share-2022-amidst-fall#:~:text=Despite%20this%2C%20GSS%2B%20volumes%20held,1bn%20total.

2 Although, GBPs formulated by ICMA have so far been widely used around the world, according to Brühl (2021) these guidelines are far from providing a precise classification. On the other hand, The European Green Bond Standard (EUGBS) is expected to create a voluntary European high-quality standard for both private and sovereign issuers (within or outside the EU) to help fund sustainable investments.

view, shareholders may perceive pro-environmental investments as less profitable or infeasible and impact financial performance and price/value negatively. Otherwise, Stakeholder Theory considers not just the interests of shareholders and equally weighs the concerns of other stakeholders as well. In this context, according to this approach stakeholders' interests must be better aligned with environmentally and socially liable firms following more sustainable business models and relying on sustainable financing/funding schemes. A significant number of studies show that such firms enjoy higher profit margins, lower cost of capital and benefit from favorable regulatory and tax treatment, which all contribute to overall firm value (Wang et al., 2020; Zhou and Cui, 2019; Baulkaran, 2019; Taghizadeh-Hesary et al., 2021; Zhang et al., 2021; Jiang et al., 2022). As the investor community's requirements for more responsible and sustainable business practices and models strengthen over time, causing the demand for green bonds and hence their premium (more than conventional bonds of the same issuer or peers) increase, resulting in lower funding costs for green bond issuers (Tang and Zhang, 2020; Kanamura, 2020; Fatica et al., 2021; Teti et al., 2020; Han and Li, 2022). Externally verified green bonds by independent reviewers further increase the premium by reducing informational costs and by relieving fears of greenwashing (Dorfleitner et al., 2022; Jones et al., 2020). Moreover, authenticity and institutional theories also support green funding schemes as companies commit themselves to business practices that alleviate the general public's social and environmental concerns (Maltais and Nykvist, 2021). Investors who purchase green bonds are able to support environmentally sustainable projects while also receiving a return on their investment. Overall, green bonds provide opportunities for a win-win solution for both investors and firms looking to support sustainable development.

Several empirical studies provide proof on the weak relationship between the yields on green bonds and returns on equities and commodities. Han and Li's (2022) findings suggest that the diversification benefits of green bonds mainly result from higher yields and lower volatility in US and European markets. Due to observed low or negative correlations, green bonds may offer significant diversification benefits, especially for active investors. In addition, the hedging opportunities and safe-haven potential of green bonds may prove to be useful in times of financial market turbulence, e.g. during the COVID-19 pandemic (Nguyen et al., 2021; Ferrer et al., 2021; Jin et al., 2020; Guo and Zhou, 2021; Naeem et al., 2021; Pham, 2021).

Figure 2 shows that overall "sustainable" debt issuance (including green bonds) reached $858.5 billion in 2022, below 24 % from the previous year.

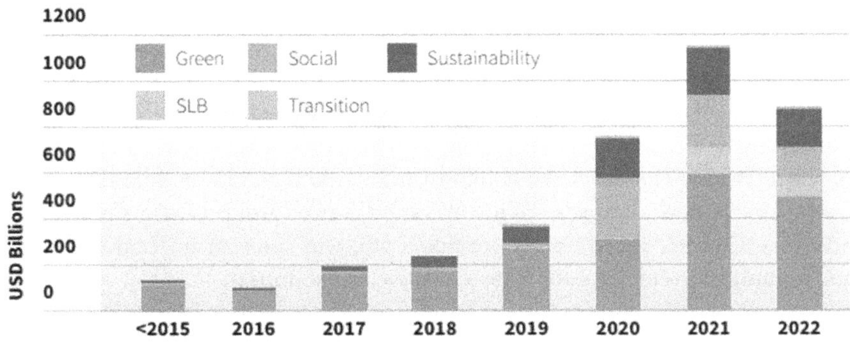

Figure 2: Green, social and sustainability volumes
Source: Climatebonds, 2022

One of the advantages of green bonds over conventional fixed income securities is the improved image of the investor (socially and environmentally responsible investing) and the issuer in the eyes of various stakeholder groups in addition to competitive pricing as reflected in higher premiums and hence lower cost of capital for issuers (Wisniewski and Zielinski, 2019; Sangiorgi and Schopohl, 2021). On the contrary, several papers imply that green bonds are more costly for the issuers and the main purpose for issuing these bonds may be just to signal their commitment to sustainability goals (Flammer, 2020). There is also another type of bond referred to as "climate bonds", issued to raise funding investments for the purposes of reducing emissions, increasing renewable energy facilities and/or climate change adaptation (Mackenzie and Ascui, 2009; Mathews and Kidney, 2010; Flaherty et al., 2017).

Social Bonds (SBs) are among those innovative assets that have enjoyed increasing popularity in the recent decade. The publication of Social Bond Principles by ICMA in 2017 contributed to their increasing awareness and popularity. Their growth and recognition have accelerated with the onset of the COVID-19 pandemic and the resulting necessity for new funding schemes to deal with unanticipated social and economic disruptions (Peeters et al., 2020). Proceeds from issues of social bonds are mainly used for funding projects that have a positive social impact, such as affordable/low-cost social housing programs, sustainable food systems and food security, projects to improve access to education and healthcare. Social bonds may have environmental co-benefits as well. They are also subject to third-party/independent verification to assure that funds raised are being used for the intended purpose(s). As in green bonds, the lack of exact explanation of SBs and the ambiguities regarding the appropriate remedies and reparations for failure to fulfill intended social obligations impose significant risks of "socialwashing" (Lenzi, 2021).

Investors who purchase social bonds are able to support socially impactful projects while also receiving a financial return on their investment. The nonprofit organization benefits from the ability to raise capital at a lower cost than other financing methods, and also gains access to a new group of socially-focused investors. Overall, social bonds provide a win-win solution for both investors and organizations looking to make a positive social impact.

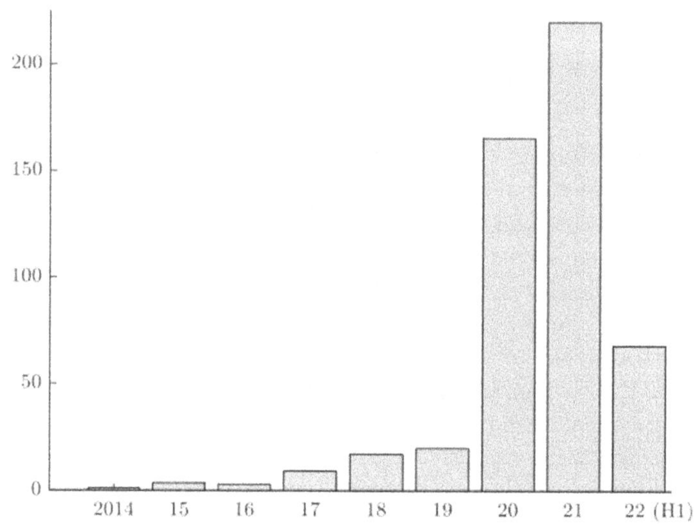

Figure 3: Issuance of social bonds
Source: Roncalli (2023)

According to CBI, the cumulative issuance of social debt amounted to $515 bn at the end of June 2022. The dynamics of social debt issuance is shown in Figure 3. There is a noticeable high growth in 2020, which is due to the issuance of social bonds to finance COVID-19 pandemic's negative impact on societies. According to CBI, the market is dominated by European (46 %) and supranational issuers (29 %). Most of social bonds are issued by the public sector (72 %) followed by financial institutions (15.7 %), development banks (7.7 %) and non-financial corporations (4.6 %).

Social Impact Bonds (SIBs) are essentially a kind of performance-pay (or outcomes-based) contractual arrangements between public or nonprofit service providers and for-profit or social investors. In this funding scheme, private agents supply funds for actions to improve targeted social outcomes (Floyd, 2017). SIBs do not assure a fixed or certain rate of return. Investors can anticipate to obtain a return, based on the savings government makes once service suppliers achieve result goals. Thus, in principle, by transferring to the private sector the financial risk of performance with respect to predetermined social targets, the government is able to decrease the costs to taxpayers (Warner, 2013).

The UK issued the first SIB (to finance a prisoner rehabilitation program) and since then has been the leader in the development of SIBs. Moreover, SIBs have been applied to several challenging social problems in various countries around the globe. They are referred to as Pay for Success activities in the US and usually as Development Impact Bonds (DIBs) in low- and middle-income countries (Tan et al., 2021). The viability of SIBs relies upon independent evaluations of their social outcomes and impacts which are very difficult to measure in practice (Jackson, 2013; OECD, 2016). In addition to difficulties in measurement and evaluation, the definition of beneficiaries and the need to take into account modifying conditions over time (Fraser et al., 2018) pose further complications.

Sustainability-Linked Bonds (SLBs) are bonds where the interest rate is tied to the issuer's sustainability performance, measured against some predetermined key performance indicators (KPIs). In general terms, as defined by ICMA (2023), these bonds' financial attributes can change according to the success of the issuer in achieving predefined sustainability/ESG targets. The issuing company sets sustainability targets that it aims to achieve over a specific period of time. If the company meets these targets, the interest rate on the bonds is reduced, resulting in lower borrowing costs for the company. If the company fails to meet these targets, the interest rate on the bonds remains the same or could even increase, resulting in higher borrowing costs. For instance, a firm may set a target to cut down its greenhouse gas emissions by 20 % within five years. If the company achieves this target, the interest rate on the Sustainability-Linked Bonds is reduced, resulting in lower borrowing costs. This incentivizes the company to improve its sustainability performance, as it can lead to lower borrowing costs and improve the company's reputation among sustainability-focused investors (Kölbel and Lambillon, 2022). Investors who purchase SLBs benefit from knowing that their investment is tied to the firm's sustainability performance. If the firm accomplishes its sustainability targets, the investor receives a financial return and can feel good about supporting a company that is committed to sustainability. Overall, SLBs provide a way to align the interests of investors and issuers towards sustainable development (Pohl et al. 2023).

SLBs are among the latest additions to this class of innovative debt instruments and since their introduction they have exhibited a dramatic growth pattern. In other words, these are bonds with a general purpose, the payments of which are aligned with the realization by the issuer of predefined, time-bound sustainability goals. The performance-based structure of SLBs significantly diverges from the use-of-proceeds structure of other sustainable bonds (Vulturius et al., 2022). In SLBs, KPIs are linked with the specific interest and/or principal payments, and they are a variant of the so-called KPI-linked bonds (Tsonkova, 2023). Specifically, the coupon interest rate on SLBs is contingent on the issuer accomplishing the prearrenged sustainability performance aim (Berrada et al., 2022). The financial structure of the SLBs may be subject to change after the issuance, usually due to the failure of the issuer to meet the predetermined targets, resulting in an increase in coupon payment (referred to as a step-up) (Giraldez and Fontana, 2022; Liberadzki et al., 2021).

Regulators also quickly recognized the potential of these instruments. For instance, in September 2020 the European Central Bank began accepting SLBs as eligible collateral in its credit and monetary policy operations.[3] Although interest in SLBs has been expanding and the market is enjoying a rapid growth, empirical research on these instruments has been relatively limited. Discussions on the risk of greenwashing and the regulatory mechanisms designed to alleviate this risk and issues related with measurement difficulties (targets to be set, determining KPIs) seem to dominate the emerging literature.

Based on the analysis of several cases of SLB issues, where the SLBs were matched with comparable conventional bonds, Liberadzki et al. (2021) confirmed existence of ESG premium resulting in lower yields for investors and hence lower cost of funding for the borrowers. In a similar study the estimated yield derived function between SLBs and non-sustainable or non-ESG bonds of the exact issuer, findings suggest that issuing an SLB yields negative average premiums, again resulting in lower borrowing costs for firms that meet predetermined sustainability targets.

Table 1 below shows the number of sustainable bonds issued.

Green Loans are bank lending schemes specifically devised to fund environmentally responsible, climate-friendly investments in assisting the

3 See also Fender et al. (2020) on the use of green bonds in foreign exchange reserve management by central banks.

Table 1: Number of sustainable/ESG bonds issued
Source: Bloomberg

	2016	2017	2018	2019	2020	2021	Total
Green bonds	275	475	572	834	1,030	1,877	5,063
Social bonds	13	43	40	76	262	482	916
Sustainability bonds	15	19	51	292	282	597	1,256
Sustainability-linked bonds	0	0	1	18	46	339	404
Total	**303**	**537**	**664**	**1,220**	**1,620**	**3,295**	**7,639**

change to a more sustainable economy. Here's an example of how green loans work: let's say that a small business wants to install solar panels on its roof to reduce its carbon footprint and lower its energy bills. The business could apply for a green loan from a financial institution to finance the installation of the solar panels. If the loan is approved, the business would receive the necessary funding to purchase and install the solar panels. The loan would be subject to a fixed interest rate and repayment terms, similar to other types of loans.

The green loan would also come with certain sustainability requirements, such as a commitment to use the energy generated by the solar panels for the business's operations, and to report on the environmental benefits of the project. This ensures that the loan profits are being used for the intended purpose and that the project is meeting its sustainability goals. The business benefits from the ability to finance its sustainability project at a lower cost than other financing methods, and also gains access to a new class of environmentally-focused lenders. The financial institution benefits from the ability to offer a new product to its customers and to support sustainable development.

Overall, green loans provide a way for businesses to finance environmentally sustainable activities while also receiving the necessary capital to grow their operations. They also provide a way for financial institutions to support sustainable development and attract environmentally-conscious customers.

Green lending activities started as early as 2005 and since then, reliance on green loans has increased to a great extent (Zhou et al., 2020). In most countries regulators (except China) do not require banks to reveal data on green loans, it is hard to conclude the size of the market accurately (Gilchrist et al., 2021). IFC's bottom-up approach to pursue existing green finance flows identifies green loans consistent with occupation nature of a project, corporation and industry. In terms of the monetary value of all syndicated loans in 2014, IFC estimated that almost

15 % ($164.7 billion) went into green finance. According to the IFC's definition, 41 % of the number of loans issued that are partly green were to the real estate sector. With regards to the allocation of loans across countries, the US had the largest share with 56.8 % followed by the UK with a share of 13 %. Turkey's estimated share was 4.2 % (IFC, 2017). Using EU classification, Gilchrist et al. (2021) estimated that, between 2004–2017, on average green loans accounted for about 55 % of total syndicated loans and the percentage of green loans increased to approximately 70 % of total during the sub-prime crisis of 2008.

Based on game-theoretic approaches, Li et al. (2018) and Huang et al. (2019) investigate the extent to which green credit financing as an intervention to promote sustainable development and environmental protection encourages firms to adopt innovative techniques. Theoretically, the authors show that these subsidies work via decreasing cost of borrowing for the enterprise, and conclude that green loans can create positive effects on the environment by reducing energy emissions. In this context, Kang et al. (2020) proposes an optimal control problem in order to assess the impact of South Korean government's Green Credit Policy on manufacturers' efforts to decrease suppliers' pollution. Results of the study indicate that by implementing an optimal strategy an effective government policy can lead reductions in environmental pollution through the entire supply chain.

Using evidence from Chinese firms Zhang (2022) concludes that China's green credit policy (GCP) significantly increases investment spending that mitigates environmental pollution. Investments oriented to pollution reduction also introduce new energy types and promote corporate social responsibility (CSR). On the other hand, these investments seem to decrease total fixed asset investments and R&D expenditures due to the financial constraint mechanism, and cause deterioration in key financial performance measures (sales growth, ROA, and ROS). Therefore, there seems a trade-off between pollution control and the financial outcomes in the case of China. Liu et al. (2019) find a significant reduction in debt financing among intemperately polluting Chinese companies following the introduction of Chinese government's GCP. They conclude that Green Credit Guidelines are effectively incorporated in bank loan approval processes and results in increased resource allocation in favor of green investments. Supporting the latter study's finding, Xing et al. (2020) shows that sustainability-focused management can significantly improve firms' loan size. Zhang et al.'s (2022) empirical findings, based on a sample of listed Chinese firms, show that while GCP is effective in expanding green innovations in general but ineffective and even disruptive for radical innovations by highly polluting companies. Liu et al.'s (2017) findings are also in line with the above studies. Specifically, using a general equilibrium model, they show that GCP has been effective in suppressing energy-intensive industries' investment spending while green security policy has been supportive of reducing the total fund flows to these industries. Lastly, He et al. (2019) obtain results suggesting that medium, small, or micro-sized enterprises' role in promoting green development is more pronounced than large enterprises. Supporting the theoretical conclusions of Kang et al. (2020), they also find that improvements in pollution control mechanisms tend to increase green economic development.

ESG Funds are investment funds that take into account ESG factors in asset allocation and portfolio choice decisions. As the interest in ESG-oriented investments has increased dramatically, ESG-themed financial products at every major investment proliferated. ESG investing products and solutions are getting ever-increasing attention from all categories of investors: large domestic and international institutional investors, wealth managers, individual investors and consultants.

The ESG Fund would use a range of ESG criteria to select companies for its portfolio. For example, the fund might screen out firms that are included in the production of fossil fuels or that have a history of environmental violations. It might also look for companies that have diverse boards of directors or that are committed to fair labor practices. If the ESG Fund is successful in selecting companies with strong ESG profiles, it may outperform traditional investment funds over the long term. This is because companies that are committed to sustainability and social responsibility may be better positioned to navigate changing market conditions and consumer preferences.

Investors who invest in ESG Funds benefit from knowing that their investments are aligned with their values and that they are supporting companies that are committed to sustainability and social responsibility. ESG Funds provide a way for investors to make a positive impact while also earning a financial return on their investment. Overall, ESG Funds provide a way to integrate sustainability and social responsibility into investment decisions, and to encourage companies to prioritize these issues in their operations.

Recent empirical findings provide proof that firms with high ESG scores yield higher excess returns and display lower volatility. Kumar et al. (2016), assessing a sample of firms covered in the Dow Jones Sustainability Index, demonstrate that companies incorporating ESG factors present lower stock price volatility and generate higher returns than their peers in the same industry. In addition, influence of ESG factors seems to vary among industries. Using a multifactor model, Peiris and Evans (2010) documents a meaningful positive correlation between profitability and valuation metrics and particular ESG rating criteria.

These findings imply that corporate social performance has positive affect on financial performance, supporting the stakeholder theory. El Ghoul et al. (2011), Eccles et al. (2014), and Gregory et al. (2014) also observed that companies with better ESG characteristics have presented less exposure to risks and enjoyed higher levels of valuation. Khan (2019) presents empirical evidence of the power of ESG performance to predict stock returns in a global context. Using governance and ESG metrics developed by himself, he found that these new metrics have significant predictive power in a global investment universe. Contrary to above studies' findings there is also substantial evidence documenting that firms with higher ESG ratings yield lower returns than those with lower ESG ratings (Luo, 2022; Pedersen et al., 2021; Bolton and Kacperczyk, 2021). La Torre et al.'s (2020) results also do not support previous evidence, at least for companies included in Euro Stoxx 50 index.

Another interesting strand of the literature on ESG-based investments comprises studies focusing on ESG momentum with the aim of understanding how stock markets price ESG characteristics (Khan et al., 2016; Giese et al., 2019; Nagy et al., 2016; Giese and Nagy, 2018). In this respect, Khan et al. (2016) and Giese et al. (2019) results demonstrate a statistically meaningful predictive power of ESG momentum for stock returns. Nagy et al. (2016) shows that the performance of a standard portfolio (market price weighted) with higher weights on positive ESG momentum companies is significantly higher than the performance of the benchmark and a comparable portfolio that put more weight on companies with high static ESG scores. Supporting these findings, Gieze and Nagy's (2018) results imply that market's reaction to ESG info for firms that do not have very low or very high ESG ratings, was more pronounced and asymmetric in the sense that reaction to ESG improvements were stronger than to downgrades.

Within an emerging market investment context, Sherwood and Pollard (2018) attempt to assess whether incorporation of ESG information improve portfolio performance and provide any significant diversification benefits. Their findings imply that ESG-based emerging market equities offer opportunities for earning higher risk-adjusted returns than non-ESG equities. Verheyden et al. (2016) also report similar results, namely higher returns against lower risks and diversification potential for both global and developed market portfolios. Cerqueti et al.' (2021) findings also point to enhanced diversification benefits of higher ESG stocks at both the macro and micro grades. Although their findings do not indicate a significant difference between sustainability and conventional stock indices in terms of risk-return performance, Jain et al.

(2019) nevertheless points to diversification and hedging potential offered by sustainable indices.

Recently, divergence of ratings by different ESG rating providers for the same company has attracted attention. In addition, confusion and ambiguities on various ESG methodologies and reporting standards have been addressed by academics and practitioners (Chatterji et al., 2016; Amel-Zadeh and Serafeim, 2018; Dimson et al., 2020; Berg et al., 2022; Serafeim and Yoon, 2022). Using ESG ratings produced by different data providers, Brandon et al. (2021) found that there is a positive relationship between equity returns and ESG rating disagreement (for a sample of firms included in the S&P 500 Index). Specifically, higher ESG rating discrepancy is associated with a risk premium. This finding supports the idea that incorporation of ESG disagreement in pricing models can result in improved investment performance. In line with above studies' findings Popescu et al. (2021), based on an evaluation of widely used sustainability measurement methods, note that carbon dioxide emissions and ESG metrics have several deficiencies, most importantly their failure to precisely measure the real-world sustainability impact of ESG-oriented investments.

Impact Investing is an investment approach or strategy that seeks to generate social and environmental impact, as well as generate returns/profits. The term "impact investing" was invented in 2007 by The Rockefeller Inc.. The Rockefeller Brothers Fund defines impact investments as "investments that both deliver market-grade returns and produce significant and mensurable impact on the Fund's task to forward social change that contributes to a more just, sustainable, and peaceable world[4]". The global impact investment market size has increased rapidly as large and small traditional impact investors have been connected by consecrated funds and instruments from the really huge investment management firms. In oppose to other investment styles, impact investing is typically straighter and focuses on accomplishing a particular affect on a social or environmental matter (Hill, 2020).

The impact investment would provide the necessary capital for the company to scale its operations and reach more people in need of clean water. In return for its investment, the investor would receive a financial return, but would also be able to track the environmental and social impact of the investment. This impact might be measured in terms of the number of people who gain access to

4 https://www.rbf.org/mission-aligned-investing/impact-investments#:~:text=The%20Fund%20defines%20impact%20investments,%2C%20sustainable%2C%20and%20peaceful%20world.

clean water as an outcome of the company's operations. This provides a way for the investor to track the impact of the investment and to ensure that it is aligned with their values.

Impact investing provides a way for investors to use their capital to make a positive impact in the world while also earning a financial return. It also enables companies working to address social and environmental challenges to access the necessary capital to scale their operations and make a greater impact. Overall, impact investing provides a way to align financial goals with social and environmental impact, and to support the development of solutions to some of our times' most challenging problems.

Impact investments attract a diverse range of investors who share a common interest in generating positive social and environmental outcomes alongside financial returns. Here are some key categories of investors that participate in impact investing: *Institutional investors* include pension funds, insurance companies, endowments, foundations, and sovereign wealth funds. These large-scale investors have significant capital and long-term investment horizons, allowing them to allocate funds to impact investments. Institutional investors often have fiduciary duties to consider the long-term sustainability and social impact of their investments, making impact investing an attractive option. *High Net Worth Individuals* (HNWIs) are affluent individuals with substantial investable assets. HNWIs who are socially conscious seek to align their investments with their values, making impact investing an appealing choice. These individuals may have a personal commitment to social and environmental causes and are willing to dedicate a portion of their wealth to impact-oriented ventures. Family offices are private wealth management firms that cater to wealthy families. *Family offices* often have the flexibility to customize investment strategies based on the family's values and long-term goals. Many family offices are increasingly incorporating impact investing into their portfolios as a means to preserve wealth while making a positive difference. *Development Finance Institutions* (DFIs) or *Development Banks* are specialized banking institutions usually established by governments or international organizations to promote economic development and address social challenges in developing countries. DFIs invest in impact-focused projects and businesses in sectors such as clean energy, microfinance, and infrastructure. Their primary goal is to foster sustainable economic growth and poverty reduction. *Retail investors* are individuals who invest in financial markets directly or through mutual funds, exchange-traded funds (ETFs), or other investment vehicles that is facilitated by some intermediary. Impact investing has become more accessible to retail investors through the development of impact-focused mutual funds and ETFs. These investment products allow individuals to participate in impact investing with relatively small investment amounts. *Impact-focused Funds and Intermediaries* are specialized impact-focused investment funds and intermediaries that play a crucial role in connecting investors with impact opportunities. These funds and intermediaries conduct due diligence, provide investment expertise, and manage impact portfolios on behalf of investors. They serve as a bridge between investors and impactful ventures, facilitating capital flows into sustainable and socially responsible projects. The landscape of impact investors continues to evolve, and there is a growing interest in impact investing across a broader range of investors. Governments, corporations, and philanthropic organizations are also increasingly exploring impact investing as a means to align their financial resources with their mission and values (Global Impact Investing Network, 2023).

3. Benefits and Drivers of Sustainable Financial Instruments

3.1 Advantages for Issuers

Sustainable financial instruments offer several advantages for issuers who choose to incorporate sustainability into their financing strategies. Here are some key advantages:

By issuing sustainable financial instruments, issuers can tap into a rapidly expanding investor base that prioritizes sustainability. Many institutional investors, asset managers, and individual investors are actively seeking investment opportunities aligned with their ESG values and sustainability goals. By offering sustainable financial instruments, issuers can attract these investors and potentially expand their investor pool.

Sustainable financial instruments can help issuers diversify their investor base beyond traditional investors. These instruments appeal to socially responsible investors, impact investors, and ESG-focused funds, bringing in new sources of capital. Diversification of investors can enhance the resilience of an issuer's funding strategy and reduce reliance on a specific investor segment. Embracing sustainability through the issuance of sustainable financial instruments can enhance an issuer's reputation and improve investor perception. It signals the issuer's commitment to responsible and sustainable business practices, demonstrating its awareness of environmental and social considerations. This can lead to increased trust from investors and stakeholders, positively impacting the issuer's brand image and long-term relationships with investors.

Sustainable financial instruments can provide issuers with a competitive edge in the market. As sustainable finance becomes increasingly mainstream, issuers that offer sustainable instruments may differentiate themselves from competitors. It can demonstrate leadership in sustainability and attract investors who prioritize ESG factors. This competitive advantage may lead to improved access to capital, lower borrowing costs, and increased market share. Incorporating sustainability into financial instruments allows issuers to better manage ESG-related risks. By evaluating and disclosing ESG factors, issuers can identify potential risks and take appropriate measures to mitigate them. For example, addressing climate-related risks can help protect the issuer's assets and operations from physical and transition risks, ensuring long-term sustainability and resilience.

Sustainable financial instruments can assist issuers in meeting evolving regulatory requirements related to sustainability. Regulators in many jurisdictions are introducing frameworks and disclosure requirements that encourage or mandate ESG considerations. By issuing sustainable financial instruments, issuers can align themselves with these regulations and demonstrate compliance, reducing the risk of regulatory penalties and reputational harm. Sustainable financial instruments, such as green bonds, provide a specific funding mechanism for green and sustainable projects. Issuers can use the proceeds from these instruments to finance environmentally beneficial initiatives, such as renewable energy projects or energy-efficient infrastructure. This access to dedicated funding channels can facilitate the development of sustainability-focused projects and contribute to achieving sustainability targets.

It's important to note that while there are advantages to issuing sustainable financial instruments, issuers should carefully consider their sustainability commitments and ensure alignment with their overall business strategy. Transparency and credibility in reporting and impact measurement are crucial to maintain investor trust and deliver on sustainability promises.

3.2 Advantages of Sustainable Financial Instruments for Investors

Sustainable financial instruments offer several advantages for investors who choose to incorporate sustainability into their investment strategies. Here are some key advantages for investors:

Sustainable financial instruments allow investors to align their investment portfolios with their values and sustainability goals. They offer opportunities to invest in projects and companies that have positive ESG impacts. Investors can address global challenges, such as climate change, social inequality, and resource depletion, while generating financial returns. Incorporation of ESG factors into investment decisions can enhance risk management and potentially improve the risk-return profile of investment portfolios. By considering ESG risks and opportunities, investors can gain insights into potential risks that may impact financial performance, such as regulatory changes, reputational risks, or supply chain disruptions. This proactive risk management can help protect investments and potentially lead to better long-term returns.

Sustainable financial instruments provide access to a range of investment opportunities in sectors with high growth potential. For example, renewable energy, clean technology, sustainable agriculture, and social infrastructure are areas that are expected to experience significant growth as societies transition to more sustainable practices. Investing in these sectors through sustainable financial instruments allows investors to participate in the growth of these markets. Sustainable financial instruments offer investors enhanced diversification benefits. By including sustainable assets, investors can spread their investment risk across different sectors, geographies, and asset classes. This diversification can help reduce exposure to specific market risks and ameliorate overall risk-adjusted portfolio returns.

Sustainable financial instruments focus on investments that aim for long-term value creation. By considering ESG factors, investors can identify companies and projects that are well-positioned to navigate environmental and social challenges, adapt to changing regulations, and capture emerging market opportunities. This long-term perspective can contribute to sustainable wealth creation and resilience in investment portfolios. Sustainable financial instruments align with the growing investor demand for ESG-focused investments. As more investors prioritize sustainability, these instruments provide access to investment opportunities that are in line with market trends and investor preferences. The increasing popularity of sustainable finance has led to the development and proliferation of innovative products and a broader range of choices for investors. Sustainable financial instruments often include impact measurement and reporting, allowing investors to evaluate the positive outcomes of their investments. Investors can track and assess the environmental and social impact generated by their investments, providing a sense of transparency and accountability. This information can be valuable for investors who want to understand and communicate the tangible results of their sustainable investments.

It's worth noting that investors should conduct proper due diligence and consider factors beyond sustainability when making investment decisions. They should assess the financial viability, management quality, and overall risk profile of sustainable financial instruments to ensure they align with their investment objectives.

3.3 Regulatory and Policy Drivers

There are several benefits and drivers of sustainable financial instruments for regulatory and policy drivers. Here are some key points:

3.3.1 Benefits for Regulatory and Policy Drivers

Sustainable financial instruments help regulatory and policy drivers align financial flows with broader sustainability goals. By promoting investments that support environmental protection, social development, and good governance, these instruments contribute to achieving policy objectives related to sustainable development, climate change mitigation, social inclusion, and responsible business practices. Sustainable financial instruments encourage the mobilization of private capital towards sustainable investments. They provide a framework for attracting funds from investors who prioritize ESG factors and facilitate, the flow of capital to sectors and projects that promote sustainable outcomes. This helps to reduce the funding gap for sustainable projects, as public funds alone may not be sufficient to address global sustainability challenges.

Regulatory and policy drivers play a crucial role in shaping the market for sustainable financial instruments. They establish guidelines, frameworks, and standards that provide clarity and transparency to issuers and investors. By creating a supportive regulatory environment, these drivers promote market development, foster investor confidence, and encourage the issuance and investment of sustainable financial instruments.

Regulatory and policy drivers often emphasize the importance of reporting and disclosure of ESG information. They require issuers of sustainable financial instruments to provide reliable and standardized ESG data, ensuring transparency and comparability. This enhances market integrity and investor confidence, allowing investors to make informed decisions based on comprehensive and comparable information.

3.3.2 Drivers for Regulatory and Policy Initiatives

Regulatory and policy drivers are increasingly recognizing the urgency of addressing environmental and social challenges. They are motivated by the need to achieve sustainability goals, such as those outlined in international frameworks such as the SDGs and the Paris Agreement on climate change. Sustainable financial instruments provide a means to mobilize private capital and financial resources towards these goals. Policy drivers are aware of the risks associated with unsustainable practices and are committed to mitigating these risks. By promoting sustainable financial instruments, they aim to integrate ESG considerations into investment decisions, reducing the potential for negative impacts on the society, environment, and the economy. This risk mitigation approach helps safeguard the stability and resilience of financial systems.

Regulatory and policy drivers recognize the potential of sustainable finance to stimulate economic growth and create jobs. By promoting investments in sustainable sectors and projects, they aim to unlock innovation, drive the transition to a low-carbon economy, and foster sustainable business practices. Sustainable financial instruments provide a mechanism to channel capital into areas that have the potential for long-term economic growth and competitiveness.

Regulatory and policy drivers seek to protect investors by assuring access to reliable and accurate information. By establishing disclosure requirements and standards for sustainable financial instruments, they promote investor protection and reduce the risk of greenwashing or misleading claims. This helps build trust in sustainable finance and ensures that investors can make well-informed decisions. Many regulatory and policy drivers are influenced by international commitments and agreements. For example, the countries that have ratified the Paris Agreement on climate change may introduce policies and initiatives to align financial systems with the goals of the agreement. Similarly, commitments to the SDGs may drive policy drivers to promote sustainable finance as a means to advance sustainable development.

In summary, regulatory and policy drivers see sustainable financial instruments as a way to align financial flows with policy objectives, mobilize private capital, develop sustainable markets, enhance reporting and disclosure, mitigate risks, stimulate economic growth, protect investors, and fulfill international commitments. By creating an enabling environment for sustainable finance, these drivers aim to drive positive change and contribute to a more sustainable and resilient future.

4. Conclusion

Sustainable financial instruments are innovative tools designed to mobilize capital toward environmentally and socially responsible projects and initiatives. They have emerged as a powerful force in aligning financial goals with sustainable development objectives. These instruments include green bonds, impact investing funds, sustainability-linked loans, social impact bonds, and more.

By integrating sustainability criteria into investment decisions, these instruments promote transparency, accountability, and responsible financial practices. Sustainable financial instruments not only benefit investors but also drive positive change on a broader scale. They facilitate the scaling of renewable energy projects, stimulate the growth of sustainable industries, and promote inclusive economic development.

However, challenges remain. Standardization and transparency are essential to ensure the credibility and effectiveness of sustainable financial instruments. Harmonized frameworks and measurement methodologies are needed to provide consistent and comparable information about the environmental and social impacts of investments. The future of finance lies in integrating sustainability as a fundamental consideration. Sustainable financial instruments provide a roadmap for creating a financial system that drives positive environmental and social outcomes while generating competitive returns. By embracing these instruments and fostering their adoption, we can harness the power of finance to build a more sustainable and inclusive world.

References

Amel-Zadeh, A., & Serafeim, G. (2018). Why and how investors use ESG information: evidence from a global survey. *Financial Analysts Journal*, 74(3). https://doi.org/10.2469/faj.v74.n3.2

Barua, S., & Chiesa, M. (2019). Sustainable financing practices through green bonds: What affects the funding size? *Business Strategy and the Environment*, 28(6), 1131–1147. https://doi.org/10.1002/bse.2307

Baulkaran, V. (2019). Stock market reaction to green bond issuance. *Journal of Asset Management*, 20, 331–340. https://doi.org/10.1057/s41260-018-00105-1

Berg, F., Kölbel, J. F., & Rigobon, R. (2022). Aggregate confusion: The divergence of ESG ratings. *Review of Finance*, 26(6), 1315–1344, https://doi.org/10.1093/rof/rfac033

Berrada, T., Engelhardt, L., Gibson, R., & Krueger, P. (2022). The economics of sustainability linked bonds. *ECGI Working Paper Series in Finance*, Working Paper No. 820. http://ssrn.com/abstract_id=4059299

Bolton, P., & Kacperczyk, M. (2021). Do investors care about carbon risk?. *Journal of Financial Economics*, 142(2), 517–549. https://doi.org/10.1016/j.jfineco.2021.05.008

Brandon, R.G., Krueger. P., & Schmidt, P. S. (2021). ESG rating disagreement and stock returns. *Financial Analysts Journal*, 77(4), 104–127. https://doi.org/10.1080/0015198X.2021.1963186

Brühl, V. (2021). Green finance in Europe – Strategy, regulation and instruments. *Intereconomics*, 56, 323–330.

Cerqueti, R., Cicirettib, R., Dalòc, A., & Nicolosid, M. (2021). ESG investing: A chance to reduce systemic risk. *Journal of Financial Stability*, 54, 100887. https://doi.org/10.1016/j.jfs.2021.100887

Chatterji, A.K., Durand, R., Levine, D.I., & Touboul, S. (2016). Do ratings of firms converge? Implications for managers, investors and strategy researchers. *Strategic Management Journal*, 37, 1597–1614. https://doi.org/10.1002/smj.2407

Climate Bonds Initiative. (2022). *Sustainable debt global state of the market*. https://www.climatebonds.net/files/reports/cbi_sotm_2022_03e.pdf

Dimson, E., Marsh, P., & Staunton, M. (2020). Divergent ESG ratings. *Journal of Portfolio Management*, 47(1), 75–87. https://doi.org/10.3905/jpm.2020.1.175

Dorfleitner, G., Utz, S., & Zhang, R. (2022). The pricing of green bonds: External reviews and the shades of green. *Review of Managerial Science*, 16, 797–834. https://doi.org/10.1007/s11846-021-00458-9

Eccles, R.G., Ioannou, I., & Serafeim, G. (2014). The impact of corporate sustainability on organizational processes and performance. *Management Science*, 60(11), 2835–2857. https://doi.org/10.1287/mnsc.2014.1984

El Ghoul, S., Guedhami, O., Kwok, C.Y., & Mishra, D.R. (2011). Does corporate social responsibility affect the cost of capital?. *Journal of Banking & Finance*, 35(9), 2388–2406. https://doi.org/10.1016/j.jbankfin.2011.02.007

Fatica, S., Panzica, R., & Rancan, M. (2021). The pricing of green bonds: Are financial institutions special?. *Journal of Financial Stability*, 54. https://doi.org/10.1016/j.jfs.2021.100873

Fender, I., McMorrow, M., Sahakyan, V., & Zulaica, O. (2020). Reserve management and sustainability: The case for green bonds?, *BIS Working Papers*, No 849.

Ferrer, R., Benítez, R., & Bolós, V.J. (2021). Interdependence between green financial instruments and major conventional assets: A wavelet-based network analysis. *Mathematics*, 9, 900. https://doi.org/10.3390/math9080900

Flaherty, M., Gevorkyan, A., Radpour, S., & Semmler, W. (2017). Financing climate policies through climate bonds–A three stage model and empirics. *Research in International Business and Finance*, 42, 468–479. https://doi.org/10.1016/j.ribaf.2016.06.001

Flammer, C. (2020). Green bonds: Effectiveness and implications for public policy. *Environmental and Energy Policy and the Economy*, 1, 95–128. https://doi.org/10.1086/706794

Floyd, D. (2017). Social impact bonds: An overview of the global market for commissioners and policymakers. *Briefing on Social Impact Bonds*, Centre for Public Impact.

Fraser, A., Tan, S., Lagarde, M., & Mays, N. (2018). Narratives of promise, narratives of caution: A review of the literature on social impact bonds. *Social Policy & Administration*, 52(1), 4–28. https://doi.org/10.1111/spol.12260

Giese, G., & Nagy, Z. (2018). *How markets price ESG, have changes in ESG scores affected stock prices?*. MSCI Research Insight.

Giese, G., Lee, L.E., Melas, D., Nagy, Z., & Nishikawa, L. (2019). Foundations of ESG investing: How ESG affects equity valuation, risk, and performance. *Journal of Portfolio Management*, 45(5), 69–83. https://doi.org/10.3905/jpm.2019.45.5.069

Gilchrist, D., Yu, J., & Zhong, R. (2021). The limits of green finance: A survey of literature in the context of green bonds and green loans. *Sustainability*, 13(2), 478. https://doi.org/10.3390/su13020478

Giraldez, J., & Fontana, S. (2022). Sustainability-linked bonds: The next frontier in sovereign financing. *Capital Markets Law Journal*, 17(1), 8–19. https://doi.org/10.1093/cmlj/kmab033

Global Impact Investing Network. (2023). Online: https://thegiin.org/impact-investing/need-to-know/#what-is-impact-investing

Gregory, A., Tharyan, R., & Whittaker, J. (2014). Corporate social responsibility and firm value: Disaggregating the effects on cash flow, risk and growth. *Journal of Business Ethics*, 124, 633–657. https://doi.org/10.1007/s10551-013-1898-5

Guo, D., & Zhou, P. (2021). Green bonds as hedging assets before and after COVID: A comparative study between the US and China. *Energy Economics*, 104, 105696. https://doi.org/10.1016/j.eneco.2021.105696

Gutterman, A. S. (2021). *Sustainable finance and impact investing*. Business Expert Press, LLC, NY, ISBN: 978-1-63742-002-7.

Han, Y., & Li, J. (2022). Should investors include green bonds in their portfolios? Evidence for the USA and Europe. *International Review of Financial Analysis*, 80. https://doi.org/10.1016/j.irfa.2021.101998

He, L., Zhang, L., Zhong, Z., Wang, D., & Wang, F. (2019). Green credit, renewable energy investment and green economy development: Empirical analysis based on 150 listed companies of China. *Journal of Cleaner Production*, 208, 363–372. https://doi.org/10.1016/j.jclepro.2018.10.119

Hill, J. (2020). *Environmental, Social and Governance (ESG) investing a balanced analysis of the theory and practice of a sustainable portfolio*. Academic Press, ISBN:978-0-12-818692-3.

Huang, Z., Liao, G., & Li, Z. (2019). Loaning scale and government subsidy for promoting green innovation. *Technological Forecasting and Social Change*, 144, 148–156. https://doi.org/10.1016/j.techfore.2019.04.023

International Capital Market Association. (2023). Sustainability-linked bond principles: voluntary process guidelines, June 2023. Online: https://www.icmagroup.org/assets/documents/Sustainable-finance/2023-updates/Sustainability-Linked-Bond-Principles-June-2023-220623.pdf

International Finance Corporation. (2017). Green finance. A bottom-up approach to track existing flows. Online: https://documents1.worldbank.org/curated/en/788041573021878350/pdf/Full-Report.pdf

Jackson, E.T. (2013). Evaluating social impact bonds: Questions, challenges, innovations, and possibilities in measuring outcomes in impact investing. *Community Development*, 44(5), 608–616, https://doi.org/10.1080/15575330.2013.854258

Jain, M., Sharma, G.D., & Srivastava, M. (2019). Can sustainable investment yield better financial returns: A comparative study of ESG indices and MSCI indices. *Risks*, 7(1), 15. https://doi.org/10.3390/risks7010015

Jiang, K., Chen, Z., & Chen, F. (2022). Green creates value: Evidence from China. *Journal of Asian Economics*, 78, 101425. https://doi.org/10.1016/j.asieco.2021.101425

Jin, J., Han, L., Wu, L., & Zeng, H. (2020). The hedging effect of green bonds on carbon market risk. *International Review of Financial Analysis*, 71, 101509. https://doi.org/10.1016/j.irfa.2020.101509

Jones, P., & Comfort, D. (2020). The COVID-19 crisis and sustainability in the hospitality industry. *International Journal of Contemporary Hospitality Management*, 32(10), 3037–3050. http://doi:10.1108/IJCHM-04-2020-0357

Jones, R., Baker, T., Huet, K., Murphy, L., & Lewis, N. (2020). Treating ecological deficit with debt: The practical and political concerns with green bonds. *Geoforum*, 114, 49–58. https://doi.org/10.1016/j.geoforum.2020.05.014

Kanamura, T. (2020). Are green bonds environmentally friendly and good performing assets?. *Energy Economics*, 88. https://doi.org/10.1016/j.eneco.2020.104767

Kang, H., Jung, S.Y., & Lee, H. (2020). The impact of Green Credit Policy on manufacturers' efforts to reduce suppliers' pollution. *Journal of Cleaner Production*, 248, 119271. https://doi.org/10.1016/j.jclepro.2019.119271

Khan, M. (2019). Corporate governance, ESG, and stock returns around the world. *Financial Analysts Journal*, 75(4), 103–123. https://doi.org/10.1080/0015198X.2019.1654299

Khan, M., Serafeim, G., & Yoon, A. (2016). Corporate sustainability: First evidence on materiality. *Accounting Review*, 91(6), 1697–1724. https://doi.org/10.2308/accr-51383

Kölbel, J., & Lambillon, A.P. (2022). Who pays for sustainability? An analysis of sustainability-linked bonds. *Swiss Finance Institute Research Paper* No. 23(7). http://dx.doi.org/10.2139/ssrn.4007629

Kumar, N.C.A., Smith, C., Badis, L., Wang, N., Ambrosy, P., & Tavares, R. (2016). ESG factors and risk-adjusted performance: A new quantitative model. *Journal of Sustainable Finance & Investment*, 6(4), 292–300. https://doi.org/10.1080/20430795.2016.1234909

La Torre, M., Mango, F., Cafaro, A., & Leo, S. (2020). Does the ESG index affect stock return? Evidence from the Eurostoxx50. *Sustainability*, 12(16), 6387. https://doi.org/10.3390/su12166387

Lebelle, M., Jarjir, S.R., & Sassi, S. (2022). The effect of issuance documentation disclosure and readability on liquidity: Evidence from green bonds. *Global Finance Journal*, 51(2), 100678. http://doi:10.1016/j.gfj.2021.100678

Lenzi, D. (2021). Corporate social bonds: A legal analysis. *European Company and Financial Law Review*, 18(2), 291–320. https://doi.org/10.1515/ecfr-2021-0014

Li, Z., Liao, G., Wang, Z., & Huang, Z. (2018). Green loan and subsidy for promoting clean production innovation. *Journal of Cleaner Production*, 187, 421–431. https://doi.org/10.1016/j.jclepro.2018.03.066

Liberadzki, M., Jaworski, P., & Liberadzki, K. (2021). Spread analysis of the sustainability-linked bonds tied to an issuer's greenhouse gases emissions reduction target. *Energies*, 14(23), 7918. https://doi.org/10.3390/en14237918

Lindenberg, N. (2014). *Definition of green finance.* German Development Institute.

Liu, J.Y., Xia, Y., Fan, Y., Lin, S.M., & Wu, J. (2017). Assessment of a green credit policy aimed at energy-intensive industries in China based on a financial CGE model. *Journal of Cleaner Production*, 163, 293–302. https://doi.org/10.1016/j.jclepro.2015.10.111

Liu, X., Wang, E., & Cai, D. (2019). Green credit policy, property rights and debt financing: Quasi-natural experimental evidence from China. *Finance Research Letters*, 29, 129–135. https://doi.org/10.1016/j.frl.2019.03.014

Luo, D. (2022). ESG, liquidity, and stock returns. *Journal of International Financial Markets, Institutions & Money*, 78, 101526. https://doi.org/10.1016/j.intfin.2022.101526

Mackenzie, C., & Ascui, F. (2009). Investor leadership on climate change: An analysis of the investment community's role on climate change, and snapshot of recent investor activity. United Nations Global Compact. http://d2m27378y09r06.cloudfront.net/viewer/?file=wp-content/uploads/climate.pdf

Maltais, A., & Nykvist, B. (2021). Understanding the role of green bonds in advancing sustainability. *Journal of Sustainable Finance & Investment*, 11(3), 233–252. https://doi.org/10.1080/20430795.2020.1724864

Mathews, J.A., & Kidney, S. (2010). Climate bonds: Mobilizing private financing for carbon management. *Carbon Management*, 1(1), 9–13. https://doi.org/10.4155/cmt.10.15

Mihálovits, Z., & Tapaszti, A. (2018). Green bond, the financial instrument that supports sustainable development: Opportunities and barriers. *Public Finance Quarterly*, 63(3), 303–318.

Mocanu, M., Constantin, L.G., & Cernat-Gruici, B., (2021). Sustainability bonds: An international event study. *Journal of Business Economics and Management*, 22(6). https://doi.org/10.3846/jbem.2021.15372

Monk, A., & Perkins, R. (2020). What explains the emergence and diffusion of green bonds?. *Energy Policy*, 145, 111641. https://doi.org/10.1016/j.enpol.2020.111641

Naeem, A., Farid, S., Ferrer, R., & Jawad, H.S. (2021). Comparative efficiency of green and conventional bonds pre- and during COVID-19: An asymmetric multifractal detrended fluctuation analysis. *Energy Policy*, 153. https://doi.org/10.1016/j.enpol.2021.112285

Nagy, Z., Kassam, A., & Lee, L. (2016). Can ESG add alpha? An analysis of ESG tilt and momentum strategies. *Journal of Investing*, 25(2), 1133–124. https://doi.org/10.3905/joi.2016.25.2.113

Nguyen, T.T.H., Naeem, M.A., Balli, F., Balli, H.O., & Vo, X.V. (2021). Time-frequency comovement among green bonds, stocks, commodities, clean energy, and conventional bonds. *Finance Research Letters*, 40, 101739. https://doi.org/10.1016/j.frl.2020.101739

Ning, Y., Cherian, J., Sial, M.S., Alvarez-Otero, S., Comite, U., & Zia-Ud-Din, M. (2023). Green bond as a new determinant of sustainable green financing, energy efficiency investment, and economic growth: A global perspective. *Environmental Science and Pollution Research*, 30, 61324–61339. https://doi.org/10.1007/s11356-021-18454-7

OECD. (2016). Understanding Social Impact Bonds. Online: https://www.oecd.org/cfe/leed/UnderstandingSIBsLux-WorkingPaper.pdf

Pedersen, H., Fitzgibbons, S., & Pomorski, L. (2021). Responsible investing: The ESG-efficient frontier. *Journal of Financial Economics*, 142(2), 572–597. https://doi.org/10.1016/j.jfineco.2020.11.001

Peeters, S., Schmitt, M., & Volk, A. (2020). Social bonds can help mitigate the economic and social effects of the COVID-19 Crisis. *EMCompass*, Note 89.

International Finance Corporation, Washington, DC. http://hdl.handle.net/10986/34853

Peiris, D., & Evans, J. (2010). The relationship between environmental social governance factors and U.S. Stock Performance. *Journal of Investing*, 19(3), 104–112. https://doi.org/10.3905/joi.2010.19.3.104

Pham, L. (2021). Frequency connectedness and cross-quantile dependence between green bond and green equity markets. *Energy Economics*, 98, 105257. https://doi.org/10.1016/j.eneco.2021.105257

Pham, L., & Huynh, T. L. D. (2020). How does investor attention influence the green bond market?. *Finance Research Letters*, 35, 101533. https://doi.org/10.1016/j.frl.2020.101533

Pohl, C., Schüler, G., & Schiereck, D. (2023). Borrower-and lender-specific determinants in the pricing of sustainability-linked loans. *Journal of Cleaner Production*, 385, 135652. https://doi.org/10.1016/j.jclepro.2022.135652

Popescu, I., Hitaj, C., & Benetto, E. (2021). Measuring the sustainability of investment funds: A critical review of methods and frameworks in sustainable finance. *Journal of Cleaner Production*, 314, 128016. https://doi.org/10.1016/j.jclepro.2021.128016

Roncalli, T. (2023). *Handbook of sustainable finance*. CC BY license. Online: http://www.thierry-roncalli.com/download/HSF.pdf.

Sangiorgi, I., & Schopohl, L. (2021). Why do institutional investors buy green bonds: Evidence from a survey of European asset managers. *International Review of Financial Analysis*, 75, 101738. https://doi.org/10.1016/j.irfa.2021.101738

Serafeim, G., & Yoon, A. (2022). Stock price reactions to ESG news: The role of ESG ratings and disagreement. *Review of Accounting Studies*. https://doi.org/10.1007/s11142-022-09675-3

Sherwood, M.W., & Pollard, J. L. (2018). The risk-adjusted return potential of integrating ESG strategies into emerging market equities. *Journal of Sustainable Finance & Investment*, 8(1), 26–44. https://doi.org/10.1080/20430795.2017.1331118

Taghizadeh-Hesary, F., Yoshuni, N., & Phoumin, H. (2021). Analyzing the characteristics of green bond markets to facilitate green finance in the post-COVID-19 world. *Sustainability*, 13(10), 5719. https://doi.org/10.3390/su13105719

Tan, S., Fraser, A., McHugh, N., & Warner, M.E. (2021). Widening perspectives on social impact bonds. *Journal of Economic Policy Reform*, 24(1), 1–10. https://doi.org/10.1080/17487870.2019.1568249

Tang, D.Y., & Zhan, Y. (2020). Do shareholders benefit from green bonds?. *Journal of Corporate Finance*, 61, 101427. https://doi.org/10.1016/j.jcorpfin.2018.12.001

Teti, M., Schatz, E., & Liebenburg, L. (2020). Methods in the time of COVID-19: The vital role of qualitative inquiries. *International Journal of Qualitative Methods*, 19, 1–5, https://doi.org/10.1177/1609406920920962

Tsonkova, V. D. (2023). Sustainability-linked bonds as a part of the sustainable debt market–state, opportunities and challenges. *KNOWLEDGE-International Journal*, 57(1), 35–43.

Verheyden, T., Eccles, R.G., & Feiner, A. (2016). ESG for all? The impact of ESG screening on return, risk, and diversification. *Journal of Applied Corporate Finance*, 28(2), 47–55. https://doi.org/10.1111/jacf.12174

Vulturius, G., Maltais, A., & Forsbacka, K. (2022). Sustainability-linked bonds – their potential to promote issuers' transition to net-zero emissions and future research directions. *Journal of Sustainable Finance & Investment*. https://doi.org/10.1080/20430795.2022.2040943

Wang, S., Wang, H., Wang, J., & Yang, F. (2020). Does environmental information disclosure contribute to improve firm financial performance? An examination of the underlying mechanism. *Science of the Total Environment*, 714, 136855. https://doi.org/10.1016/j.scitotenv.2020.136855

Warner, M.E. (2013). Private finance for public goods: Social impact bonds. *Journal of Economic Policy Reform*, 16(4), 303–319. https://doi.org/10.1080/17487870.2013.835727

Wiśniewski, M., & Zieliński, J. (2019). Green bonds as an innovative sovereign financial instrument. *Ekonomia I PrawoEconomics and Law*, 18(1). https://doi.org/10.12775/EiP.2019.007

Xing, C., Zhang, Y., & Wang, Y. (2020). Do banks value green management in China? The perspective of the green credit policy. *Finance Research Letters*, 35, 101601. https://doi.org/10.1016/j.frl.2020.101601

Zhang, D. (2022). Does the green loan policy boost greener production?– Evidence from Chinese firms. *Emerging Markets Review*, 51, Part B, 100882. https://doi.org/10.1016/j.ememar.2021.100882

Zhang, R., Li, Y., & Liu, Y. (2021). Green bond issuance and corporate cost of capital. *Pacific-Basin Finance Journal*, 69, 101626. https://doi.org/10.1016/j.pacfin.2021.101626

Zhang, J., Luo, Y., & Ding, X. (2022). Can green credit policy improve the overseas investment efficiency of enterprises in China?. *Journal of Cleaner Production*, 340, 130785. https://doi.org/10.1016/j.jclepro.2022.130785

Zhou, X., & Cui, Y. (2019). Green bonds, corporate performance, and corporate social responsibility. *Sustainability*, 11(23), 6881. https://doi.org/10.3390/su11236881

Zhou, X., Tang, X., & Zhang, R. (2020). Impact of green finance on economic development and environmental quality: A study based on provincial panel data from China. *Environmental Science and Pollution Research*, 27, 19915–19932. https://doi.org/10.1007/s11356-020-08383-2

Çiydem ÇATAK

The Confusion over the Terminology of Sustainable, ESG, Socially Responsible and Impact Investing

Abstract: Although they have different meanings, the terms "sustainable investing", "socially responsible investing", "environmental, social and governance investing" and "impact investing" are often used interchangeably in the literature. This study aims to expand knowledge about these concepts by reviewing previous literature. It defines the differences and areas of convergence between these different investment approaches while drawing clearer boundaries between them. One could say that sustainable investing is an umbrella term that covers all these forms of investment. Environmental, social and governance investing (ESG) refers to the process of measuring a company's environmental, social and governance activities in the context of traditional financial indicators. Financial returns are the main objective of ESG investing. On the other hand, socially responsible investing (SRI) involves the selection or exclusion of investments based on certain moral standards. Impact investing is about giving investors the opportunity to invest in a company or organization that adds social value and thus creates an impact.

Keywords: Sustainable Investing, ESG Investing, Socially Responsible Investing, Impact Investing

1. Introduction

Sustainability is undoubtedly one of the most important and popular terms today. When strategies are developed today, sustainability is almost always the leitmotif behind them. However, the term is much more than a fad. It is a process of change and transformation and provides a clear direction for the future. Sustainability is like a compass that society and business can use to find ways to a better future. Economic performance must therefore not only be oriented towards one's own short-term interests, but must be linked to the goal of always acting in an ecologically responsible and socially just manner.

There is not yet a single definition of what exactly sustainable investments is, but some define them as investing in companies with environmental or ethical standards, others as participating in large energy projects such as sustainable wind or solar power. Some sustainable indices and funds exclude companies involved in industries such as weapons of war, alcohol or tobacco production, while others exclude companies that allow the employment of children or make their money from gambling or pornographic content. It is not clear which investments are sustainable investments and what should be included and excluded. There is no framework for these inclusion and exclusion rules. As there is no standardized regulation, it is often difficult for investors to understand which kind of filters are actually used when selecting sustainable investments. Also, it could be said that there is no particular "good or bad" when it comes to investments that take some criteria into account, because sustainable investments are diverse and cover a broad spectrum. Sustainability is often about different personal values. Therefore, the criteria are usually assessed according to specific environmental, social and governance criteria or values created for society. Ultimately, everyone needs to decide for themselves which investment is sustainable for them.

Along with the term "sustainable investing", new terms with related meanings have entered our lives. The terms "environmental, social and governance investing", "socially responsible investing" and "impact investing" are often used synonymously in the literature, although they are actually different terms. Sustainable investing is a more general term and refers to an investment approach that takes social, environmental, socially responsible and ethical aspects into account when making an investment decision. On the other hand, ESG investing is an investment approach that considered some ESG factors like energy consumption, pollution, human rights, board independence for evaluating corporate behavior and screening potential investments. Socially responsible investments take it a step further than ESG investments. It entails the inclusion or removal of assets based on certain moral principles. The other one is impact investing, in which impact investing must bring real social benefits. In other words, they should contribute companies or organizations to achieve specific goals that are beneficial to society or the environment.

In the following section, value-based investing and traditional investing are defined and a comparison is made between value-based investing and traditional investing. Section 3 then identifies overlaps and distinctions between sustainable, environmental, social and governance, socially responsible and impact investing and summarizes which approaches are used synonymously in the literature and for what purpose. Finally, a conclusion is drawn in Section 4.

2. Traditional Investing vs. Value-based Investing

Sustainable, environmental, social and governance investing, socially responsible and impact investing are prevalent in today's investment world and are favored by investors who do not seem to care about sacrificing a particular return as long as they can preserve certain values with their investments. Value-based investing is a term that encompasses a variety of investment approaches and as the name suggests, reflects values, whether those of society, the environment or religion. Among the issues that investors are typically concerned about are diversity, nuclear energy, clean technology, employee health and safety, and animal welfare.

Value-based investing first came into our lives for religious reasons, and years ago some people began to consider social reasons in their investments, excluding companies that produce weapons or alcohol or are involved in the slave trade from their portfolios. It later became widespread, and the PAX Investment Fund, the first financial instrument for socially aware investing, was founded in 1971 by individuals boycotting companies that supported the Vietnam War and supplied military goods and products for the conflict (Yan, Ferraro and Almandoz, 2019). Later, more funds and even indices were launched, and interest in value-oriented investments grew day by day. The results of the Morgan Stanley Institute for Sustainable Investing's Sustainable Signals 2022 survey show that 85 % of asset managers and 83 % of asset owners today say they are already implementing or plan to implement sustainable investing, which is one of the value-based investment approaches, in whole or in part in their portfolios (Morgan Stanley, 2022).

As more and more investors choose value-based investing, companies that want to grow are also forced to behave more responsibly. While value-based investing helps investors stand up for the values they believe in, behaving more responsibly brings many advantages also to businesses. It is assumed for example that socially responsible companies often tend to perform well (Goukasian and Whitney, 2008; Asemah, Okpanachi and Edegoh, 2013). It is expected that better social performance will increase reputation approval in the capital market, reduce the likelihood of environmental punishment and legal costs, increase profits and productivity due to innovation, and increase employee loyalty and all of which help companies achieve better financial performance (Stojanovic, Milosevic, Arsic, Urosevic and Mihaljovic, 2020). On the other hand, there are also some disadvantages of value-based investing from the point of view of investors and companies. From the investor's perspective, value-based investing makes it more difficult to have a more diversified portfolio. It could also be that focusing not only on the financial but also on the social performance of investments can reduce investment returns. When value becomes more important than financial performance, it can put investors in a difficult position. The other disadvantage is that it is often difficult to verify that companies actually deliver what they claim. Also checking always whether companies really have the values that they declare to the public is a time-consuming, labor-intensive and continuous process. On the other hand, value-based investments come with some burdens from the

Table 1: A comparison between value-based investing and traditional investing

	Value-based Investing	**Traditional Investing**
The strategy	Adding value to the environment, society and/or people + Profit maximization	Profit maximization
Approach	An evidence-informed approach	An evidence-based approach
Basis	Beliefs and values	Financial benefits
Selection process	Investments are not made in every company, industry, or sector or investment product	Can include any company, industry, or sector or investment product
Analysis	Based on the management structure, workplace safety, energy policy, human capital development and etc.	Based on price-earnings ratio, technical analysis, fundamental analysis, earnings per share, return on assets, return on equity, etc.
Reports	Corporate Governance Reports, Sustainability reports, Corporate Social Responsibility reports etc.	Balance Sheet, Income Statement, Cash Flow Statement etc.

companies' perspective, e.g. being more socially responsible is not easy and it is costly.

A comparison between traditional financing, where financial benefits are obtained without taking into account the contribution that the investment makes to the environment, society and/or people, and value-based investment, where in addition to the financial benefits, it is also taken into account that this investment creates added value for the environment, society and/or people, has been made above. As can be seen in Table 1, the value-based investing differs from traditional investing according to the strategy, approach, basis, selection process, the analysis and reports that the investors consider.

Traditional investing is based on profit maximization also the only goal is getting more return without taking consideration all other things. On the other hand value-based investing basierd of not only profit maximization it is also important to adding value to the environment, society and/or people. Value investing takes an evidence-informed approach, using the best available information to decide how to invest. In contrast, traditional investing takes an evidence-based approach that relies on analysis conducted according to carefully applied methods. This can be extensive and complicated. The basis for value-based investing is beliefs and values. Traditional investments, however, are based on financial benefits. The selection process for these two types of investments is also completely different. While value-oriented investments are not made in every company, industry, sector or investment product, traditional investments can be made in every company, industry, sector or investment product. Since investments are made in most companies, diversification is high for traditional investments and low for value-based investments. Value-based investing focuses on management structure, workplace safety, energy policy, human capital development, etc., while traditional investing uses price-earnings ratio, technical analysis, fundamental analysis, earnings per share, return on assets, return on equity, etc. Corporate governance reports, sustainability reports, corporate social responsibility reports, etc. are considered as reports for value-based investments. For traditional investments, by contrast, the balance sheet, income statement, cash flow statement, etc. are taken into account.

3. Intersections and Separations

As mentioned earlier, there are overlaps and differences between the terms "sustainable investing", "socially responsible investing", "environmental, social and governance investing" and "impact investing". While it cannot be said that they are completely separate, it can be said that they are mutually evolving investments. As shown in Figure 1 sustainable investing is comprehensive term that involve ESG investing, socially responsible investing and impact investing.

ESG investing is a framework that take environmental, social and governance criteria into account when deciding how to allocate assets and risks in order to achieve sustainable, long-term financial returns (Boffo and Patalano, 2020). ESG investments are made in companies that better meet these three main criteria – environmental, social and governance – but there is no standard rule to determine this "better". In the absence of a standard rule, investments are made according to the most appropriate approach. This means that the companies that meet the ESG criteria most in their sector will be the most attractive. This approach rewards companies from any sector that show a stronger commitment to environmental, social and governance issues. Ideally, this creates competitive pressure towards greater sustainability. ESG also differs from socially responsible investing and impact investing in this respect. There are no standardized criteria for ESG investing, so it depends heavily on who decides what is considered "good" or "bad". On the other hand, socially responsible investing and impact investing are more standardized compared to ESG investing. For example, it is well known that socially responsible investing excludes companies from investing in certain areas such as gambling, alcohol or weapons. Impact investing, on the other hand, looks at a company's specific, measurable impact on a particular issue, such as climate change, gender investments, etc. Unlike ESG investing, where companies are judged on how they interact with the environment, society and governance, impact investing considers companies that actively address a specific issue or problem and add value to society.

ESG investments are traditional investments. Therefore, financial returns are the main source of value for investors who focus on ESG. Impact investing, on the other hand, considers all three types of benefits – financial, social and environmental – and can even prioritize social and environmental values as long as there is a financial return. Because ESG metrics outcomes are based on publicly reported data, ESG tend to be found in the public markets, while impact investing is widely used in the private market (Belaisch, 2019).

Socially responsible investing is a form of investment that lies between ESG investing and impact investing and consider both financial returns and moral values in investments decisions. Berry and Junkus (2013) state that defining socially responsible investing is easy when using an exclusionary SRI filter. The exclusionary approach selects certain companies based on products or a certain corporate behavior when selecting investments for a portfolio. For example, a socially responsible investor may not include a particular company in its portfolio if it is involved in violations of labor standards such as child labor or exploitation. The integrative approach, on the other hand, is more difficult because it weights an investment in a company according to whether its behavior is more or less socially responsible. Clearly, this approach involves a high degree of subjectivity. The investor has to decide which positive or negative behaviors of the company to focus on and how much importance to attach to each activity. The exclusionary approach is more standardized than the inclusionary approach, as the types of assets that can be included in the portfolio are more or less obvious.

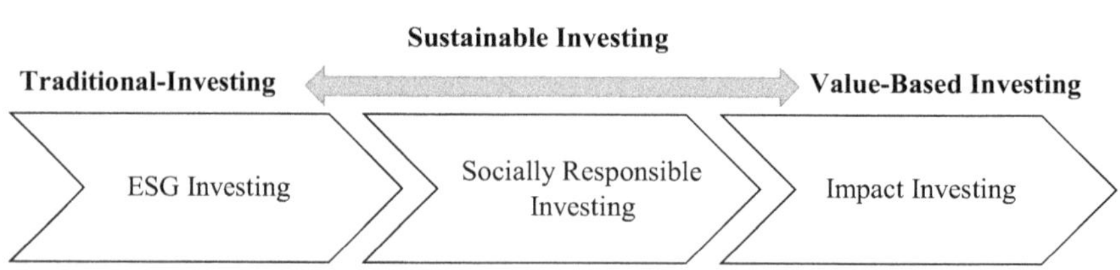

Figure 1: The seperation between all the types of investments

The use of investor money is closely linked to the value-based principles of impact investing. One could say that impact investing takes into account the way a company impacts the world and that investors who want to make impact investments only invest in companies that have a positive social or environmental impact. Impact investors are often able to use funds for purposes that are not directly targeted by public financial markets, such as community development and poverty reduction. Impact investing also tends to have more influence on the execution and management of portfolio companies than other forms of investment such socially responsible investing. Impact investing differs from socially responsible investing in that it seeks positive aspects to invest in rather than trying to eliminate perceived negative aspects. It usually takes place in the private market, whereas SRI and ESG investing usually relate to publicly traded assets. A summary comparison of all these types of investments is shown in Table 2.

Table 2: An overview of ESG, socially responsible and impact investing

	ESG-Investing	**Socailly Responsible Investing**	**Impact Investing**
Criterion	Objective	Subjective	Subjective
Nature	Somewhat complicated	Simple	Complicated
Accessibility	Easy	Mid-Level	Limited
Diversification	Very high	High	Low
Measurement	Backward-looking	Backward-looking	Forward looking
Transparency	Low	Mid-Level	High
Customization	Not possible	Not possible	Possible
Risk	As risky as traditional investments	As risky as traditional investments	Higher risks than traditional investments

Caplan, Griswold and Jarvis (2013) refer to all the concepts of socially responsible investing, mission-related investing, impact investing and environmental, social and governance-related investing as responsible investing and distinguish between the three main categories of responsible investing, i.e. SRI, ESG and impact investing approaches, by stating that they serve very different purposes. They argue that SRI and impact investing use financing and investments to express institutional values or to further the institution's mission. In contrast, ESG investing aims to improve investment performance and thereby provide additional resources to support the mission.

In the literature, these terms are often used interchangeably. As can be seen in Table 3, there is confusion about these types of investments and even experts and some institutions and organizations find it difficult to distinguish between them. Of course, there are some areas where all of these investment types overlap. It would also be wrong to assume that there is no intersection, because it has been said that they complement each other. For example, all of them could be classified as sustainable investments because they have some impact on the economy as a whole from a sustainability point of view. Perhaps not all of them are perfect in terms of sustainability, but these types of investments could be considered to provide a way forward and an acceptable balance for investors. The HSBC (2018) report for example uses the terms "sustainable investing" and "ESG investing" interchangeably and points out that a sustainable global economy needs to develop through individual action into an institutional transformation where environmental, social and governance considerations become not only a moral but also a business imperative. On the other hand, the Boffo and Patalano (2020) identifies ESG investing as a form of sustainable investing and notes that all forms of sustainable investing have increased significantly in the last few years as more and more institutional investors and funds are adopting different approaches to ESG investing. Although sustainable investing is a broader term than ESG-oriented investing, Deliotte (2020) also uses ESG investing and sustainable investing synonymously. The Global Sustainable Investment Alliance (GSIA) (2020), on the other hand, states that sustainable investing is an investment approach that takes into account environmental, social and governance factors, and in order to make the global reports as comprehensive as possible, they use a broad definition of sustainable investing, which includes seven core approaches, namely ESG integration, corporate engagement and shareholder action, standards-based screening, negative/exclusionary screening, best-in-class/positive screening, sustainable thematic investing, impact investing and community investing for sustainable investment. The term "sustainable investing" is equated with, among others, the terms "responsible investing" and "socially responsible investing", while recognizing that there are differences and regional variations in its meaning and use.

Rizzi, Pellegrini and Battaglia (2018) bring all these approaches, such as social impact investing and socially responsible investing, together under the term "social finance" and define them as a set of alternative lending and investment approaches for financing projects and companies that are intended to have a positive impact on society, the environment or sustainable development while generating financial returns. Niggemann and Brägger (2011) use the terms "socially responsible investing" and "impact investing" interchangeably, as impact investing aims for both a financial and a social return. They also use the terms "mission-based investing", "blended value investing" and "programme-based investing" instead of "socially responsible" and "impact investing" and refer to all of these terms as closely related. Gomes (2020) describes SRI as ethical finance and also uses the term SRI instead of ESG investing and impact investing, noting that SRI refers to investor decisions that combine financial objectives with environmental, social and governance concerns in general. In another study, Townsend (2020) states that ESG investing and impact investing are the key components of SRI. He states that the three pillars of SRI are value-based avoidance screening, proactive sustainability-focused analysis called "ESG investing" and impact investing.

Eurosif (2018) uses the abbreviation SRI for "Sustainable and Responsible Investing" and defines it as a long-term investment approach that integrates ESG factors into the research, analysis and selection process of securities within an investment portfolio. They argue that SRI combines fundamental analysis with ESG factor ratings to generate long-term returns for investors and benefit society by influencing corporate behavior. They distinguish between impact investing and incidental impact investing and categorize SRI and ESG research as incidental impact investing. The target companies of incidental impact investing usually meet the needs of the market and have a sustainable or reasonable business model. Impact investing, on the other hand, is intentional, meaning that target companies consciously address social or environmental issues and at the same time have economically sustainable business models. MSCI (2018) uses ESG investing synonymously with sustainable investing, socially responsible investing, mission-related investing or screening. They categorize impact investing as a common ESG investment objective and socially responsible investing as a common ESG investment approach. In addition, they define SRI as an umbrella term that can be used to describe a values-based investment approach that aims to reduce exposure to negative externalities. They also use "values-based investing" interchangeably with "ethical investing" or "standards-based investing".

Table 3: Literature review

Study	**Author(s)/ Institution (s)**	**Year of the study**	**Objective**	**Which terms are used interchangeably?**
Socially Responsible and Sustainable Investing: A Review and Appraisal	Camilleri	2017	Presents the opportunities and challenges for SRI	All terms used interchangeably
Sustainable, Responsible, and Impact Investing and Islamic Finance: Similarities and Differences	CFA Institute	2019	Expand knowledge and provide investment professionals with an introduction to Islamic finance and SRI approaches, emphasizing the ethical orientation of both approaches	Sustainable, socially responsible and impact investing are used synonymously. Even the abbreviation for socially responsible investing "SRI" is used for sustainable, responsible and impact-oriented investing
An introduction to Sustainable Investing	FTSE Russell	2020	Define sustainable investing and explain why interest in this approach is growing and how investors can implement a portfolio with a sustainability perspective	Sustainable investments and ESG investments are used synonymously
Can Sustainable Investing Save the World? Reviewing the Mechanisms of Investor Impact	Kölbel, Heeb, Paetzold, and Busch	2020	Try to find out how sustainable investments contribute to social goals and conduct a literature review	Use sustainable investments and ESG investments interchangeably and define sustainable investments as investments that take into account environmental, social and governance (ESG) information

Sustainable Investing: Fast-forwarding its Evolution	KPMG	2020	Examines in detail sustainable investing and its impact on the alternative investment industry	The criterion of SRI, negative screening, is used as it is also a criterion for ESG investments. The exclusion of shares that are not in line with the investor's values is given as an example of ESG instead of SRI. SRI and ESG investments are also used synonymously
Sustainable Investing: How to Do It	Schoenmaker	2018	Describe the process of sustainable investment	Sustainable investing and ESG investing are used synonymously. It is noted that sustainable investments represent a shift from passive investments to active investments supported by ESG ratings
A Guide to Socially Responsible Investing	Whitechurch Securities Limited	2019	Explain the development of investments, why they are becoming increasingly important	Ethical investing, ESG investing and impact investing are all components of socially responsible investing, and the term SRI encompasses all of these types of investments

4. Conclusion

Traditional investment strategies focus on maximizing returns without considering social, environmental, governance or socially responsible aspects. Sustainable investments, i.e. value-based investments, take into account environmental, social and ethical criteria. Not only making a profit with an investment, but also supporting something good is sustainable investing in the narrower sense. However, the terms related to sustainable investing are unclear and are mostly used synonymously in the relevant literature and are not clearly distinguished from each other.

ESG investing, socially responsible investing and impact investing, which are all forms of sustainable investing, are not the same thing and never have been. ESG investing is about investing for good and no sector, company or fund is excluded from investment portfolios. They provide meaningful data on companies' performance in relation to environmental, social and governance criteria. SRI, on the other hand, uses a screening process that allows investors to allocate investments based on socially responsible measures. Impact investing is simply what the name says: investing that has a positive impact on a specific issue. Impact investors do not focus on the direct return of their investments, but place the same, if not greater, emphasis on impact. All these forms of investment could be called complementary investments, which add an additional aspect to value-based investments.

References

Asemah, E. S., Okpanachi, R. A., and Edegoh, L. O. N. (2013). Business Advantages of Corporate Social Responsibility Practice: A Critical Review. New Media and Mass Communication, ISSN 2224-3267 (Paper) ISSN 2224-3275 (Online).

Belaisch, A. (2019). Can Social Investment Be for Profit? An Analysis of the Principles of Impact Finance, Institute of Global Affairs, London School of Economics and Political Science, https://www.lse.ac.uk/iga/assets/documents/research-and-publications/AB-For-profit-social-finance.pdf

Berry, T. C., and Junkus, J. C. (2013). Socially Responsible Investing: An Investor Perspective. Journal of Business Ethics, 112, pp. 707–720, DOI: 10.1007/s10551-012-1567-0.

Boffo, R., and Patalano, R. (2020). "ESG Investing: Practices, Progress and Challenges", OECD Paris.

Camilleri, M. A. (2017). Socially Responsible and Sustainable Investing. In Corporate Sustainability, Social Responsibility and Environmental Management, pp. 61–77. Cham, Switzerland: Springer Nature.

Caplan, L., Griswold, J. S., and Jarvis, W. F. (2013). From SRI to ESG: The Changing World of Responsible Investing. Commonfund Institute.

CFA Institute. (2019). Sustainable, Responsible, and Impact Investing and Islamic Finance: Similarities and Differences, https://www.cfainstitute.org/-/media/documents/survey/sri-investing-and-islamic-finance.pdf

Deliotte. (2020). Advancing Environmental, Social, and Governance Investing-A Holistic Approach for Investment Management Firms, https://www2.deloitte.com/content/dam/insights/us/articles/5073_Advancing-ESG-investing/DI_Advancing-ESG-investing.pdf

Eurosif. (2018). European SRI Study, https://www.eurosif.org/wp-content/uploads/2021/10/European-SRI-2018-Study.pdf

FTSE Russell. (2020). An Introduction to Sustainable Investing, https://content.ftserussell.com/sites/default/files/an_introduction_to_sustainable_investing_final.pdf

Gomes, O. (2020). Optimal Growth under Socially Responsible Investment: A Dynamic Theoretical Model of the Trade-off between Financial Gains and Emotional Rewards. International Journal of Corporate Social Responsibility, 5, https://doi.org/10.1186/s40991-020-00049-z

Goukasian, L., and Whitney, L. K. (2008). Corporate Socially Responsible Firms Perform Well! Evidence from Financial and Operating Performances. Available at SSRN: https://ssrn.com/abstract=972649 or http://dx.doi.org/10.2139/ssrn.972649

GSIA. (2020). Global Sustainable Investment Alliance, Global Sustainable Investment Review. https://www.gsi-alliance.org/wp-content/uploads/2021/08/GSIR-20201.pdf

HSBC. (2018). Sustainable Financing and ESG Investing Report, https://www.hsbc.com/-/files/hsbc/news-and-insight/2018/pdfs/180911-hsbc-sustainable-financing-and-esg-investing-report.pdf?download=1

Kölbel, J. F., Heeb, F., Paetzold, F., &, Busch, T. (2020). Can Sustainable Investing Save the World? Reviewing the Mechanisms of Investor Impact. Organization & Environment, 33(4), pp. 554–574, https://journals.sagepub.com/doi/pdf/10.1177/1086026620919202

KPMG. (2020). Sustainable Investing: Fast-forwarding its Evolution, https://assets.kpmg.com/content/dam/kpmg/xx/pdf/2020/02/sustainable-investing.pdf

Morgan Stanley. (2022). Sustainable Signals Opportunities for Asset Managers to Meet Asset Owner Demands, https://www.morganstanley.com/assets/pdfs/CRC-5066630-GSF_Sustainable_Signals_AM_AO_2022_report_FINAL.pdf

MSCI. (2018). Introducing ESG Investing, https://www.msci.com/documents/1296102/7943776/ESG+Investing+brochure.pdf/bcac11cb-872b-fe75-34b3-2eaca4526237

Niggemann, G. and Brägger, S. (2011). Socially Responsible Investments (SRI), Wealth Management Research, https://thegiin.org/assets/documents/pub/introducing-impact-investing-ubs.pdf

Rizzi, F., Pellegrini, C. and Battaglia, M. (2018). The Structuring of Social Finance: Emerging Approaches for Supporting Environmentally and Socially Impactful Projects. Journal of Cleaner Production, 170, pp. 805–817.

Schoenmaker, D. (2018). Sustainable Investing: How to Do It, Policy Contribution Issue n°23 | November 2018, https://www.bruegel.org/sites/default/files/wp_attachments/PC-23_2018.pdf

Stojanovic, A., Milosevic, I., Arsic, S., Urosevic, S., and Mihaljovic, I. (2020). Corporate Social Responsibility as a Determinant of Employee Loyalty and Business Performance. Journal of Competitiveness, 12(2), pp. 149–166. https://doi.org/10.7441/joc.2020.02.09

Townsend, B. (2020). From SRI to ESG: The Origins of Socially Responsible and Sustainable Investing, https://www.bailard.com/wp-content/uploads/2020/09/History-Socially-Responsible-Investing-and-ESG-Investing.pdf

Whitechurch Securities Limited. (2019). A Guide to Socially Responsible Investing, https://www.whitechurch.co.uk/whitechurch-co-uk/_img/Brochures/Ethical%20Guide%20-%20SRI.pdf

Yan, S., Ferraro, F., and Almandoz, J. (2019). The Rise of Socially Responsible Investment Funds: The Paradoxical Role of the Financial Logic. Administrative Science Quarterly, 64(2), pp. 466–501, https://blog.iese.edu/ferraro/files/2021/10/The-Rise-of-Socially-Responsible-Investment-Funds-The-Paradoxical-Role-of-the-Financial-Logic.pdf

Ömer Faruk TAN

The Impact of Climate Policy Uncertainty on ESG Scores: Evidence from Latin American Countries

Abstract: Addressing sustainability issues has become a critical part of firm's finance strategy. The classical definition of maximizing the wealth of shareholders has transformed with sustainability, taking into account the interests of other stakeholders. In addition, increased serious governmental efforts to reduce environmental footprints in the face of rising abnormal climate events have forced firms to alter their strategies in order to deal with climate-induced policy uncertainty. This study aims to examine whether climate policy uncertainty (CPU) affects the environmental, social and governance (ESG) ratings of 97 companies in six Latin American countries (Argentina, Brazil, Chile, Colombia, Mexico and Peru) for the period between 2005 and 2019. The results show that CPU has a positive and statistically significant effect on ESG in Latin America, implying that firms employ ESG scores to protect themselves from CPU risk. The findings of the study are consistent with those of the existing literature. To the best of our knowledge, this study is the first to analyze the relationship between the CPU index and ESG scores for Latin American firms.

Keywords: ESG, Climate Policy Uncertainty, Latin American Countries

1. Introduction

In the last decade, the subject of climate change has become a critical global issue due to the increasing number of climate related disasters. Sustainable policies that force firms to reduce emissions and transition to renewable energy are supported by many countries (Fox and Alldred, 2020). The 2015 Paris Agreement marked a turning point where all participating countries agreed to cooperate to address the escalating unpredictability of climate (Hoang, 2023). However, the implementation of new climate policies has put pressure on firms, as these rules primarily aim to mitigate emissions, particularly emissions from firms' production (Bartram et al., 2022).

Environmental, social and governance (ESG) issues have gradually gained popularity in practice and academia in recent years. The term "ESG" was first introduced in June 2004 by the United Nations Global Compact, which urged firms to take into account their performance in these areas while conducting business (Drempetic et al., 2020). The United Nations (UN), International

Financial Reporting Standards Foundation (IRFS), and various investment institutions have collaborated to promote ESG and raise awareness in the wider community (Lokuwaduge and Heenetigala, 2017). As a result of their joint efforts, ESG is being increasingly adopted and applied in new areas of research and practice. This expansion is expected to continue into the future (Wang et al., 2023). Sustainability is undeniably the future of business, demanding firms' commitment to lowering their emissions to an acceptable level. However, changing an emissions scheme requires a significant shift in a firm's strategy, as most corporate resources are dedicated to their current approach (Kump, 2021). As climate uncertainty increases and investors become more sensitive to it, firms have become more transparent in terms of their sustainability and explain their ESG criteria in greater detail. The disclosure of sustainability information, which indicates a company's dedication towards being eco-friendly, is critical in meeting market players' demand for Corporate Social Responsibility (CSR). During times of higher climate uncertainty, the importance of sharing information regarding ESG practices improves (Hoang, 2023).

This study examines the relationship between climate uncertainty and ESG disclosures to determine whether companies tend to disclose more ESG criteria in times of higher climate uncertainty. Specifically, it analyzes the impact of climate uncertainty on the ESG disclosure of 97 Latin American companies between 2005 and 2019. According to the International Bar Association (2022), the adoption of ESG criteria is increasing in Latin America and most ESG-related practices are in the environmental, compliance, banking and corporate areas, and approximately 80 % of firms have incorporated ESG in their internal practices. The ESG and climate change regulations for each country are listed in the Appendix of this chapter. Gavriilidis (2021) creates a climate policy uncertainty (CPU) index based on Baker et al. (2016)'s uncertainty index. Due to its recent development, few studies in the extant literature consider the CPU index (Hoang, 2022; Ren et al., 2023; Shang et al., 2022; Ye, 2022; Zeng et al., 2022; Zhang et al., 2022). The first study to examine the relationship between the CPU index and ESG scores was conducted by Hoang (2023) for US companies. This study is, as far as is known, the first to analyze the relationship between the CPU index and ESG ratings for Latin American companies. The rest of this paper is structured as follows. Section 2 explains the literature review and data and methodology are presented in Section 3. The empirical results are presented in Section 4 and finally, the conclusions are presented in Section 5.

2. Literature Review and Hypothesis Development

The development of the CPU index by Gavriilidis (2021) has sparked interest in the impact of CPU on various financial issues such as s energy sources, airline industry, corporate policy. Apergis et al. (2022) explore the effects of CPU on individuals' travel patterns, utilizing the CPU index and US air travel data between 2000 and 2019. Applying causality testing between CPU and US air travel, the findings indicate that CPU has a significant impact on air travel demand to all destinations included in the study. Zeng et al. (2022) analyze the impact of CPU on the wind carbon neutral concept index (CNCI) volatility in China and reveal that CPU has a significant effect on CNCI. Also, Bouri et al. (2022) investigate how the CPU affects green and brown energy stocks and demonstrate that the CPU is a significant factor in determining the performance of green energy stocks compared to brown energy stocks. Additionally, Shang et al. (2022) show that crude oil prices have a positive impact on non-renewable energy consumption, while CPU has a negative impact on consumption in the US over the quarterly data from 2000Q1 to 2021Q3. Wang et al. (2023) analyze data from 557 companies listed in Shanghai and Shenzhen stock exchanges and find that environmental uncertainty negatively affects ESG performance. Although economic growth does not have a significant impact on non-renewable energy consumption, it does have a positive effect on the demand for renewable energy. This positive effect is in contrast to the dampening effect that crude oil prices have on renewable energy demand. In the long run, CPU also has a positive impact on renewable energy demand. When it comes to the impact of environmental uncertainty on firm ESG performance, investor sentiment plays a role in the mediating path between environmental uncertainty and green innovation, which in turn masks the direct impact of environmental uncertainty on ESG performance. This means that firms with high levels of green innovation are more capable of handling environmental uncertainty and tend to have better ESG performance levels. Ye (2022) demonstrates that climate news risk, as measured by the Wall Street Journal climate news index, influences uncertainty in the short, medium, and long term, with the effect being most pronounced in the short run and gradually diminishing thereafter for the US firms.

Following studies consider relationship between uncertainty and firm policy. For example, Ren et al. (2023) examine how CPU affects the financialization of Chinese listed A-share companies between 2007 and 2019. According to their results, an increase in the CPU leads to a decrease in the financialization of companies, with energy-intensive companies being the most affected. Although uncertainty negatively affects the size of firms, the impact depends on the different types of assets. Hoang (2022) explores the impact of CPU on research and development (R&D) investment of heavy emitter firms in the US. Their findings indicate that because of technology and infrastructure concerns, CPU has a negative effect on R&D investment of heavy emitters. This negative impact varies with firm maturity, sentiment, and managerial ability. In another study by Ren et al. (2022), CPU is shown to influence investment decisions using data from 128 Chinese companies in the energy sector from 2007 to 2019. The study demonstrates that the impact of CPU on firm investment is nonlinear, meaning it varies depending on the level of uncertainty. CPU does not seem to significantly impact investments in high-level uncertainty situations; however, it negatively affects investments in low-level uncertainty scenarios. The mining industry is greatly affected by CPU while the electricity, heating, gas, and water sectors benefit positively. Furthermore, Azimli (2023) examines whether US firms with stronger CSR engagement can reduce the negative effect of CPU on their valuation. According to the findings, increased CPU negatively influences firm value, whereas higher CSR-engagement positively effects firm value. More importantly, increased CSR engagement may compensate for the negative impact of CPU on firm value. Finally, Hoang (2023) finds that US firms tend to disclose more ESG information when there is an increase in CPU. Firms utilize ESG reporting as a means to protect themselves from potential risks associated with policy uncertainty. Additional analyzes indicate that firms with more alert audit committees, tighter financial constraints, earnings management problems, higher greenhouse gas emissions, increased utilization of renewable energy, and a better understanding of climate risks experience a more pronounced positive impact from CPU. Based on the literature, the following hypothesis is formulated:

Hypothesis: The impact of the CPU index on ESG scores are positive

3. Data and Methodology

This study investigates the impact of CPU on ESG scores in Latin American countries. The sample comprises firms in Argentina, Brazil, Chile, Colombia, Mexico, and Peru between 2005 and 2019. A total of 97 companies that have ESG scores included. Firm-level data are taken from Thomson Reuters DataStream and the CPU Index Gavriilidis (2021) is obtained from its website[1]. There are some limitations in firm selection. Firms in the financial industry, sports, utility firms and real estate investment trusts are excluded from the sample. Firms with

---

1 https://www.policyuncertainty.com/climate_uncertainty.html

at least four years of consecutive data are selected to be eligible for the panel data methodology (Bond, 2002; Hu and Izumida, 2008). Since the listed firms have different initial public offerings (IPO), an unbalanced panel regression method is utilized to test the hypothesis (Aksoy-Hazır and Tan, 2023). After processing the data, the final sample includes unbalanced data from 97 firms with 769 observations. Table 1 shows the sector classifications of the firms together with the number of observations.

Table 1: Sectoral classification

Sectors	**Obs.**	%	**Sectors**	**Obs.**	%
Aerospace & Defense	10	1.3	Homebuilding & Construction Supplies	10	1.3
Automobiles & Auto Parts	4	0.52	Hotels & Entertainment Services	4	0.52
Beverages	41	5.33	Machinery, Equipment & Components	23	2.99
Chemicals	19	2.47	Media & Publishing	17	2.21
Household Electronics	4	0.52	Metals & Mining	105	13.65
Construction & Engineering	8	1.04	Non-Alcoholic Beverages	10	1.3
Construction Materials	56	7.28	Oil & Gas	57	7.41
Consumer Goods	13	1.69	Paper & Forest Products	23	2.99
Discount Stores	8	1.04	Passenger Transportation Services	15	1.95
Distilleries	18	2.34	Personel & Household Services	10	1.3
Diversified Mining	12	1.56	Pharmaceuticals	18	2.34
Diversified Retail	34	4.42	Professional & Commercial Services	4	0.52
Food & Drug Retailing	25	3.25	Software & IT Services	16	2.08
Food & Tobacco	82	10.66	Specialty Retailers	20	2.6
Freight & Logistic Services	15	1.95	Telecommunication Services	50	6.5
Highway Operators	7	0.91	Transport Infrastructure	31	4.03
			Total	**769**	**100**

To investigate the effects of CPU on ESG, the study of Hoang (2023) is followed.

$$ESG_{i,t} = \beta_o + \beta_1 CPU + YEAR + \ni_{it}; \quad (1)$$

$$ESG_{i,t} = \beta_o + \beta_1 CPU + \beta_2 SIZE_{i,t} + \beta_3 LEV_{i,t} + \beta_4 Q_{i,t} + \beta_5 EBITDA_{i,t} + YEAR + \ni_{it}; \quad (2)$$

In this study, the ESG combined score is used as an independent variable. Environmental (E), social (S), governance (G) and other sub-criteria are also used as independent variables. The CPU is used as the main dependent variable, which is constructed by Gavriilidis (2021). The CPU index is calculated monthly. Since the financial data are annual, the CPU index is calculated as the annual average. In the reduced model (1), CPU is only used as a dependent variable to capture its impact on ESG. In the extended equation (2), firm-specific control variables are added, namely the natural logarithm of total assets, leverage, Tobin's Q and cash flow (Azimli, 2023; Hoang, 2023; Ren et al., 2022; Vural-Yavaş, 2021; Wang et al., 2023). Table 2 below lists the definitions of each variable.

Table 2: Definition of variables

Explanatory Variables	**Definitions**
Climate Policy Uncertainty	Annual average of CPU Index
ESG Combined Score	Overall ESG performance score
Environmental Pillar Score	The average of resource use, emissions, and environmental innovation score
Social Pillar Score	The average of work force, human rights, community, and product responsibility scores
Governance Pillar Score	The average of management, shareholders, and CSR strategy scores.
SIZE	Natural logarithm of total assets
LEV	The ratio of total debts to total assets
Tobin's Q	Market value of equity / book value of equity
EBITDA	Earnings Before Interest and Taxes + Depreciation and Amortization

4. Empirical Findings and Discussions

Table 3 shows the descriptive statistics of the variables. The table presents summary statistics for ESG score, CPU Index and Environmental, Social and Governance score, as well as its sub-categories and sub-dimensions. It also includes information on the firm-level control variables.

The empirical results for models (1) and (2) are presented in Table 4. First the suitability of the pooled ordinary least squares (POLS), fixed effects (FE), and random effects (RE) models are determined. The F-test and the Breusch-Pagan LM test show that the FE and RE models are more appropriate to use than

Table 3: Descriptive statistics

Variables	Obs.	Mean	Std. Dev.	Min.	Max.
ESG	769	45.296	21.878	0.98	89.83
Environmental Score	769	41.787	28.176	0	96.05
Social Score	769	48.480	27.413	0.44	96.86
Governance Score	769	50.615	22.138	0.43	96.07
CSR Strategy Score	769	42.377	33.315	0	98.78
Community Score	769	51.923	30.505	0.64	99.54
Emissions Score	769	47.151	23022,00	0.95	100
Environmental Innovation Score	769	18.295	26.784	0	98.08
Human Rights Score	769	40.078	36.050	0	99.28
Management Score	769	51.672	27.992	0.27	99.42
Resource Use Score	769	46.936	32.496	0	99.74
Shareholders Score	769	52.591	28.442	0.54	99.42
Workforce Score	769	55.275	30.476	0.14	99.56
Climate Policy Uncertainty	769	125.409	36.999	66.038	192.001
SIZE	769	18.069	2.595	11.717	25.680
LEVERAGE	769	0.2933	0.178	0	1.521
TOBIN'S Q	769	116.388	1.224	0.017	18.679
EBITDA	769	0.123	0.147	-1.354	2.662

the POLS model. According to the result of the Hausman test, the FE model is determined to be the best-fitting model. Next, an analysis of the FE model is conducted to assess its validity, and diagnostic tests for heteroscedasticity, autocorrelation, and serial correlation are performed. As these issues are prevalent, the robust standard error estimator known as Driscoll and Kraay's test is utilized. Furthermore, the variance inflation factor (VIF) is calculated to test the model's multicollinearity, the VIF value for each variable is determined to be less than 10 (Guizani, 2017).

In Table 4, columns (1) and (2) show the reduced form with FE. Column (3) includes the baseline model and control variables. Even though the FE model is determined to be the most suitable, columns (4) and (5) show the results based on RE. According to the analysis, the coefficient of CPU is statistically significant and positive at 1 % level, indicating that CPU and ESG scores have a positive correlation. For every unit increase of the CPU, ESG disclosure rises by 0.022 standard deviation. This result supports the hypothesis of this study and is consistent with the findings of a previous study in the existing literature (Hoang, 2022), which found that Latin American companies also increase their

Table 4: Empirical results

	FE	FE	FE	RE	RE
	1	2	3	4	5
CPU	0.09003***	0.20817***	0.14263***	0.19904***	0.20147***
	(0.018)	(0.023)	(0.022)	(0.039)	(0.028)
SIZE			6.75040***		
			(0.605)		
LEV			-3.02519		
			(2.538)		
TOBIN'S Q			0.76477***		
			(0.219)		
EBITDA			0.61900		
			(1.604)		
Constant	YES	YES	YES	YES	YES
Year	NO	YES	YES	YES	YES
Sector	NO	NO	NO	NO	YES
Country	NO	NO	NO	YES	YES
Observations	769	769	769	769	769
Number of groups	97	97	97	97	97
Prob > F	0.000	0.000	0.001		
Prob > chi2				0.000	0.000
Hausman			0.001		
R-squared	0.0811	0.1844	0.240	0.2835	0.2835
Driscoll-Kraay standard errors in parentheses. *** p<0.01, ** p<0.05, * p<0.1					

ESG disclosure in times of CPU. Firms demonstrate greater commitment to ESG policies when uncertainty increases. SIZE and Tobin's Q show a positive relationship with ESG scores and have statistically significant and positive results at 1 % level (Hoang, 2023; Wang et al., 2023) Leverage has a negative and statistically insignificant relationship with ESG (Wang et al., 2021), which is consistent with the findings of Husted and Sousa-Filho (2019), who also find insignificant results for Latin American firms. Finally, EBITDA has a positive but insignificant relationship to ESG scores.

In addition to the ESG score, it is also examined subcategories and subdimensions. Table 5 presents the results of these analysis. According to the results, the CPU is positive and statistically significant at 1 % level for the individual E, S, and G variables. For the environmental criteria, during periods of uncertainty, firms try to increase their capacity to reduce the use of materials

Table 5: Empirical results for subcategories and subdimensions

	E			
	Environmental	**Resource Use**	**Emission**	**Environmental Innovation**
	1	**2**	**3**	**4**
CPU	0.26145***	0.17941***	0.15648***	0.4961***
	(0.0162)	0.012	(0.013)	(0.045)
Control variables	YES	YES	YES	YES
Constant	YES	YES	YES	YES
Year	YES	YES	YES	YES
Observations	769	769	769	769
Number of groups	97	97	97	97
Prob>F	0.000	0.000	0.000	0.000
R-squared	0.356	0.324	0.267	0.159
	S			
	Social	**Workforce**	**Human Rights**	**Community**
	5	**6**	**7**	**8**
CPU	0.27952***	0.18739***	0.43744***	0.03539
	(0.015)	(0.018)	(0.040)	(0.031)
Control variables	YES	YES	YES	YES
Constant	YES	YES	YES	YES
Year	YES	YES	YES	YES
Observations	769	769	769	769
Number of groups	97	97	97	97
Prob>F	0.000	0.000	0.000	0.000
R-squared	0.266	0.138	0.228	0.162
	G			
	Governance	**CSRStrategy**	**Management**	**Shareholders**
	9	**10**	**11**	**12**
CPU	0.19677***	0.28954***	0.24112***	-0.01286
	(0.023)	0.031	(0.020)	(0.054)
Control variables	YES	YES	YES	YES
Constant	YES	YES	YES	YES

(*Continued*)

Table 5: Continued

	G			
	Governance	**CSRStrategy**	**Management**	**Shareholders**
Year	YES	YES	YES	YES
Observations	769	769	769	769
Number of groups	97	97	97	97
Prob>F	0.000	0.000	0.000	0.000
R-squared	0.215	0.281	0.167	0.020
Driscoll-Kraay standard errors in parentheses. *** p<0.01, ** p<0.05, * p<0.1				

to find efficient solutions for supply chain management, reduce environmental emission in the production and operations process (Vural-Yavaş, 2021) and reduce the environmental costs to create new market opportunities through new environmental technologies. For the social criteria, firms try to increase the effectiveness of job satisfaction, a healthy and safe workplace, respect to fundamental human right conventions under uncertainty. Finally, for the governance criteria, under climate uncertainty, firms make contribution to improve their corporate governance principles and CSR strategy.

5. Conclusion

Decisions taken by companies in sustainable finance policies have become crucial for investors in recent years. The implementation of ESG criteria for firms has gained importance since its introduction in 2004. In addition, the implementation of various climate agreements such as the 1992 United Nations Framework Convention on Climate Change, the 1997 Kyoto Protocol, and the 2015 Paris Agreement has highlighted the significant environmental implications of business activities (Hoang, 2023). The importance of ESG criteria has also increased. This study analyzes the impact of the CPU on the ESG ratings of 97 Latin American companies in Argentina, Brazil, Chile, Colombia, Mexico, and Peru between 2005 and 2019. This is, so far as is known, the first study conducted for Latin American countries. The findings indicate that in times of increased CPU, firms want to increase their ESG scores to improve their transparency towards their investors. They want to invest in ESG criteria to reduce the negative impact of uncertainty. Taken together, the results suggest that regulators and investors should pay more attention to the relationship between CPU and ESG scores. There are also some limitations of this study. First, the COVID-19 period is not taken into account. Second, macroeconomic variables such as interest rates, inflation and gross domestic product were not included in the analysis. Future studies can then analyze the impact of the pandemic. In addition, ownership structure, financial constraints, board of directors and management skills could be included for subgroup analysis.

References

Aksoy-Hazır, Ç., & Tan, O. F. (2023). The impact of geopolitical risk on cash holdings policy: Evidence from an emerging market. *Managerial Finance*. https://doi.org/10.1108/MF-01-2022-0024

Apergis, N., Gavriilidis, K., & Gupta, R. (2022). Does climate policy uncertainty affect tourism demand? Evidence from time-varying causality tests. *Tourism Economics*, 1–15. https://doi.org/10.1177/13548166221110540

Azimli, A. (2023). The impact of climate policy uncertainty on firm value: Does corporate social responsibility engagement matter? *Finance Research Letters, 51*. https://doi.org/10.1016/j.frl.2022.103456

Baker, S. R., Bloom, N., & Davis, S. J. (2016). Measuring economic policy uncertainty. *Quarterly Journal of Economics, 131*(4), 1593–1636. https://doi.org/10.1093/qje/qjw024.Advance

Bartram, S. M., Hou, K., & Kim, S. (2022). Real effects of climate policy: Financial constraints and spillovers. *Journal of Financial Economics, 143*, 668–696. https://doi.org/10.1016/j.jfineco.2021.06.015

Bond, S. R. (2002). Dynamic panel data models: A guide to micro data methods and practice. *Portuguese Economic Journal, 1*(2), 141–162. https://doi.org/10.1007/s10258-002-0009-9

Bouri, E., Iqbal, N., & Klein, T. (2022). Climate policy uncertainty and the price dynamics of green and brown energy stocks. *Finance Research Letters, 47*. https://doi.org/10.1016/j.frl.2022.102740

Drempetic, S., Klein, C., & Zwergel, B. (2020). The influence of firm size on the ESG score: Corporate sustainability ratings under review. *Journal of Business Ethics, 167*(2), 333–360. https://doi.org/10.1007/s10551-019-04164-1

Fox, N. J., & Alldred, P. (2020). Re-assembling climate change policy: Materialism, posthumanism, and the policy assemblage. *British Journal of Sociology, 71*(2), 269–283. https://doi.org/10.1111/1468-4446.12734

Gavriilidis, K. (2021). Measuring climate policy uncertainty. *SSRN Electronic Journal*. https://doi.org/10.2139/ssrn.3847388

Guizani, M. (2017). The financial determinants of corporate cash holdings in an oil rich country: Evidence from Kingdom of Saudi Arabia. *Borsa Istanbul Review, 17*(3), 133–143.

Hoang, H. V. (2023). Environmental, social, and governance disclosure in response to climate policy uncertainty: Evidence from US firms. In *Environment, Development and Sustainability*. https://doi.org/10.1007/s10668-022-02884-5

Hoang, K. (2022). How does corporate R&D investment respond to climate policy uncertainty? Evidence from heavy emitter firms in the United States. *Corporate Social Responsibility and Environmental Management*, *29*(4), 936–949. https://doi.org/10.1002/csr.2246

Hu, Y., & Izumida, S. (2008). Ownership concentration and corporate performance: A causal analysis with Japanese panel data. *Corporate Governance: An International Review*, *16*(4), 342–358. https://doi.org/10.1111/j.1467-8683.2008.00690.x

Husted, B. W., & Sousa-Filho, J. M. de. (2019). Board structure and environmental, social, and governance disclosure in Latin America. *Journal of Business Research*, *102*, 220–227. https://doi.org/10.1016/j.jbusres.2018.01.017

International Bar Association Forum. (2022). *ESG survey results report : ESG in Latin America*.

Kump, B. (2021). When do threats mobilize managers for organizational change toward sustainability? An environmental belief model. *Business Strategy and the Environment*, *30*(5), 2713–2726. https://doi.org/10.1002/bse.2773

Lokuwaduge, C. S. D. S., & Heenetigala, K. (2017). Integrating environmental, social and governance (ESG) disclosure for a sustainable development: An Australian study. *Business Strategy and the Environment*, *26*(4), 438–450. https://doi.org/10.1002/bse.1927

Ren, X., Li, W., Duan, K., & Zhang, X. (2023). Does climate policy uncertainty really affect corporate financialization? *Environment, Development and Sustainability*. https://doi.org/10.1007/s10668-023-02905-x

Ren, X., Shi, Y., & Jin, C. (2022). Climate policy uncertainty and corporate investment: Evidence from the Chinese energy industry. *Carbon Neutrality*, 1–14. https://doi.org/10.1007/s43979-022-00008-6

Shang, Y., Han, D., Gozgor, G., Mahalik, M. K., & Sahoo, B. K. (2022). The impact of climate policy uncertainty on renewable and non-renewable energy demand in the United States. *Renewable Energy*, *197*(April), 654–667. https://doi.org/10.1016/j.renene.2022.07.159

Vural-Yavaş, Ç. (2021). Economic policy uncertainty, stakeholder engagement, and environmental, social, and governance practices: The moderating effect of competition. *Corporate Social Responsibility and Environmental Management*, *28*(1), 82–102. https://doi.org/10.1002/csr.2034

Wang, K.-H., Xiong, D.-P., Mirza, N., Shao, X.-F., & Yue, X.-G. (2021). Does geopolitical risk uncertainty strengthen or depress cash holdings of oil enterprises? Evidence from China. *Pacific-Basin Finance Journal*. https://doi.org/https://doi.org/10.1016/j.pacfin.2021.101516

Wang, W., Sun, Z., Wang, W., Hua, Q., & Wu, F. (2023). The impact of environmental uncertainty on ESG performance: Emotional vs. rational. *Journal of Cleaner Production, 397*. https://doi.org/10.1016/j.jclepro.2023.136528

Ye, L. (2022). The effect of climate news risk on uncertainties. *Technological Forecasting and Social Change, 178*. https://doi.org/10.1016/j.techfore.2022.121586

Zeng, Q., Ma, F., Lu, X., & Xu, W. (2022). Policy uncertainty and carbon neutrality: Evidence from China. *Finance Research Letters, 47*(PB), 102771. https://doi.org/10.1016/j.frl.2022.102771

Zhang, D., Wang, C., & Dong, Y. (2022). How does firm ESG performance impact financial constraints? An experimental exploration of the COVID-19 pandemic. *European Journal of Development Research, 0123456789*. https://doi.org/10.1057/s41287-021-00499-6

Appendix

Country	ESG Related Regulations	Description	Climate Change Related Regulations
Argentina	N/A	There is currently no specific national regulation for ESG reporting by companies. However, some companies in Argentina are voluntarily adopting mainly environmental practices	Renewable Energy and Energy Efficiency Law (Law 27.191)
Brazil	BC Resolution No. 139/ 2021 and BC Instruction Standard No. 153/2021	In September 2021, a package of solutions and requirements on ESG disclosure was launched. There are other financial instrument regulations such as the criteria for granting rural loans.	National Policy on Climate Change (PNMC)
Chile	Ministry of Finance launched a Taxonomy to promote green investments	Taxonomy is presented as a tool to define a common language between what is understood as environmentally sustainable. In addition, ISO 26000 is voluntary, but has been implemented by 50 % of the multinationals. It consists of providing companies with guidelines and orientation for adopting socially responsible behavior with their environment, considering the social and environmental impacts they may produce.	Law on General Bases of the Environment (Law 19300)

Colombia	Green Taxonomy and External Circulars 008 and 020 adopted by SFC in 2022	Promotes and facilitates the channeling of resources towards sustainable investments and defines the primary guidelines for the development of green finance. instructions on the content of the prospectus for environmental, social, and/or industry and knowledge economy bonds. Companies have also adopted standards such as ISO26,000 on a voluntary basis.	There is significant weight in laws on environmental protection issues. Law 1931 of 2018
Mexico	Sustainable Finance Committee. such as: (1) Sustainable Taxonomy; (2) Leveraging Capital Mobilization Opportunities (3) ESG Risk Measurement (4) Disclosure of Information and Adoption of ESG Standards	CNBV (regulator of banking and public companies) will present aggregated results of these diagnostics and will conduct a pilot application of the taxonomy with the participation of voluntary financial institutions, with three main objectives: climate change, financial inclusion and gender inclusion.	Compendium of 13 laws and regulations derived from the different standards (NOM, NMX) applicable to each environmental area; water, soil, air, rural development, waste, among others.

(Continued)

Table 5: Continued

Country	ESG Related Regulations	Description	Climate Change Related Regulations
Peru	N/A	There is currently no specific regulation for CSR reporting by companies. However, some companies in Peru are voluntarily adopting sustainability reporting practices.	The purpose of the Framework Law on Climate Change is to establish the principles to reduce the country's vulnerability to climate change, take advantage of the opportunities of low-carbon growth and comply with the international commitments assumed by the State.

Source: This data is taken from https://www.kreston.com/article/esg-committee-update/

Firm-Year Observations		
Country	**Obs.**	**%**
Argentina	50	6,50
Brazil	290	37,71
Chile	69	8,97
Colambia	47	6,11
Mexico	252	32,77
Peru	61	7,93
Total	**769**	**100**

Sena YILMAZ ARSLAN

Sustainable Markets and Abnormal Weather: Exploring the Impact of Climate Risks on Sustainable Investing in Turkey

Abstract: Global warming, as a result of climate change, has important economic and financial effects on society. But these effects are not fully explored yet. The risks related to climate change are categorized into physical and transition risks. Since Turkey is one of the countries currently impacted by the physical dangers of climate change, the study's objective is to advance awareness of the financial effects of those risks. Specifically, this study explores how investor preferences and attitudes toward sustainable investments are affected by physical climate risks in the context of the Salience Theory. Physical climate risks are measured using temperature anomalies and precipitation anomalies. The trading volume of the BIST Sustainability Index is used as a proxy for sustainable investing. The results indicate that there is no relationship between abnormal weather and the trading volume of the BIST Sustainability Index, implying that abnormal weather does not lead to a change in investors' decisions.

Keywords: Sustainability, Climate Change, Climate Finance, Climate Risk, Physical Risk

1. Introduction

One of the significant challenges of today's world is climate change. The warming of the planet will have economic and financial implications which are yet not well understood in society because of the long-term nature and the abstract concept of the topic which makes it difficult to predict the risks and their consequences. Nevertheless, the consequences of climate are not only in the future, they have started to impact economies today. Investors, financial institutions, and governments must have a thorough understanding of climate change's effects on financial markets to be able to make informed decisions that will reduce risks and take advantage of opportunities. The risks related to climate change are categorized by the Task Force on Climate-related Financial Disclosures (TCFD) into transition risks and physical risks. The risks of shifting to a low-carbon economy that result from changes in market conditions, technology, policy, or law are referred to as transition risks. Physical risks are related to risks caused by climate events or shifts in climate patterns (TCFD, 2017).

Turkey is one of the countries which is already affected by the physical risks of climate change. The rising number of climate disasters, draughts, and high temperatures are showing the beginning of this challenge. According to the G20 Climate Risk Atlas temperatures can rise to 2.7°C by 2050 in Turkey if the current high carbon pathway remains. In this worst-case scenario in 2050 Turkey will face agricultural droughts 37 % more frequently, heatwaves will last 4242 % longer, and overall climate change will lead to a loss of 2.26 % in GDP (CMCC, 2021).

Concerning the above-explained development, interest in sustainable investments, as an umbrella term containing green investments, is rising as finance plays a pivotal role in the climate change challenge. Therefore, academic research concentrates on comprehending how climate change will affect financial markets. On the one hand, the literature which examines the influence of climate and weather phenomena on different dimensions of financial decisions shows mainly that climate risks lead to investment decisions in favor of sustainable investing (Ardia et al., 2022; Choi et al., 2020; Marshall et al. 2021). On the other hand, research demonstrates that the prices of assets that are subject to climate risks fall after exposure to these risks (Bernstein et al., 2019; Bertolotti et al., 2019; McCoy and Walsh, 2018). In this regard, local weather events are used as a proxy for climate change. As physical climate risks in the form of weather events or natural disasters attract great attention and are therefore salient, an important part of the literature is based on the salience theory. Salience is the phenomenon wherein the information in a specific part of the environment will be given greater importance in subsequent decisions when one's attention is unevenly focused therein as compared to other parts of the environment (Bordalo et al., 2012). In this context, investors are expected to adapt their investment decision to climate change after severe events related to climate change because such salient events come to mind more easily.

Hereof, the purpose of this study is to investigate how climate risks and increased concerns about climate change affect financial decisions, with a specific focus on sustainable firms in the case of Turkey. Specifically, the study seeks to answer the following research questions; What is the relationship between climate risks and sustainable investing in Turkey? So, this study explores how investor preferences and attitudes toward sustainable investments are affected by physical climate risks. Physical climate risks are measured using abnormal weather developments as these are omnipresent in the perception of investors and are therefore regarded as salient information. Regarding this, the relationship between the trading volume of the BIST Sustainability Index and abnormal weather is examined using data on temperature anomalies and precipitation anomalies. The salience of these weather anomalies is tested using Google Trends data for climate change.

The contributions made should be of wide interest in understanding sustainable investment as there is a growing trend toward sustainable investing, which is expected to play an increasingly crucial role in financial markets. Furthermore, the unchartered area regarding the consequences of the financial implications of climate change will be illuminated. The research is also contributing to the behavioral finance literature as it shed light on the influence of salience information on investors' behavior empirically. Finally, although there is a growing body of literature on the effects of climate change on financial markets, to our knowledge, this study is the first to investigate the relationship between climate risks and sustainable investing in Turkey. The USA is the primary subject of prior research that attempts to determine how climate change may affect financial markets. By examining this relationship, the study makes a unique contribution to the literature on sustainable finance and behavioral finance in Turkey.

2. Salience Theory

Tversky and Kahneman (1974) argue that people use several heuristics and biases to evaluate the probability of risky situations to reduce the complexity of the decision-making process. In general, heuristics describe the phenomena of quick decision-making using what first comes to mind (Gennaioli and Shleifer, 2010). This does not mean that people are not capable of complex and analytical decision processes but due to cognitive limitations, people focus only on some available aspects regarding the decision. Such reasoning is referred to as "local thinking" as only one portion of relevant information in the decision-making process is used (Bordalo et al., 2012).

The Salience Theory of choice under risk (Bordalo et al., 2012) is based on the availability bias defined by Tversky and Kahneman (1974). According to the availability bias the risk assessment is done based on how easily related information is brought to mind rather than using all the available information. One of the factors which affect the availability is salience as it makes information easily retrievable and recent occurrences are expected to be more available.

In this regard, salience is a cognitive psychological concept that enables humans to focus their limited cognitive resources on a relevant subset of available data. This available data will be overemphasized in the following judgments. So, according to the salience theory, decision-makers favor the upside of a risky option when it is salient and act in a risk-seeking manner. Conversely, they favor the downside when it is salient and act in a risk-averse manner (Bordalo et al., 2012).

In the context of climate finance, the salience framework is used to explain the relationship between climate change and financial decisions and the underlying decision process of investors. Climate change and the climate risks that come with it are seen as salient when analyzed in the context of natural disasters or abnormal weather. Such salient events are expected to change investors' behavior (Bernstein et al., 2019; Choi et al., 2020; Marshall et al. 2021; McCoy and Walsh, 2018).

3. Literature Review

Despite the negative effects of climate change on the economy, climate finance literature is only newly emerging. The financial implications of climate change are analyzed using a wide set of different perspectives. Overall, the empirical literature on climate finance quantifies the relationship between climate and the economy. In this regard, the relationship between several climate risks which are mainly divided into climate and transition risks, and the pricing of different assets is examined. It is also important to mention that climate risks are at the attention of investors relatively new. Therefore, the analyzes made mainly focus on more recent data, time series which are longer than 15 years are not suitable in this context (Giglio et al., 2021).

The literature which analyzes the impact of climate risks on asset prices reveals that prices of assets that are exposed to climate risks both physical and transition are negatively affected. One of the analyzed markets is the housing market. Bernstein et al. (2019) show that the sea level rise led to a discount in coastal property prices in the US which are expected to be exposed to sea level rise. According to McCoy and Walsh (2018), house prices face price shocks in wildfire risk zones in the year following wildfires. Rehse et al. (2019) compare the trading volume and the bid-ask spread of stocks of Real Investment Trusts in and outside of the affected area by Hurricane Sandy. Their result shows that the trading volume decreases and the bid-ask spread increases in the affected area. Bertolotti et al. (2019) show that around extreme weather events US electric utility security prices drop and their volatility increases.

Some researchers analyze the effect of climate risks on financial decisions with a more comparative perspective. Here, climate phenomena are used as natural experiment situations. The main idea is that with the rise of concerns about climate change investors change their preferences in favor of green investments. It is expected that concerns about climate change rise with the occurrence of climate disasters or abnormal weather which are regarded as salient information. Some studies underline this assumed relationship by using data on Google Searches or the coverage of the climate change topic in the media (Ardia et al., 2022; Choi et al., 2020; Marshall et al., 2021). Major US newspapers are used by Ardia et al. (2022) to create a daily proxy for assessing unexpected rises in climate change worries. By using this proxy, the authors demonstrate that when concerns about climate change rise, green company stock performance outperforms that of brown company stock performance. Choi et al. (2020) analyze the effects of abnormally high temperatures on stock prices for a range of cities worldwide. Their results suggest that in times of high temperatures investors prefer climate-friendly stocks because their belief in global warming changes. Marshall et al. (2021) examine whether climate disasters influence the inflows into mutual funds dividing the funds into green and brown funds in eight US states. Inflows into green funds are larger in times of the occurrence of climate disasters.

The literature which directly examines investor preferences and attitudes regarding climate finance shows that investors consider climate risks in their decisions. Dessaint and Matray (2017) illustrate how the occurrence of a hurricane increases the risk perceived by managers in the US, resulting in an increase in cash holdings. The survey on institutional investors worldwide by Krueger et al. (2020) supports prior empirical evidence. The majority of their respondents confirm that climate risks are important for their investment decisions.

To conclude, the newly emerging climate finance literature aims to capture the financial implications of climate change in two ways. First, the literature shows that climate risks negatively influence the prices of assets that are exposed to those risks. Second, the literature shows that with the rise of concerns regarding climate change especially after natural disasters related to climate change investors' preference towards sustainable investments rise. Additionally, it should be noted that the literature mainly focuses on the USA.

4. Data and Methodology

In this section, the obtained data regarding the BIST Sustainability Index, the Google Search Volume Index and the weather, the variables created, and the linear regression models of the study will be explained respectively.

4.1. BIST Sustainability Index

The BIST Sustainability Index (XUSRD) is a benchmark index that tracks the performance of companies listed on the Istanbul Stock Exchange that meet certain sustainability criteria. The constituents of the index are voluntary companies whose ESG score, which is calculated by Refinitiv, is at least 50. According to Borsa Istanbul, one of the aims of the index is to indicate how the constituents handle sustainability challenges like global warming, the draining of natural resources, health, security, and employment (Borsa Istanbul, n.d.). In this regard, XUSRD is used as a proxy for the overall sustainability investment in the Turkish market as it contains among others environmental considerations. Trading volume is chosen in particular as it reflects the level of investor interest. So, the monthly trading volume of XUSRD for the time frame from December 2014 to December 2022 is used as the dependent variable. The time frame was chosen because XUSRD was launched on 4th November 2014. The data is obtained from the Finnet 2000 Plus database.

4.2. Google Search Volume Index

Google Trends provides data on Google Searches on a particular topic or a particular search term. The Search Volume Index (SVI) for the topic "Global Warming[1]" for Turkey in the analyzed time frame is obtained from Google Trends. The SVI for a topic rather than on a search term is chosen as the data is aggregated for different searches on the same topic and the data is cleaned for misspellings, different languages, etc. The SVI data does not show the absolute search volumes but is a normalized index showing the interest in a topic on a scale from 0 to 100. This data is used as a proxy for general interest in Turkish society for climate change.

4.3. Weather

As a measure of physical climate risk, the monthly average temperatures (°C) and the monthly total precipitation ($mm = kg \div m^2$) for all weather stations in Turkey are obtained from the Turkish State Meteorological Service. The data for temperature and precipitation are chosen as they are among other environmental indicators used in the measurement of climate change by the Republic of Turkey Ministry of Environment, Urbanization and Climate Change (Republic of Turkey Ministry of Environment, Urbanization and Climate Change, n.d.).

---

1 Turkish: "Küresel Isınma".

Temperature is directly related to climate change and is an indicator of a changing situation according to the pressures of global warming. Furthermore, temperature is a salient information that investors face in their daily lives. So, according to the Salience Theory positive-signed temperature anomalies are expected to strengthen the beliefs of investors in global warming related to climate change. To calculate the temperature anomalies, first, the average monthly temperature for the whole of Turkey is calculated using the monthly average temperature data of all weather stations in Turkey. Second, the long-term average temperature for each month is subtracted from the calculated average monthly temperature for each matching month to get the monthly temperature anomaly (*temp_an*). The long-term average temperature for each month is the average temperature measured in the time frame 1991–2020. This temperature is regarded as the "normal temperature" by the meteorological service. Deviations from these temperatures are regarded as anomalies (Turkish State Meteorological Service, n.d.a).

The second measure used is the total precipitation. Precipitation is also very strongly related to climate change. The combination of changes in the precipitation regime and temperature increases can cause extreme hydrological events such as floods and droughts. Especially in the case of Turkey, there are severe risks of droughts and long-term desertification, which are directly related to precipitations. In this regard, negative-signed precipitation anomalies, which are assumed to be salient, are expected to lead to changes in investors' choices regarding sustainable investments. The preparation of the precipitation anomaly variable (*precip_an*) is similar to the temperature anomaly. Here, the long-term average precipitation (1991–2020) is used. So, for both weather variables, the long-term deviation is calculated. These deviations/anomalies are briefly referred to as abnormal weather in the following.

4.4. Methodology

The relationship between the Google search volume index on global warming and abnormal weather and the relationship between the trading volume of the BIST Sustainability Index and abnormal weather will be examined using linear regression. Table 1 provides the summary statistics for the variables discussed above that will be used in the analysis.

Table 1: Summary statistics

Variable	Obs.	Mean	Std. Dev.	Min	Max
Vol	97	232.86	332.86	27.80	1914.96
temp_an	97	0.65	1.46	-5.46	3.10
precip_an	97	-2.32	19.61	-51.41	63.01
svi	97	4.44	9.99	0.5	100

In the first step, the relationship between the interest in the topic of global warming using *svi* and abnormal weather using *temp_an* and *precip_an* is analyzed. It is assumed that the general Google searches on this topic reflect the attitude of investors. Further, it is expected that temperature anomalies are positively related to the SVI because high temperatures are associated with global warming. Precipitation anomalies are expected to be negatively related to global warming as low precipitation leads to droughts. This analysis is performed to test the salience of the extreme weather variables. The following regression analysis is performed;

$$svi(i,t) = \beta 0 + \beta 1 \ x \ temp\_an(i,t) + \beta 2 \ x \ precip\_an(i,t) + \epsilon$$

In the second step, the relationship between the trading volume of XUSRD and the abnormal weather variables is examined. It is expected that temperature anomalies positively affect the trading volume (*vol*) because investors prefer sustainable investments because their concerns about global warming rise when temperatures rise. The same relationship is expected with precipitation anomalies in a negative way because negative precipitation anomalies lead to droughts. The regression formula is as follows;

$$vol(i,t) = \beta 0 + \beta 1 \ x \ temp\_an(i,t) + \beta 2 \ x \ precip\_an(i,t) + \epsilon$$

5. Results

The findings from four regression analyzes are reported in this section in two parts. In the first part, the relationship between the abnormal weather variables and Google Searches and the relationship between abnormal weather variables and the trading volume of XUSRD are presented. As a result of the insignificant results in the first part, in the second part, two further regression analyzes are conducted using two dummy variables that try to capture extreme weather.

5.1. Google Searches, Abnormal Weather, and Trading Volume

The results of regression analyzes are presented in Table 2. The first regression tries to capture the relationship between the interest in global warming and abnormal weather. Contrary to the expectation the effect of the weather on the interest in the topic of global warming and thus climate change is only partially significant. There seems to be no effect of abnormal temperatures on the Google searches made on the topic. But for the precipitation anomaly, there is a negatively significant relationship as expected.

The results of regression between the trading volume of XUSRD and the extreme weather are insignificant. There seems to be no relationship between the trading volume and the weather anomalies. This result is no surprise with respect to the results of the first regression as it can be seen that weather anomalies do not lead to a significant rise in interest in global warming at all. So, it cannot be assumed, that investors' concerns about global warming rise. Therefore, the hypothesis regarding the second regression becomes irrelevant.

Table 2: Regression results – Google searches, abnormal weather, and trading volume

	(1) svi	**(2) vol**
temp_an	0.248	11.30
	(0.35)	(0.47)
precip_an	-0.103*	-2.938
	(-1.94)	(-1.66)
N	97	97
R-sq	0.046	0.037
adj. R-sq	0.025	0.016

t statistics in parentheses
* $p < 0.1$, ** $p < 0.05$, *** $p < 0.01$

5.2 Extreme Weather and Trading Volume

The first question which comes to mind regarding these unexpected results is whether the weather anomalies are not "salient enough". To answer this question further regression analyzes are done with new variables regarding the weather. The new variables are calculated as dummies with the aim to capture more "extreme" weather rather than overall anomalies.

The temperature dummy (*temp_dummy*) is created using the temperature anomaly variable. Here, the anomaly data which deviates more than one standard deviation from the mean is marked as "1", assuming that higher anomalies are more salient.

The precipitation dummy (*precip_dummy*) is created using the precipitation anomaly variable. In this case, a slightly different methodology is used. The

Table 3: Regression results – Google searches, extreme weather, and trading volume

	(1) svi	(2) vol
temp_dummy	-2.686	38.76
	(-0.90)	(0.38)
precip_dummy	5.844**	55.61
	(2.26)	(0.63)
N	97	97
R-sq	0.052	0.008
adj. R-sq	0.032	-0.013

t statistics in parentheses
* p < 0.1, ** p < 0.05, *** p < 0.01

dummy variable is created using the meteorological methodology percent of normal index (PNI). The PNI is calculated as a percentage by dividing the average precipitation by the long-term average precipitation. If the PNI is equal or above to 70 % there is a risk of medium-grade meteorological drought and therefore observations with a PNI equal or above to 70 % are marked as "1" (Turkish State Meteorological Service, n.d.b).

The results of the regression with the dummy variables can be seen in Table 3. The regression of *temp_dummy* and *precip_dummy* with *svi* verifies the results of the first part showing that the effect of extremely low precipitation increases searches on the topic of global warming with a higher significance. The relationship between extreme weather and trading volume is insignificant similar to the results of the first part. Further, the low R-squared values indicate that weather anomalies have barely explain variations in investment decisions. However, for models which assess human behavior like in this study low R-squared values are acceptable (Ozili, 2022). Other publications in this field (Choi et al., 2020; Marshall et al. 2021) show also R-squared values below 0.05.

To conclude, there seems to be no relationship between weather anomalies and sustainable investing in Turkey. Nevertheless, it can be assumed that this is not due to the lack of salience. Similar studies in the literature (Bernstein et al., 2019; Choi et al., 2020; Marshall et al. 2021; McCoy and Walsh, 2018) show contrary results compared to the findings of this study. Their results show that consistent with the salience theory attention to climate change rises with the realization of events related to climate change. At the same time, the realization of such events leads to a change in investment behaviors in favor of sustainable investment alternatives. It should be noted that the mentioned papers mostly use samples from the USA. This study is the first to analyze the impact of climate risks on sustainable investment for Turkey. As Turkey is an emerging country the dynamics which influence investment behaviors could be different to a developed country like the USA. Possible other reasons for the reported unexpected results will be discussed in the following conclusion.

6. Conclusion

According to the salience theory people will overemphasize available data in the decision-making process due to cognitive limitations. In the context of this paper, it is assumed that abnormal weather is salient and therefore leads to changes in investment decisions in favor of sustainable investment based on prior research (Bernstein et al., 2019; Choi et al., 2020; Marshall et al., 2021; McCoy and Walsh, 2018). In the first part, the relationship between abnormal weather and the trading volume of the XUSRD is examined. Abnormal weather is measured with two variables showing the monthly temperature anomalies and the monthly precipitation temperature anomalies for the analyzed time frame. But the results of this study are not like expected. The regression results reveal that there is no relationship between abnormal weather and the trading volume of XSURD implying that abnormal weather does not lead to a change in investors' decisions. This result is supported by regression of abnormal weather and Google Searches on the topic of global warming. The impact of abnormal weather on the search volume is only partially and slightly significant indicating that weather anomalies do not rise attention to global warming. In the second part, the same regression analyzes are done with dummy variables which are formed to measure extreme weather rather than just the deviation from the normal. The aim is to test the salience of weather. The findings of the second part, verify the first part. No relationship between extreme weather and the trading volume of XUSRD is found. But the regression with the SVI demonstrates that extremely low precipitation significantly influences Google Searches on global warming.

There are several possible reasons for the unexpected findings of this paper. Firstly, the main assumption regarding the salience of abnormal weather is not totally verified. The results indicate that precipitation is salient but temperature is not. This could be explained by the fact that drought is more visible and that droughts are one of the most severe climate risks which Turkey faces. In future research, the effects of more salient weather phenomena like natural disasters could be examined. Nevertheless, it can be seen that rising concerns about droughts do not lead to a change in investment decisions. Secondly, it is possible that XUSRD investors are not investing in companies listed on this index due to environmental considerations. The sustainability index captures also social and governmental topics, leading to the question of which factors determine the decision to choose sustainable investment alternatives. Future studies can conduct surveys or interviews on this topic. Finally, it should be mentioned that climate change and sustainable investment are relatively new concepts and are newly popular in society. So, analyzes are only suitable for more recent time frames. Statistical significance may be captured on this topic in the future with the use of larger time series.

References

Ardia, D., Bluteau, K., Boudt, K., & Inghelbrecht, K. (2022). Climate change concerns and the performance of green vs. brown stocks. *Management Science*, Article mnsc.2022.4636. Advance online publication. https://doi.org/10.1287/mnsc.2022.4636

Bernstein, A., Gustafson, M. T., & Lewis, R. (2019). Disaster on the horizon: The price effect of sea level rise. *Journal of Financial Economics, 134*(2), 253–272. https://doi.org/10.1016/j.jfineco.2019.03.013

Bertolotti, A., Basu, D., Akallal, K., & Deese, B. (March 2019). *Climate risk in the US electric utility sector: A case study.* https://doi.org/10.2139/ssrn.3347746

Bordalo, P., Gennaioli, N., & Shleifer, A. (2012). Salience theory of choice under risk. *The Quarterly Journal of Economics, 127*(3), 1243–1285. https://doi.org/10.1093/qje/qjs018

Borsa Istanbul. (n.d.). Sustainability Indices. Retrieved May 27, 2023, from https://www.borsaistanbul.com/en/sayfa/2227/sustainability-indices

Choi, D., Gao, Z., & Jiang, W. (2020). Attention to global warming. *The Review of Financial Studies, 33*(3), 1112–1145. https://doi.org/10.1093/rfs/hhz086

CMCC. (2021). G20 Climate Risk Atlas: Turkey.

Dessaint, O., & Matray, A. (2017). Do managers overreact to salient risks? Evidence from hurricane strikes. *Journal of Financial Economics, 126*(1), 97–121. https://doi.org/10.1016/j.jfineco.2017.07.002

Gennaioli, N., & Shleifer, A. (2010). What comes to mind. *The Quarterly Journal of Economics, 125*(4), 1399–1433.

Giglio, S., Kelly, B., & Stroebel, J. (2021). Climate finance. *Annual Review of Financial Economics, 13*(1), 15–36. https://doi.org/10.1146/annurev-financial-102620-103311

Krueger, P., Sautner, Z., & Starks, L. T. (2020). The importance of climate risks for institutional investors. *The Review of Financial Studies, 33*(3), 1067–1111. https://doi.org/10.1093/rfs/hhz137

Marshall, B. R., Nguyen, H. T., Nguyen, N. H., Visaltanachoti, N., & Young, M. (2021). Do climate risks matter for green investment? *Journal of International Financial Markets, Institutions and Money, 75*, 101438. https://doi.org/10.1016/j.intfin.2021.101438

McCoy, S. J., & Walsh, R. P. (2018). Wildfire risk, salience & housing demand. *Journal of Environmental Economics and Management, 91*, 203–228. https://doi.org/10.1016/j.jeem.2018.07.005

Ozili, Peterson K., The Acceptable R-Square in Empirical Modelling for Social Science Research (June 2022). Social research methodology and publishing results, http://dx.doi.org/10.2139/ssrn.4128165

Rehse, D., Riordan, R., Rottke, N., & Zietz, J. (2019). The effects of uncertainty on market liquidity: Evidence from Hurricane Sandy. *Journal of Financial Economics, 134*(2), 318–332. https://doi.org/10.1016/j.jfineco.2019.04.006

Republic of Turkey Ministry of Environment, Urbanization and Climate Change. (n.d.). Environmental Indicators. Retrieved May 27, 2023, from https://cevreselgostergeler.csb.gov.tr/en

TCFD. (June 2017). *Recommendations of the task force on climate-related financial disclosures.*

Turkish State Meteorological Service. (n.d.a). Aylık Sıcaklık Analizi. Retrieved May 27, 2023, from https://www.mgm.gov.tr/veridegerlendirme/sicaklik-analizi.aspx?s=a#sfB

Turkish State Meteorological Service. (n.d.b). Kuraklık Analizi. Retrieved May 27, 2023, from https://www.mgm.gov.tr/veridegerlendirme/kuraklik-analizi.aspx?d=yontemsinif#sfB

Tversky, A., & Kahneman, D. (1974). Judgment under uncertainty: Heuristics and biases. *Science, 185*(4157), 1124–1131.

Carsten-Henning SCHLAG

Corporate Social Responsibility and Its Importance in the World of Sustainability

Abstract: The aim of this chapter was to critically discuss the concept of Corporate Social Responsibility (CSR) from both theoretical and applied perspectives. The current understanding of CSR aims to capture a complex phenomenon that includes societal, environmental, and economic dimensions, among others. Prioritizing one dimension over another is not conducive to sustainability. The European Commission (2011) has set clear signals with its CSR definition and political initiatives. CSR activities provide benefits to companies that ultimately translate into improved success. These benefits include gaining a competitive advantage over their competitors. However, the numerous political initiatives of the past decade should not overshadow the need for a critical examination of CSR. The study addresses three aspects in this regard: the foremost role and task of companies for society, the accusation of "greenwashing," and the withdrawal of state institutions from financing and influencing the social or cultural sphere.

Keywords: Corporate Social Responsibility, Competitive Advantage, Sustainability

1. Introduction

Due to numerous corporate scandals, economic-ethical issues have become an integral part of today's sociopolitical discourse. This applies not only to currently much-discussed environmental or climate-related problem areas. Recently, a scandal from the international financial sector once again made headlines worldwide. In mid-March 2023, the economic collapse of the major bank Credit Suisse had to be prevented by the Swiss government with over 200 billion Swiss francs. The bank was sold to another bank with the support of government funds. Numerous misconducts by the corporate management and mismanagement had destroyed the trust in the long-standing bank, which had existed since 1856, within a few years. Investors lost their assets, and many employees were at risk of losing their jobs. The collapse of such a bank, which was among the 30 largest banks in the world, would have had fatal consequences for the entire Swiss economy and could have triggered massive effects in the international financial sector.

The subsequent sociopolitical discussion about the social role of internationally operating companies touches upon the topic area of companies, society, and values, which is addressed in this study. However, demands for socially responsible companies are not an invention of the 21st century (Gröneweg and Matiaske, 2018). The historical roots of socially motivated activities by companies can be traced back to ancient Roman law, as seen by Latapi Agudelo et al. (2019). Even back then, entrepreneurial initiatives established hospitals and orphanages for the elderly and the needy (Latapi Agudelo et al., 2019). With the spread of Christianity, the ideas of socially engaged companies further developed in the following centuries, both in Europe and the USA. In Germany, in particular, entrepreneurial engagement for the social environment has a long tradition. An early example of this was provided by the Fugger family, which founded a social settlement for needy citizens of the city of Augsburg as early as the 16th century (Gröneweg and Matiaske, 2018). During the industrialization in the 19th century, renowned entrepreneurs such as Alfred Krupp, Ernst Abbé, or Robert Bosch practiced entrepreneurial engagement for the social environment.

In the scientific literature, the social responsibility of companies, or CSR, was initially discussed primarily in the Anglo-Saxon context. Latapi Agudelo et al. (2019), who provide a systematic literature review of the development of CSR, attribute the beginning of the academic discussion on CSR to the early 1930s. Following that, there was a lively debate in academic journals, books, and magazines. According to Hiss (2007), the debate has become even more intense since the 1990s. In practice, CSR has evolved from a theoretical concept to an integral part of entrepreneurial actions (Hopkins, 2006). In the political sphere, numerous initiatives to promote CSR activities were launched at the national and international levels in the early 2000s. The European Commission (2011) emphasizes that companies can align their CSR concept with important internationally recognized principles and guidelines. Notable examples include the OECD Guidelines for Multinational Enterprises, the ten principles of the United Nations Global Compact, the ISO 26000 standard on social responsibility, the International Labour Organization's Declaration on Multinational Enterprises and Social Policy, and the UN Guiding Principles on Business and Human Rights. Furthermore, the European Commission developed a CSR strategy for the member countries of the European Union in 2011, which is in line with the aforementioned guidelines.

Overall, CSR receives considerable attention in academia, politics, and business practice, and has even become somewhat of a buzzword. However, there is a lack of clear understanding in the public about what CSR actually means in specific cases. Often, the term CSR is interpreted differently in various contexts. Before delving into a detailed explanation of CSR, it is important to establish a precise definition of the term. In general usage, CSR is often mistakenly used synonymously with sustainability. However, in theory, the concept of CSR is more narrowly defined. CSR essentially refers to the concrete contribution of a company to sustainable business practices (BMAS, n.d.). More recently, the term Corporate Responsibility (CR) has also been used interchangeably with CSR. By avoiding the word "social" or the German word "sozial," the focus is shifted away from the mistaken assumption that CSR solely pertains to the social dimension of corporate sustainability (BMAS, n.d.). Instead, the economic dimension of the topic is emphasized. In this regard, CSR is distinguished from the term Corporate Citizenship (CC). CC exclusively refers to the social engagement of companies beyond their core business activities. According to BMAS (n.d.), CC encompasses the area of charitable engagement by companies (e.g., sponsorship, donations, and foundation activities). Heblich and Gold (2010) describe CC as a phenomenon in which companies present themselves as good corporate citizens by collaborating advantageously and in the long term with the local community.

The aim of this chapter is to present and critically reflect on the concept of CSR from both a theoretical and applied perspective. The perspective is not specifically focused on business administration, but also explicitly addresses values and ethics in entrepreneurial actions. Additionally, macroeconomic considerations are incorporated into the argumentation. The structure of this chapter is as follows: Following the introduction, the second chapter presents the relevant theoretical and empirical foundations on the topic. The third chapter addresses the question of how companies can utilize their social engagement to enhance their competitiveness and gain specific competitive advantages over their rivals. Chapter four and five give an overview about CSR in politics and practice. The sixth chapter concludes with a discussion that includes a summary and interpretation of the findings. Furthermore, recommendations for practice and an outlook are provided.

2. Corporate Social Responsibility (CSR)

CSR refers to the social responsibility of companies, i.e., the responsibility of companies for the impact of their business actions or the physical existence of the organization on society and the environment. These impacts can be social, ecological, and economic in nature. This section presents relevant theoretical and empirical foundations on the topic of "Companies, Society, and Values." It begins with theoretical foundations and the understanding of the concept of CSR. Subsequently, various reasons for companies to engage in CSR activities are discussed from the perspective of the companies and illustrated with examples.

2.1. Theoretical Foundations

Tanner et al. (2018) discuss three approaches that constitute the essential theoretical foundations for understanding CSR: organizational sustainability, Carroll's Pyramid Model (1979, 1991), and Freeman's Stakeholder Theory (1994). Corporate responsibility is associated with the concept of sustainability or sustainable behavior of organizational members. According to concept of Elkington (1994), organizational sustainability encompasses three areas characterized by economic, environmental, and social objectives (Tanner et al., 2018). Only when all three areas are pursued on an equal footing and in parallel, can long-term and sustainable success be achieved by organizations. According to some authors, the equal implementation of the three areas often falls short in practical application. Tanner et al. (2018) emphasize that in practice, the economic goals of companies clearly take precedence, while social and environmental goals often receive only limited commitments.

Carroll's Pyramid Model (1979, 1991) specifically addresses the social responsibility of companies (Tanner et al., 2018). The model integrates the two components of values and ethics into the originally purely economic perspective. Carroll (1991) distinguishes four levels of social responsibility for companies: economic, legal, ethical, and philanthropic. The model, as depicted in Figure 1, assumes a pyramid shape for CSR. The economic responsibility of companies, i.e., organizations should strive to operate at least cost-covering, forms the foundation of CSR. The market-driven incentive for the organization is profit-making, which is achieved through offering products and services that satisfy customer needs (Carroll, 1991).

The second level is the legal responsibility of companies. Society expects organizations to comply with legal provisions (e.g., requirements, laws, regulations) (Tanner et al., 2018). This level already reflects a certain inclination towards considering ethical standards and moral requirements at the societal level (Carroll, 1991). The third level encompasses the broader ethical responsibility of companies. It pertains to the societal expectation that organizations act fairly and ethically, beyond what is necessary or within the legal framework (Tanner et al., 2018). Ethical demands on companies change over time as the legal framework is modified due to evolving societal beliefs (Carroll, 1991). The fourth and highest level of the pyramid model describes the philanthropic responsibility and charitable engagement (e.g., sponsoring food banks in cities) of the company to improve the general quality of life in society (Tanner et al., 2018). Carroll (1979) emphasizes that the societal responsibility of companies extends beyond the economic and legal levels. The four levels influence each other according

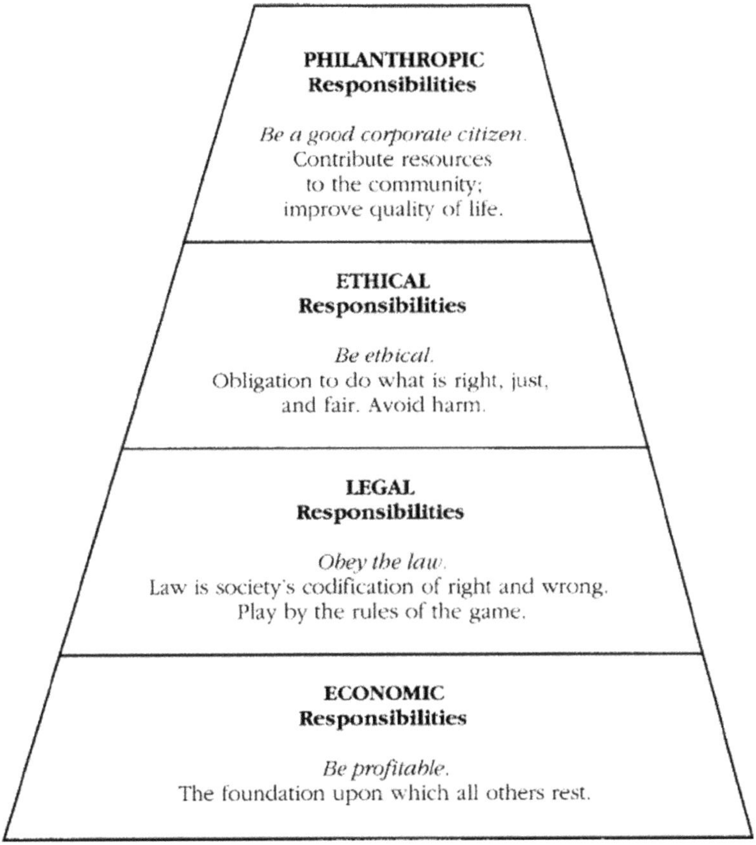

Figure 1: Carroll's Pyramid Model
Source: Carroll, 1991

to Carroll (1991) and are difficult to separate in practice. In recent years, both the ethical and philanthropic levels have gained importance. Society increasingly expects companies to assume comprehensive social responsibility and demands this, for example, regarding environmentally sustainable production of goods and services.

The third approach mentioned by Tanner et al. (2018) is Stakeholder Theory of Freeman (1994). According to this approach, the long-term economic success of an organization or business depends on the extent to which the interests of stakeholder groups, such as shareholders, customers, suppliers, competitors, employees, communities, local associations, and environmentalists, are taken into account or how well the enterprise can maintain and expand relationships and contacts with these diverse interest groups (Tanner et al., 2018). The Stakeholder Theory thus extends the so-called Shareholder Theory. This theory, advocated by economist and Nobel laureate Milton Friedman in the 1970s, states that a company is only accountable to its financial stakeholders (e.g., shareholders, owners), meaning the primary goal of the company is to generate profit for the shareholders (Friedman, 1970).

2.2. Conceptual Definitions

The WBCSD (World Business Council for Sustainable Development) defines CSR as "…continuing commitment by business to behave ethically and contribute to economic development while improving the quality of life of the workforce, their families as well as of the local community and society at large" (WBCSD, 2000, p. 10). The OECD (Organization for Economic Co-operation and Development) regards CSR as "business contribution to sustainable development" (OECD, 2001, p. 13). Accordingly, corporate behavior should not only ensure returns for shareholders, wages for employees, and goods and services for consumers but also address social and environmental concerns and values. According to the European Commission (2001), the social responsibility of companies is a concept "…that serves as a basis for companies to integrate social and environmental concerns into their business operations and their interactions with stakeholders on a voluntary basis. Acting in a socially responsible manner means not only complying with legal provisions but also investing 'more' beyond mere legal compliance in human capital, the environment, and relationships with other stakeholders" (European Commission, 2001, p. 7). This definition aligns with Carroll's (1979) idea that CSR goes beyond the economic responsibility of companies. The profitability of a company is rather understood as a framework or starting point for CSR (Tanner et al., 2018). Additionally, it explicitly addresses stakeholders, not just shareholders, of the companies.

The European Union's (EU) strategy for promoting CSR, formulated in 2001, has undergone significant revision since then. In the "Europe 2020" strategy, the European Commission committed to renewing the EU strategy for promoting CSR (European Commission, 2011). The global financial and economic crisis of 2008/2009 was also a reason for the redefinition. The resulting social consequences diminished trust in companies to some extent, and the public has since become more aware of companies' social and ethical performance (European Commission, 2011). Since 2011, the European Commission has used a modified definition of CSR. According to this definition, CSR is defined as "the responsibility of companies for their impact on society" (European Commission, 2011, p. 7). The European Commission further states: "This responsibility can only be fully met if companies respect applicable laws and established agreements between social partners. In order for companies to fully meet their social responsibility, they should have a process in place that allows for the integration of social, environmental, ethical, human rights, and consumer concerns into business operations and core strategies in close collaboration with stakeholders" (European Commission, 2011, p. 7).

2.2.1 Reasons for Conducting CSR Activities

Zerbini (2017) discusses various reasons why organizations or companies should conduct CSR activities. Firstly, CSR activities are considered a competitive advantage for the company, which can improve the organization's reputation in the long term (Resource-Based View). This specific aspect regarding competitive advantages is further explored in the application part of this work. CSR activities are also seen as a means of entrepreneurial self-fulfillment (Stewardship Theory). According to this perspective, managers of the company carry out CSR activities "...because they believe it is the right thing to do, also if their decision will affect firm performance negatively" (Zerbini, 2017, p. 2). Furthermore, CSR is carried out to meet the expectations of other market participants, in order to establish a certain alignment or consensus (Institutional Theory). Ultimately, CSR is implemented to substantially serve the diverse interests of stakeholders (Stakeholder Management Theory) (Tanner et al., 2018).

The European Commission (2011) also provides arguments for conducting CSR activities, but focuses more on internal motivations. It views CSR activities as a strategic approach to improving the competitiveness of companies. Accordingly, this can promote risk management, cost savings, as well as enhance access to capital, customer relationships, human resource management, and innovation capacities of companies. CSR requires a certain interplay of internal and external stakeholders, enabling companies to better adapt to the ever-changing expectations of society. From this, companies can derive direct benefits by accessing new markets and generating long-term growth opportunities.

2.3 Dimension of CSR

The European Commission (2001) distinguishes two dimensions when aligning CSR activities: the internal dimension, where CSR activities are understood in relation to intraorganizational processes and the employees of the company, and the external dimension, which encompasses all CSR activities directed at actors outside the company (Tanner et al., 2018).

2.3.1 Internal Dimension of CSR

Regarding the internal dimension, socially responsible actions within companies primarily concern the workforce, i.e., the employees. This involves investments in human capital, occupational safety, health protection, coping with organizational change, as well as environmental compatibility and the management of natural resources (European Commission, 2001). The company's own employees are key stakeholders who should receive special attention in terms of CSR activities. The needs of employees regarding occupational safety standards and health protection are, therefore, core areas of CSR activities. The areas of responsibility of human resource management, such as improving equal opportunities, facilitating work-life balance, job security, or professional development, which significantly influence employee motivation and overall satisfaction, also constitute part of internally oriented CSR activities, according to the European Commission (2001) (Tanner et al., 2018).

Furthermore, adaptability in organizational change is seen as an important component of internal CSR activities (European Commission, 2001). This area concerns the interests of various stakeholders (e.g., employees, shareholders). Change processes always involve certain uncertainties. For successful implementation of, for example, restructuring measures, it is beneficial to reduce the uncertainty experienced by those affected through comprehensive stakeholder participation. This requires continuous and transparent information as well as timely consultation with all stakeholders (Tanner et al., 2018). According to the European Commission (2001), companies can mitigate the social and local impacts of restructuring by engaging in regional economic development partnerships or active labor market policies, such as social plans. Finally, environmental compatibility and the management of natural resources within an organization are also part of the internal dimension of CSR activities. This includes reducing resource consumption, environmental pollution, and waste production, as stated by the European Commission (2001). More efficient resource utilization strengthens profitability and improves the competitiveness of companies.

2.3.2 External Dimension of CSR

The European Commission (2001) points out that the social responsibility of companies does not end at factory gates or in modern office spaces. It extends into local and regional communities and involves a wide range of stakeholders beyond employees and shareholders, including business partners, suppliers, customers, and authorities. Furthermore, the financial and economic globalization of the past forty years has highlighted the importance and necessity of global governance, particularly in terms of upholding human rights and international labor standards. Activities related to global environmental and climate protection have also gained significance. Voluntary CSR activities of companies can make a significant contribution in these areas (European Commission, 2001).

3. Competitive Advantages through CSR

According to Zerbini (2017), one important reason why organizations or companies engage in CSR activities is to develop competitive advantages. This means that there are explicit incentives for companies to engage in socially responsible practices beyond the usual business and legal requirements. For instance, Hardt (1995) and Reinhardt (1998) emphasize the competitive advantages that can be gained through CSR activities related to environmental responsibility. Russo and Fouts (1997) also highlight the positive relationship between environmental CSR activities and firm performance.

3.1 Key Findings from Meta-studies

Two meta-studies conducted by Loew and Clausen (2010) and Perrini et al. (2011) analyzed various primary studies that examined the relationship between CSR activities and resulting competitive advantages. While Perrini et al. (2011) provided a comprehensive review of literature spanning the last four decades, the meta-study by Loew and Clausen (2010) focused on the period after 2003. Loew and Clausen (2010) state that studies from 2003 onwards adopted the current understanding of CSR, influenced by the European Commission (2001), to determine competitive advantages. According to this understanding, CSR primarily focuses on the environmental and social responsibility within the core business activities of companies, whereas corporate citizenship activities (such as donations, volunteering, and sponsorship) that reflected the understanding of CSR until the late 1990s, are now considered as only one aspect of CSR. Perrini et al. (2011) concluded from their analysis of existing studies that there is little doubt that CSR can be advantageous for companies. The following are the main findings from Loew and Clausen (2010). The authors considered that competitive advantages resulting from CSR are composed of advantages gained in different areas of CSR activities. These include factors such as good working conditions, environmental protection within the company, ecological product responsibility, and responsible procurement. Loew and Clausen (2010) analyzed nine primary studies conducted between 2003 and 2009. They summarized the mentioned competitive advantages as follows: cost efficiency (energy and material efficiency), risk reduction, improvement of risk management, building and protecting reputation and brands, employee motivation, attraction and retention of talent, fostering innovation, strengthening customer relationships, developing new business through new products or entering new markets, and enhancing investor relations (investor dialogue or financial communication).

3.2 In-depth Analysis of Specific Areas

Loew and Clausen (2010) state that the cost reduction advantages identified in the studies mostly stem from specific environmental protection measures. This involves reducing the overall operating costs of companies through conscious and controlled consumption and use of energy and other input factors as capital and labor for the production of goods and services. In the long term, there are potential savings through resource-efficient production along the entire value chain of companies. Promoting reputation and strengthening the brand are often cited competitive advantages induced by CSR. Stakeholders' decisions to support a company or purchase a product are no longer based solely on economic factors. Nowadays, people want to identify with the company or product in order to invest in the company or make a purchase (Nguyen, 2013). Companies that take social responsibility appeal to certain stakeholders, such as investors, customers, and employees, on an emotional level. The intended positive effects of CSR contributions on building and protecting the company's reputation, strengthening the brand, risk reduction, and risk management are closely related to whether and to what extent CSR activities are viewed as a strategic advantage by companies (Branco and Rodrigues, 2006; McWilliams and Siegel, 2010; Surroca et al., 2010). A systematically approached CSR management can have a positive impact. Heblich and Gold (2010) argue that companies use CSR as a strategic tool to secure their long-term business foundation. Loew and Clausen (2010) further argue that the size of the company ultimately plays a significant role. For large and internationally operating corporations, reputation is a crucial control variable that affects, among other things, business success. For small and medium-sized enterprises (SMEs), this advantage provided by CSR may be less relevant in terms of significance.

Competitive advantages regarding employee motivation and the attraction and retention of professionals and executives can be generated, particularly by considering employee interests. CSR has a positive influence on a company's reputation. The higher or more established the reputation, the more attractive the company becomes to skilled professionals. However, the CSR activities of a company not only affect potential employees but also benefit existing employees. Positive working conditions such as family-friendliness, fairness, flexibility, occupational health and safety, etc. increase employee loyalty, thereby avoiding personnel turnover. Employee orientation generally enhances employee satisfaction and motivation, both of which are important factors for business success (Nguyen, 2013). Loew and Clausen (2010) state that for SMEs, attracting and retaining skilled professionals and motivating their employees are particularly important.

Furthermore, CSR activities can generate competitive advantages when they contribute to fostering innovation, strengthening customer relationships, developing new business through new products or entering new markets, and improving investor relations. The expertise induced by CSR activities within the company, along with highly motivated professionals, are important resources for companies to potentially develop innovative products. These can help overcome the challenges of a globalized economy by tapping into new markets. CSR strengthens the relationship with customers as responsible actions of a company are increasingly considered in the purchasing decision for a product. A systematic CSR management that transparently communicates these activities can increase the attractiveness of companies to investors. Therefore, it appears possible that CSR activities improve companies' access to capital (Nguyen, 2013).

4. CSR in Politics

The topic of CSR has gained significant attention in the socio-political debate in recent years. At the international level, important initiatives and measures have been adopted and implemented by organizations such as the UN, EU, OECD, and ISO. The European Commission (2001) addressed the European framework for corporate social responsibility in its Green Paper, sparking a broad discussion on the topic. The United Kingdom was a pioneer in Europe, appointing a CSR Minister in the mid-2000s to establish a unified framework for social and environmental reporting of companies and the labeling of CSR activities in the UK (Beile et al., 2010). In November 2010, the ISO published the ISO 26000, a guidance standard providing recommendations on how organizations should behave responsibly. The application of this guidance is voluntary. In Germany, the standard was published as DIN ISO 26000 and serves as an internationally accepted reference framework applicable to various types of organizations, not just businesses (BMAS, 2011). The standard defines seven fundamental principles for exercising social responsibility, including accountability, transparency, ethical behavior, respect for stakeholder interests, adherence to the rule of law, respect for international behavior standards, and respect for human rights (BAMS, 2011). These principles should be applied to the core areas of social responsibility, as defined by the ISO: organizational governance, fair operating practices, human rights, consumer issues, labor practices, the environment, and community involvement and development (BAMS, 2011).

In 2011, the European Commission revised its definition of CSR and presented an updated EU strategy (2011–2014) for corporate social responsibility (European Commission, 2011). At the end of 2014, the European Commission documented the CSR strategies implemented by individual EU member states until September 2014, and in 2019, it published an update on the progress report (European Commission, 2019). In Germany, the "CSR Action Plan" of the federal government, introduced in 2010, serves as the basis for CSR initiatives (Deutscher Bundestag, 2016). Since then, the federal government has been pursuing a systematic CSR strategy. To develop this national strategy and facilitate further progress, the Federal Ministry of Labour and Social Affairs (BMAS) established the National CSR Forum in January 2009, which consists of experts from business, trade unions, non-governmental organizations (NGOs), and politics (Deutsche Bundesregierung, 2010). The forum convenes twice a year and can be described as a multi-stakeholder body (BMAS, n.d.). The CSR Action Plan aimed to better integrate CSR into companies and public administration, engage SMEs in CSR, increase the visibility and credibility of CSR, optimize the political framework for CSR, and contribute to the social and environmental shaping of globalization (Deutsche Bundesregierung, 2010, p. 6). These strategies are still valid and continue to be pursued, with some of them already fully implemented. Key steps in the further development of the national CSR strategy include supporting SMEs, strengthening international alignment (EU, G20, ILO), and the formation of the "Berlin CSR Consensus on Corporate Responsibility in Supply and Value Chains" in 2018, which describes management and leadership principles for responsible supply chain management (BMAS, n.d.). The latter describes management and leadership principles for responsible supply chain management. To make CSR initiatives more widely known to the public and businesses, the German federal government initiated the internet portal "CSR in Deutschland" (CSR in Germany) as an important milestone. It is a website managed by the Federal Ministry of Labour and Social Affairs (BMAS) that consolidates and provides centralized access to all CSR content of the government (Deutscher Bundestag, 2016).

At the international level, the OECD revised its Guidelines for Multinational Enterprises in 2011, incorporating human rights and due diligence as additional topics (BMAS, n.d.). In Europe, the EU adopted Directive 2014/95/EU in 2014, which regulates the assumption of corporate social responsibility by companies and the transparency thereof. This directive constitutes the significant legal framework for EU member states, including Germany (BMAS, n.d.). According to this directive, large companies with more than 500 employees must publish a non-financial statement from 2018 onwards (based on information from the fiscal year 2017) (European Commission, 2017). This statement is essentially a CSR report that must be prepared in accordance with the guidelines issued by the European Commission (2017). In late 2016, the German federal government adopted the "National Action Plan on Business and Human Rights," which established for the first time the responsibility of German companies to respect human rights. This was preceded by the United Nations' Guiding Principles on Business and Human Rights issued in 2011, which are based on the three pillars of state duty to protect, corporate responsibility, and access to remedy. Furthermore, in 2021, Germany enacted the Supply Chain Due Diligence Act (Lieferkettensorgfaltspflichtengesetz, LkSG), which legally regulates the responsibility of German companies to respect human rights in global supply chains (BMAS, n.d.).

5. CSR in Practice

Companies have been assuming responsibility for their social environment long before the international efforts of the UN, EU, ILO, and OECD over the past 25 years. Heblich and Gold (2010) emphasize that CSR has a long tradition in Germany, even if it was not always referred to as such. An early example was provided by the Fugger family, who established a social housing settlement for needy citizens of the city of Augsburg in the 16th century (Gröneweg and Matiaske, 2018). During the industrialization period in the 19th century, entrepreneurial engagement for the social environment was practiced by well-known entrepreneurs such as Alfred Krupp, Ernst Abbé, or Robert Bosch. They voluntarily introduced initial regulations in the areas of occupational safety and leisure compensation within their companies, which later evolved into generally applicable labor and social laws (Heblich and Gold, 2010). The German social legislation by Bismarck was particularly influenced by Alfred Krupp's General Regulation of 1872, which granted privileges to the company's employees (affordable housing, health insurance coverage) (Gröneweg and Matiaske, 2018).

Despite this sometimes very long-standing tradition of corporate social responsibility in Germany, it cannot be denied that the significance of CSR for general business practice has increased in recent years due to the aforementioned international efforts. Bleile et al. (2010) analyze the topic of CSR in relation to the involvement of employee representatives based on five case studies of companies including Norsk Hydro, Danone, Beiersdorf, Unilever, and Wilkhahn. The website "CSR in Germany" provides information on CSR activities in practice for both the interested public and companies (BMAS, n.d.). For companies seeking information, concrete information and tips for implementing CSR activities are provided for various areas of the business, such as management and governance, personnel, environmental management, procurement and supply chains, logistics and mobility, IT management, research and development, and communication. Furthermore, there are reports available on industry-specific developments and activities of companies. CSR impulses from individual companies are provided, categorized by company size. For example, detailed information on CSR impulses from BASF SE, REWE Group, and SAP SE is available for large companies (BMAS, n.d.).

The German federal government also promotes its CSR Award competition on the "CSR in Germany" website, which has been awarded in different categories (company sizes, special categories) in 2013, 2014, 2017, and 2020. In addition to the competition, the award ceremony also establishes a network of participating companies. Around 600 previous competition participants and interested individuals from various companies attended the 2nd networking meeting on April 13, 2021. Furthermore, the mentioned website features a CSR self-assessment test, which is intended to provide initial guidance for companies that have not yet established CSR management. The questions are divided into several topic areas: recognition of social responsibility within the company, communication with stakeholders, and action areas such as corporate governance, market, workplace, environment, and community (BMAS, n.d.). Especially for SMEs that are not covered by the aforementioned reporting requirement (non-financial statement), implementing voluntary CSR management offers competitive advantages by distinguishing themselves from competitors of similar company sizes. Therefore, SMEs should perceive CSR as an opportunity, not as an additional task without value for the company.

6. Discussion and Conclusion

The current understanding of CSR aims to capture a complex and multifaceted phenomenon that encompasses societal, ecological, and economic dimensions, among others. Prioritizing one dimension over another in terms of the social responsibility of companies is not conducive to long-term or sustainable perspectives. The European Commission (2011) has set clear signals with its definition of CSR (responsibility of companies for their impacts on society) and its political initiatives, as demonstrated in Section 4. It emphasizes the urgent need, from a societal and environmental policy perspective, for companies in today's globalized economy to assume social responsibility for their actions and their social environment, and to integrate CSR activities as a strategic element into their core business. CSR activities, which have both internal and external dimensions, provide benefits for the companies involved, resulting in long-term improvement in success. The potential benefits lie in the fact that CSR activities bring competitive advantages to companies compared to their competitors. These were discussed in Section 3 and ultimately represent the economic dimension of CSR.

However, the numerous national and international political initiatives of the past decade should not overshadow the need for a critical examination of the CSR concept. From a scientific perspective, a critical reflection on CSR is recommended before far-reaching recommendations are derived for policy and practice. Firstly, it is about the actual and central role and task of companies in the economic process. Section 2.1 introduced Freeman's stakeholder theory (1994), which provides an approach for the theoretical foundation of CSR. It is in clear contradiction to the shareholder theory. Liberal economists, especially Milton Friedman (1962, 1970), see the sole responsibility of a company as increasing its profit, as they should be solely accountable to their shareholders. He justifies this based on the principles of the market economy. According to Friedman, the potential threat of competition does not allow companies to assume social responsibility; they do not have the financial freedom or leeway to solve societal problems (Friedman, 1970). Furthermore, according to Friedman's argumentation, companies cannot assume societal responsibility, as this is only possible through individuals. However, the actions of individuals within companies should align with the interests of the shareholders, as managers and employees are employed by the shareholders of the company (Jonker et al., 2011). Levitt (1958) holds a similar opinion to Friedman, stating pointedly, "Welfare and society are not the corporation's business. Its business is making money, not sweet music" (Levitt, 1958, p. 47).

The economic theory advocated by Levitt and Friedman dates back to the 1960s, but it should not necessarily be considered antiquated. Undoubtedly, economic ideas and perspectives have evolved over time. Nowadays, only a few economists still adhere to the concept that social and economic goals are inherently contradictory. The economic landscape has undergone fundamental changes due to globalization, climate change, and advancements in information and communication technology. The interdependencies in production and trade between companies are much stronger today than in the 1960s and 1970s. Nevertheless, it is important not to overburden companies with tasks and responsibilities that go beyond purely financial objectives. Therefore, it seems appropriate, for example, for larger companies in the EU, which have greater financial resources, to have reporting obligations for CSR activities while exempting smaller and medium-sized enterprises (SMEs). Investments in CSR activities generally represent short-term costs for companies (Branco & Rodrigues, 2006), which, according to liberal economic thinking, must be borne either by consumers or shareholders. Higher costs, ceteris paribus, i.e., under otherwise equal conditions, initially reduce entrepreneurial profit. Many of the competitive advantages attributed to CSR activities in Section 3, such as enhancing brand reputation, employee satisfaction, and motivation, are not necessarily of a tangible nature and are therefore difficult to measure monetarily and directly attribute to activities. The benefits resulting from the positive effects of CSR activities often only occur in the medium or long term, if at all (Branco and Rodrigues, 2006). Particularly for SMEs, the focus of critical consideration often lies on the short-term costs of CSR activities.

Another aspect regarding CSR is the accusation of "greenwashing." "Greenwashing" refers to a practice where companies, especially through environmentally related CSR activities, seek to improve their image and differentiate themselves from the competition without genuinely intending to address societal issues (Jonker et al., 2011). CSR activities thus function more or less as a facade of corporate engagement in the CSR domain. It aims to create the impression of a "green" image for the company and be marketed accordingly. Müller (2007) vividly describes various reasons for greenwashing. For example, the purchase of a "green" product, which already has a better reputation, aims to generate a sense of ethical satisfaction among consumers, or a higher price may be justified through climate-neutral production. However, it is evident that strategic benefits for companies through CSR can only be realized with genuine commitment and a strategic alignment within the corporate strategy. It is also presumed that a feigned commitment will eventually be recognized by stakeholders and negatively sanctioned (Habisch, 2003). Furthermore, the image loss associated with exposing a mere pretense of engagement is likely to be greater for a company than the gains from a feigned commitment (Jonker et al., 2011).

Lastly, it should be noted that an increased assumption of social responsibility by companies carries a latent danger of gradual withdrawal of state institutions from financing and influence in the social and cultural spheres. This could negatively impact general state-funded art and cultural promotion and lead to an enhanced power position for companies with social engagement. However, corporate social engagement should never be seen as a substitute for state support but rather as a complement. It is essential to ensure that specific cultural obligations of public institutions remain unaffected and secured despite the social engagement of companies (Jonker et al., 2011).

In conclusion, every company should critically engage with the concept of CSR and the associated opportunities and risks. While CSR is not a panacea for gaining a competitive advantage over competitors, it should be understood as a long-term opportunity for companies to assume social responsibility for their stakeholders and secure their market position, and even expand it through innovative solutions (Nicole et al., 2022).

With the political initiatives for CSR activities discussed in Section 4, particularly those at the European level that include legal requirements for EU member states, the political framework for companies assuming social responsibility in Europe has been established. At least for larger companies that are subject to the introduced reporting obligation for CSR activities. The information provided on the website of the Federal Ministry of Labour and Social Affairs ("CSR in Germany") should also increasingly appeal to and encourage small and medium-sized enterprises (SMEs) to leverage the entrepreneurial potential of CSR activities. However, it should be examined – either by the Federal Ministry of Labour and Social Affairs or industry associations – whether the website is being actively used or if it is even known to companies. The level of awareness and usage of the internet portal could be determined through surveys conducted by the respective industry associations. Depending on the results, alternative channels (e.g., information sessions at trade fairs, informational discussions during company visits) may need to be explored to market the benefits of CSR and encourage more companies to voluntarily assume social responsibility. More intensive and transparent communication of CSR would certainly be helpful in embedding CSR within companies.

To address the issue of "greenwashing" more effectively from a governmental perspective, it would be helpful to have the CSR reports submitted by companies reviewed by an administrative body. This could help identify any inconsistencies that may exist. Whether these inconsistencies should have legal consequences is another aspect that cannot be conclusively answered at this point. The oversight does not necessarily have to be assigned to the Federal Ministry of Labour and Social Affairs; outsourcing to an external entity such as an NGO is also conceivable. This external entity could potentially conduct an annual analysis of CSR reports for verification and communicate the findings accordingly.

The discussion on the topic of companies, society, and values has shown that academia, politics, and companies themselves have recognized the importance of companies assuming social responsibility for the social and environmental cohesion of today's society (Lindgreen & Swaen, 2010). In the current socio-political discourse, it is important to incorporate business ethics aspects. The German government has taken up the issue and recently regulated the responsibility of German companies for respecting human rights in global supply chains through the law on corporate due diligence in supply chains (Lieferkett ensorgfaltspflichtengesetz, LkSG) (BMAS, n.d.). This is a significant milestone towards the desired societal assumption of social responsibility by companies.

As always, it is important not to excessively restrict entrepreneurial freedom through legal requirements. Market principles should never be completely disregarded. However, to some extent, it seems understandable and well-founded to use both government measures and regulations, as well as societal pressure from stakeholders, to encourage companies to adopt CSR. This is particularly relevant when a socially desirable state cannot be achieved through voluntary CSR activities alone. The national and international CSR activities in recent years indicate that progress is being made in this regard.

References

Beile, J., Feuchte, B., & Homann, B. (2010). *Corporate Social Responsibility (CSR) und Mitbestimmung: Fünf Unternehmensbeispiele*. Edition der Hans-Böckler-Stiftung, Band 248, Düsseldorf.

BMAS – Bundesministerium für Arbeit und Soziales. (2011). *Die DIN ISO 26000: Leitfaden zur gesellschaftlichen Verantwortung von Organisationen – Ein Überblick*. Accessed 02/10/2023. Available under https://www.bmas.de/SharedDocs/Downloads/DE/Publikationen/a395-csr-din-26000.pdf?__blob=publicationFile&v=2

BMAS – Bundesministerium für Arbeit und Soziales. (n.d.). *CSR in Deutschland*. Accessed 03/10/2023. Available under https://www.csr-in-deutschland.de

Branco, M. C., & Rodrigues, L. L. (2006). Corporate social responsibility and resource-based perspectives. *Journal of Business Ethics, 69*(2), 111–132. https://doi.org/10.1007/s10551-006-9071-z

Carroll, A. B. (1979). A three-dimensional conceptual model of corporate performance. *The Academy of Management Review, 4*(4), 497–505. https://doi.org/10.2307/257850

Carroll, A. B. (1991). The pyramid of corporate social responsibility: Toward the moral management of organizational stakeholders. *Business Horizons, 34*(4), 39–48. https://doi.org/10.1016/0007-6813(91)90005-G

Deutsche Bundesregierung. (2010). *Nationale Strategie zur gesellschaftlichen Verantwortung von Unternehmen (Corporate Social Responsibility – CSR) – Aktionsplan CSR.* Accessed 02/20/2023. Available under

http://rritrends.res-agora.eu/uploads/13/BMAS%202010%20Aktionsplan%20 CSR.pdf

Deutscher Bundestag. (2016). *Corporate Social Responsibility (CSR): Aktueller Stand in Deutschland.* Wissenschaftliche Dienste, Sachstand WD 5 – 3000 – 032/16. Accessed 03/08/2023. Available under https://www.bundes tag.de/resource/blob/424954/76374d447099012620a493400ba0001c/wd-5-032-16-pdf-data.pdf

Elkington, J. (1994). Towards the sustainable corporation: Win-win-win business strategies for sustainable development. *California Management Review, 36*(2), 90–100. https://doi.org/10.2307/41165746

Europäische Kommission. (2001). *Grünbuch: Europäische Rahmenbedingungen für die soziale Verantwortung der Unternehmen.* Accessed 03/03/2023. Available under http://eur-lex.europa.eu/legal-content/DE/TXT/PDF/-?uri= CELEX:-52001DC0366&from=de.

Europäische Kommission. (2011). *Mitteilung der Kommission an das Europäische Parlament, den Rat, den Europäischen Wirtschafts- und Sozialausschuss und den Ausschuss der Regionen. Eine neue EU-Strategie (2011–14) für die soziale Verantwortung der Unternehmen (CSR).* Accessed 12/12/2022. Available under http://eur-lex.europa.eu/legal-content/DE/TXT/PDF/?uri=CELEX:5201 1DC0681&from_DE_der_Kommission.pdf

Europäische Kommission. (2017). *Leitlinien für die Berichterstattung über nichtfinanzielle Informationen (Methode zur Berichterstattung über nichtfinanzielle Informationen, 2017/C 215/01).* Amtsblatt der Europäischen Union, C 215/1–20.

European Commission. (2014). *Corporate social responsibility: National public policies in the European Union – Compendium 2014.* Accessed 02/35/2023. https://digital-strategy.ec.europa.eu/en/library/corporate-social-responsibil ity-national-public-policies-european-union-compendium-2014

European Commission. (2019). *Corporate social responsibility, responsible business conduct, and business & human rights: Overview of progress.* Commission staff working document. Accessed 03/11/2023. Available under https://ec.europa. eu/docsroom/documents/34963

Freeman, R. E. (1994). The politics of stakeholder theory: Some future directions. *Business Ethics Quarterly, 4*, 409–421. https://doi.org/10.2307/3857340

Friedman, M. (1962). *Capitalism and freedom*. Chicago: University of Chicago Press.

Friedman, M. (1970). *The social responsibility of business is to increase its profits*. New York Times, 13. September, 122–126.

Gröneweg, C., & Matiaske, W. (2018). Dresscode entschlüsseln: Eine organisationstheoretische Perspektive für die CSR-Forschung. In C. Jakobeit, R. Kappel, & U. Mückenberger (Hrsg.), *Transnationale Akteure und Normbildungsnetzwerke* (pp. 143–177). Baden-Baden: Nomos.

Habisch, A. (2003). *Corporate Citizenship: Gesellschaftliches Engagement von Unternehmen in Deutschland*. Berlin: Springer.

Hart, S. L. (1995). A natural-resource-based view of the firm. *Academy of Management Review, 20*(4), 986–1014. https://doi.org/10.2307/258963

Heblich, S., & Gold, R. (2010). Corporate Social Responsibility: eine Win-Win Strategie für Unternehmen und Regionen. In H. Pechlaner & M. Bachinger (Hrsg.), *Lebensqualität und Standortattraktivität: Kultur, Mobilität und regionale Marken als Erfolgsfaktoren* (pp. 333–358). Berlin: Schmidt.

Hiss, S. (2007). Corporate Social Responsibility. Über die Durchsetzung von Stakeholder-Interessen im Shareholder-Kapitalismus. *Berliner Debatte Initial, 18*(4/5), 6–15.

Hopkins, M. (2006). What is corporate social responsibility all about? *Journal of Public Affairs, 6*(3–4), 298–306. https://doi.org/10.1002/pa.238

Jonker, J., Stark, W., & Tewes, S. (2011). *Corporate Social Responsibility und nachhaltige Entwicklung: Einführung, Strategie und Glossar*. Berlin: Springer.

Latapi Agudelo, M. A., Jóhannsdóttir, L., & Davídsdóttir, B. (2019). A literature review of the history and evolution of corporate social responsibility. *International Journal of Corporate Social Responsibility, 4*(1). https://doi.org/10.1186/s40991-018-0039-y

Levitt, T. (1958). The dangers of social responsibility. *Harvard Business Review, 36*, 41–50.

Lindgreen, A., & Swaen, V (2010). Corporate social responsibility. *International Journal of Management Reviews, 12*(1), 1–7. https://doi.org/10.1111/j.1468-2370.200900277.x

Loew, T., & Clausen, J. (2010). *Wettbewerbsvorteile durch CSR. Eine Metastudie zu den Wettbewerbsvorteilen von CSR und Empfehlungen zur Kommunikation an Unternehmen*. Accessed 12/12/2022. Available under https://www.4sustainability.de/wp-content/uploads/2021/06/Loew-Clausen-2010-Wettbewerbsvorteile-durch-CSR-Gutachten-fuerBMAS.pdf

McWilliams, A., & Siegel, D. S. (2010). Creating and capturing value: Strategic corporate social responsibility, resource-based theory, and sustainable competitive advantage. *Journal of Management, 37*(5), 1480–1495. https://doi.org/10.1177/0149206310385696

Müller, U. (2007). *Greenwash in Zeiten des Klimawandels. Wie Unternehmen Ihr Image grün färben*. Accessed 03/10/2023. Available under https://www.lobbycontrol.de/wp-content/uploads/greenwash-studie.pdf

Nguyen, H. L. (2013). *Ausbau von Wettbewerbsvorteilen durch strategische Corporate Social Responsibility*. Bachelorarbeit an der Hochschule Mittweida, University of Applied Sciences, Fakultät Medien.

Nicole, S. J., Lada, S., Ansar, R., Abdul Adis, A.-A., Fook, L. M., & Chekima, B. (2022). Corporate social responsibility and strategic management: A bibliometric analysis. *Sustainability, 14*(17), 10526. https://doi.org/10.3390/su141710526

OECD – Organization for Economic Co-operation and Development (2001). *Corporate social responsibility: partners for progress*. Paris: OECD.

Perrini, F., Russo, A., Tencati, A., & Vurro, C. (2011). Deconstructing the relationship between corporate social and financial performance. *Journal of Business Ethics, 102*, 59–76. https://doi.org/10.1007/s10551-011-1194-

Reinhardt, F. L. (1998). Environmental product differentiation: Implications for corporate strategy. *California Management Review, 40*(4), 43–73. https://doi.org/10.2307/41165964

Russo, M. V., & Fouts, P. A. (1997). A resource-based perspective on corporate environmental performance and profitability. *Academy of Management Journal, 40*(3), 534–559. https://doi.org/10.2307/257052

Surroca, J., Tribó, J. A., & Waddock, S. (2010). Corporate responsibility and financial performance: The role of intangible resources. *Strategic Management Journal, 31*(5), 463–490. https://doi.org/10.1002/smj

Tanner, G., Bamberg, E., & Gude, M. (2018). Corporate Social Responsibility: Verständnis, Bedingungen und Wirkungen. In C. T. Schmitt & E. Bamberg (Hrsg.), *Psychologie und Nachhaltigkeit* (pp. 113–126). Wiesbaden: Springer Fachmedien. https://doi.org/10.1007/978-3-658-19965-4_10

WBCSD – World Business Council for Sustainable Development. (2000). *Corporate social responsibility: Making good business sense*. Geneva: WBCSD.

Zerbini, F. (2017). CSR initiatives as market signals: A review and research agenda. *Journal of Business Ethics, 146*, 1–23. http://doi.org/10.1007/s10551-015-2922-8.

Svenja Sabine KEITEL and Mehtap ÖNER

Green Bonds and the Current Challenge of Greenwashing

Abstract: In the era of transformation, sustainability has emerged as one of the most significant concerns that penetrates various aspects of societies and economies all around the world. This chapter analyzes the role of green bonds, which have gained popularity as a way to finance environmentally related projects, processes, and technologies which in turn expected to contribute a more sustainable shared future. However, these financial instruments also present challenges as greenwashing in the context of sustainability which is generally due to the lack of standardization and transparency in defining and reporting green projects. With greenwashing companies misrepresent their activities as environmentally friendly. To mitigate greenwashing and leverage the full potential of green bonds it is important to establish a mechanism that can ensure credibility which may require external verification and sustainability assessment of companies in the issuing process of these instruments. A profound understanding of this mechanism is crucial, given the vital role instruments as green bonds are expected to play in funding sustainable investments and mitigating climate change.

Keywords: Green Bonds, Green Projects, Greenwashing, Sustainable Finance

1. Introduction

The loss of sea ice, melting glaciers, sea level rise, and more intense heat waves are just a few examples of how human-caused climate change effects the earth (NASA, 2023). Climate change is manifested mainly in weather and climate extremes and affects not only certain areas but all regions of the world. To tackle the environmental challenges, 195 countries signed up to a global agreement at the Paris Climate Change Conference in 2015 to limit the rise in the global average temperature to less than 2°C above pre-industrial levels, with a long-term goal of reducing the rise to 1.5°C (UNFCCC, 2015). Another measure to counteract climate change is the EU climate target plan 2030, which includes the goal to make Europe climate neutral by 2050 and to reduce net greenhouse gas emissions by at least 55 % by 2030 comparison to 1990. This ambitious target plan has the potential to make Europe a more sustainable and low-carbon economy (Jensen, 2020).

To struggle with environmental and climate problems-together with many of the sectors, regulators and economies-finance world has also made contribution through developing and designing various innovative financial instruments. One of them with a paramount importance is green bonds which are long term debt securities used to finance investments providing environmental sustainability. Green bonds as sustainable financial instruments can be issued by either private or public entities to provide funds for financing climate/environmentally friendly projects. If an investor-individual or institutional, public or private entity-prefers a green bond he or she will contribute to environmental sustainability while still being able to generate a return from his or her investment. Day by day, green bonds are becoming more and more in the spotlight and are gaining popularity as a financial instrument to support investments in environmentally related projects, processes and technologies (Hyun et al., 2019). However, as green bonds increase in popularity, the concept of greenwashing which refers to misleading anyone who are sensitive to environmental issues about the environmental benefits of the investments undertaken or goods and services provided, has emerged as a challenge. According to the study by Leung et al. (2022) from research department of Hong Kong Monetary Authority, it is stated that nearly one third of the companies in the global markets that issued green bonds are documented to have a poorer environmental performance following their first issue of green bonds. It should be emphasized that due to the skepticism regarding the actual environmental benefits that are expected after the issuance, the concept of greenwashing has potential to affect the credibility of green bonds. Therefore, it is important to understand interrelationship among green bonds and greenwashing.

This chapter discusses the use of green bonds as a financial instrument to mitigate the effects of the climate crisis for a more sustainable world. Firstly, green bonds will be defined in general before the respective market is analyzed in more detail with up-to-date information regarding the world green bond market. The basic differences between conventional bonds and green bonds will also be summarized. Furthermore, as one of the current challenges in this context, greenwashing will be examined more closely.

2. Green Bond as a Financial Sustainable Instrument

Green bonds are defined as "*any type of bond instrument where the proceeds or an equivalent amount will be exclusively applied to finance or re-finance, in part or in full, new and/or existing eligible green projects*" (ICMA, 2021). The first green bond was issued by the European Investment Bank in 2007 with the name of 'Climate Awareness Bond'. The aim of the issuance was to finance renewable energy and environmentally friendly projects which were expected to increase energy efficiency. Following the European Investment Bank, World Bank (WB) together with Scandinavian Bank issued green bonds in 2008 to be used in financing the projects that would tackle with climate change. Since the first issue, the value of the green bonds issued by WB has approached to $18 billion in 25 different currencies (World Bank, 2022). Public and private sector institutions have also started issuing green bonds after 2013.

Figure 1 below demonstrates the total volume of green bond issuance between the years 2014 and 2022 based on a classification for supranational, emerging and developed countries. Total green bond issuance reached a value more than half a trillion dollars for the first time at the end of 2021. However, it experienced its first drop in 2022 by a 16 % lower volume when compared to previous year. The bars with the colors of blue, red and green represents the total volume of green bond issuance for emerging countries, developed countries and supranational, respectively. Since the share of emerging countries issue is very small in the initial years, we can only see the shares of developed countries and supranational in the bars below for the years 2014 and 2015.

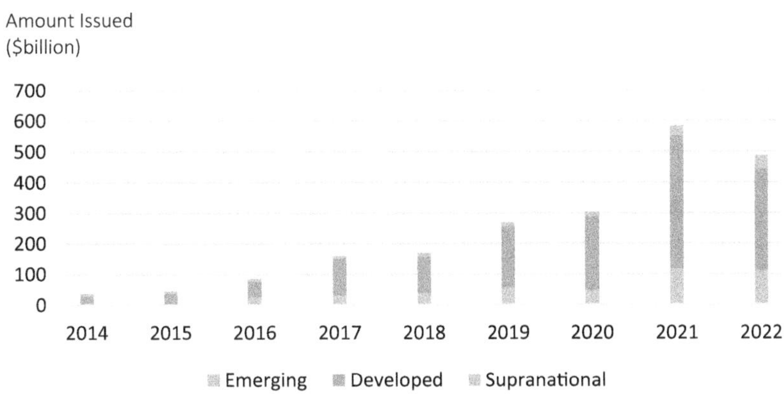

Figure 1: Volume of green bond issue based on regional development level (Billion $)

Source: Graphics were prepared by the authors with the data taken from CBI (n.d.a.) https://www.climatebonds.net/market/data/

As demonstrated in above Figure, while one fourth of the green bond issuance was realized by supranational and only 2 % by emerging countries in 2014, the percentage of shares has changed over the years. The share of supranational fell steadily to nearly 5 % until 2021. However, it increased to 9 % again in 2022. On the other hand, share in total has increased for emerging countries above 20 % in 2022. The highest share of issue has always been for developed countries whose share in the total has remained at an average of 70–75 % until 2021, while in 2022 it also fell below 70 %.

In the following sub sections, the overview of the green bonds together with its advantages and disadvantages for both investors and issuers will be discussed. Additionally, green bonds and conventional bonds will also be compared briefly.

2.1. Overview of Green Bonds

Even the general name is green bond, there is differentiation among the bonds that are traded on the green bond market. As one type, the Standard Green Use of Proceeds Bond is a classical recourse-to-the-issuer liability. The Green Revenue Bond, in contrast, is backed only by certain streams of payments such as fees, revenues, taxes, etc. (without recourse to the issuer). On the other hand, the Green Project Bond is a bond where the investor bears the risk of one or several green projects. As another type, the Secured Green Bond is a type of bond in which the net proceeds are exclusively used to finance or refinance either the specific green projects that secure the bond (Secured Green Collateral Bond) or the green projects of the issuer, originator, or sponsor that may secure all or a portion of the bond (Secured Green Standard Bond) (World Economic Forum, 2021).

Green bonds can also be classified as labeled or unlabeled. The bonds who are marked as labeled by the issuer must conform with the required Green Bond Principle (GBP). On the other hand, unlabeled bonds can be any type of bonds issued by companies whose day-to-day business is dedicated to climate-related projects, for example manufacturers of solar panels. The proceeds of these companies can be used for environmental projects, but also to cover their operating costs. These types of green bonds are not compatible with the GBP, which require that the use of the proceeds generated be allocated directly to specific environmental projects (Asia Development Bank, 2021).

The official Voluntary Process Guidelines for Issuing Green Bonds, published by the International Capital Market Association (ICMA, 2021), states that green bonds should be aligned with the four core components of the GBP which are *use of proceeds*, *process for project evaluation and selection*, *management of proceeds* and *reporting*. The GBP identifies a broad category of projects for which the bonds' proceeds can be used. They include projects which can mitigate climate change or protect natural resources. The issue of £250 million green bonds in 2014 by Unilever was an example of sustainable financing whose proceeds are

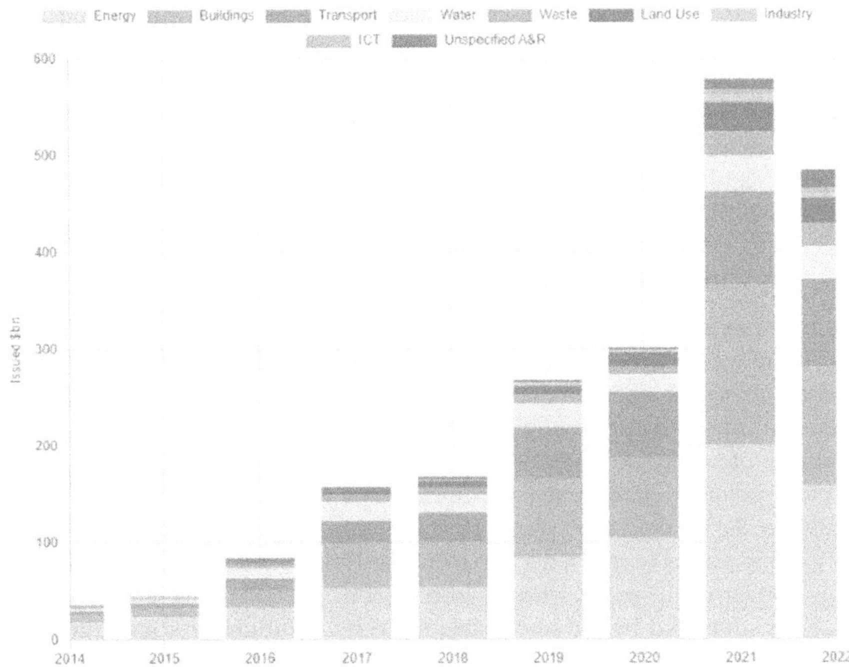

Figure 2: Use of proceeds

Source: CBI, Interactive Data Platform (CBI (n.d.b.)). https://www.climatebonds.net/market/data/#use-of-proceeds-charts

intended to be used for reduction in green gas emissions, water and waste in the factories of the company.[1]

Figure 2 above demonstrates the use of proceeds of the green bonds for the period between 2014 and 2022. As seen in the Figure 2, the largest use of proceed categories consist of energy, buildings and transport which has more than 75 % share in total green debt volume.

Regarding the remaining Green Bond Principles, for the process of project evaluation and selection, the issuer of the green bond should communicate to the investors about what the purpose of the green projects is, how the

1 For more details see "Unilever issues £250m green bond," by S. Daneshkhu and A. Bolger (March, 2014), Financial Times. https://www.ft.com/content/b3ea447a-af59-11e3-9cd1-00144feab7de

process has proceeded in which the Committee has determined that it is an eligible green project, as well as supplementary information related to the selection to the relevant project. The net proceeds of the green bond should be separate, tracked and verified by the issuer as part of an internal process related to its lending and investment activities. Transparency of the expected and/or achieved results of the projects is also essential for reporting (ICMA, 2021).

2.2. Pros and Cons of the Green Bonds

Both issuers and investors can benefit from offering or buying green bonds. As an advantage for society in general, green bonds can be seen as a tool against climate change. A study conducted by Fatica and Panzica (2021) that examined the environmental impact of green bonds showed that they reduce the carbon intensity of corporate assets. They further state that green bonds also create a more credible environmental commitment to climate-friendly corporate activities. From the issuer perspective, offering green bonds manifests itself by gaining access to a broader investor base. This is due to the fact that they now also attract investors who are interested in the environmental and social progress promoted by the sustainable projects. Additionally, commitment to sustainability through offering such instruments by firms can also be used as an opportunity to improve their corporate image (Deschryver and de Mariz, 2020; Freeburn and Ramsay, 2020). From the investor perspective, green bonds offer a sustainable financial return for them. This is due, for example, to the fact that they are used to finance future-oriented projects. Furthermore, it offers the possibility for investors to support environmental improvements (Deschryver and de Mariz, 2020).

On the other hand, green bonds also have some disadvantages since they involve relatively a cost-intensive process. Among other things, these arise from the costs of preparing and reviewing the reports as well as the costs incurred in order to meet the sustainability criteria. Furthermore, green bonds are associated with high requirements. They require further internal capacities, which are often missing. It may also have some disadvantages for investors, because it may really be difficult for them to measure the actual environmental impact of a project. Additionally, limited number of choices compared to conventional bonds for investors is another disadvantage of green bonds (Deschryver and de Mariz, 2020). As a current challenge of green bonds, some authors argue that one of the most crucial disadvantages of green bonds for investors is greenwashing (Freeburn and Ramsay, 2020).

2.3. Comparison of Green Bonds with Conventional Bonds

Even any types of bonds are defined as long term debt securities to raise capital their different types have varying features. Green bonds, as well as conventional bonds, can both be seen as financial instruments, but they differ in a number of ways as their purpose, pricing, environmental impact, reporting and transparency and also in terms of investor demand and preferences. These differences are shortly explained below:

2.3.1 Purpose

One of the basic differences between green bonds and conventional bonds is about the purposes of the investments that will be financed through the mentioned bonds. Green bonds are issued specifically to finance projects that will provide environmental benefits, such as renewable energy, energy efficiency, clean transportation, or sustainable infrastructure. Hence, the proceeds from green bonds are allocated to investments of the green projects (National Bank of Belgium, 2020; Löffler et al., 2021). On the other hand, conventional bonds are general debt instruments issued to raise capital for financing investments with various purposes which do not necessarily have a specific environmental focus (Securities and Exchange Comission, n.d.).

2.3.2 Pricing

Green bonds and conventional bonds also differ with respect to their pricing. Even the literature is relatively new and limited for green bonds, it reveals that there is no consensus in the literature related with the pricing of green bonds. However, there is an argument for a positive greenium which means that investors are willing to pay higher prices for green bonds than for conventional bonds, because green bonds have social benefits. Therefore, a lower return is accepted by investors since they contribute to environment friendly activities (Baker et al., 2022; Cheong and Choi, 2020; Zerbib, 2016). On the other hand, some other studies come to the opposite conclusion. They observe that green bonds have a higher return due to their newness and their relative risk. However, there are also studies whose findings reveal that in the case of perfect matching, there are no price differences between conventional bonds and green bonds and thus no greenium (Cheong and Choi, 2020).

2.3.3 Environmental Impact

Green bonds have a direct positive impact on the environment by financing projects that contribute to sustainability and mitigation of climate change.

These projects aim to reduce greenhouse gas emissions, promote clean energy, and protect natural resources, thereby helping to address environmental issues. However, it is often pointed out in the literature that a positive environmental impact is only credible if the green bonds are externally verified (Yeow and Ng, 2021). On the other hand, the environmental impact of conventional bonds is not inherently positive or negative. The priorities of the issuer will determine how the funds raised can be used. Therefore, use of the capital raised may or may not be consistent with sustainability goals (Securities and Exchange Comission, n.d.).

2.3.4 Reporting and Transparency

Green bonds often require issuers to be transparent and report regularly on the use of proceeds and the environmental impact of the projects financed (National Bank of Belgium, 2020; Dutordoir et al., 2022). This promotes accountability and helps investors assess the effectiveness of their investments in achieving environmental goals. A study by Dorfleitner et al. (2022) found that investors are very sensitive to information asymmetries in the green bond market, which makes it even more important for companies to be transparent about their reporting. On the other hand, reporting requirements for conventional bonds can vary and are not as strict as for green bonds. Moreover, they tend to focus on financial performance and creditworthiness rather than specific environmental metrics (Dutordoir et al., 2022).

2.3.5 Investor Demand and Preferences

Green bonds have gained popularity in recent years as investors increasingly prioritize environmental, social and governance (ESG) considerations in their investment decisions. Green bonds offer socially conscious investors the opportunity to support sustainable projects and align their portfolio with their values (National Bank of Belgium, 2020; Löffler et al., 2021). Conventional bonds are aimed at a broader investor base that does not necessarily focus on environmental factors. Investors in conventional bonds may focus on factors such as creditworthiness, yield, or liquidity without particular consideration of environmental impact (Securities and Exchange Comission, n.d.).

3. Current Challenges for the Green Bond Market: Greenwashing

Greenwashing is used by many companies to present products and activities as environmentally friendly, even though they usually have no positive impact on the environment. In this part of the chapter; firstly, a more detailed definition of greenwashing will be provided. Then, various examples in which companies have used green bonds to practice greenwashing will be discussed.

3.1. The Concept of Greenwashing

The three potential reasons for issuing green bonds are suggested to be signaling, cost of capital and greenwashing by Flammer (2021). Regarding the signaling, it is believed that with the issuance of green bonds firms can provide reliable positive signals related with its commitment to the environment. A second reason is suggested to be related with cost of capital. It is argued that if the potential green bond investors are sensitive to environmental issues, they may accept a lower return from green bonds if they believe they are environmentally friendly. As a result, green bond issuance will be a relatively cheaper source of financing for the issuers. The last reason why companies prefer green bond issuance is explained by greenwashing which is defined as '*the practice of making unsubstantiated or misleading claims about the company's environmental commitment*'. Accordingly, although companies do not take environmentally friendly actions in greenwashing, they act like that and demonstrate themselves as environmentally responsible.

Even greenwashing seems a positive choice for firms, it can damage the trust of society, who may be less willing to invest their capital in a sustainable way as in the form of green bonds. Furthermore, greenwashing can lead to reputational risks. This encourages investors to pull back their investments or funding, which has the effect of weakening the financial position of financial market participant. A recent study by Leung et al. (2022) demonstrates that the greenwashing behavior is not uncommon in the world of green bond market. The evidence reveals that nearly one third of the companies who issue green bonds for the first time are observed to experience relatively poorer performance regarding their environmental activities after issuance. Further evidence documents that players in the green bond market penalize the behavior of issuers who have greenwashing activities. However, the study suggests that through a green bond taxonomy and improved disclosure requirements related with environment, the greenwashing behavior of companies can be discouraged.

3.2. The Greenwashing Practices of Companies

The study by the New Climate Institute (2022) analyzed the climate protection promises of 25 multinational companies, such as Amazon, Apple and BMW Group. The companies' goal of "net zero" or "carbon-neutrality" was examined in more detail. Only three of the 25 companies namely; Maersk, Vodafone and Deutsche Telekom, committed to deep decarbonization of over 90 % by the target years. Furthermore, the achievability of the goals of the Paris Agreement was also examined. While 15 of the companies assessed have preliminary climate targets in their reports, the average emissions reduction commitment for their total value chain emissions between 2019 and 2030 is only 23 %. This is less than the 40–50 % reduction in global greenhouse gas emissions required between 2010 and 2030 to limit global temperature rise to 1.5°C.

One of the popular public cases in which the company admitted to greenwashing was the automaker Volkswagen. In 2015, the company disclosed that it had intentionally installed software in its diesel vehicles to make them look cleaner and more environmentally friendly. The scandal went public as the "Dieselgate" scandal. In the process, the organization covered up the fact that its vehicles were emitting nitrogen oxide pollutants far in excess of the acceptable level. This scandal had drastic consequences for the company. Among other things, the share price fell for example by 40 % within just two weeks (Jung and Sharon, 2019).

Another example of possible greenwashing is the "Clean Coal" project in China. The goal here is to reduce the environmental impact of coal-fired power generation through the use of advanced technologies. The aim is to increase the efficiency of coal combustion in order to reduce pollutant emissions (International Energy Agency, 2009). China has been able to promote clean-coal technology through green bonds (Hornby, 2017). Critics argue that despite technological advances, coal combustion is not an environmentally friendly alternative because it continues to release pollutants and greenhouse gases. Furthermore, the entire life cycle of coal, including mining and transportation, has significant environmental and health impacts. Critics also argue that the term is used as a form of greenwashing. This allows coal projects to be labeled "clean" without giving adequate consideration to their full environmental impact (BNN Bloomberg, 2021; Reuters, 2021). However, to align with international standards, China has removed the controversial coal investments in its 2020 Green Bond Catalogue (Climate Bond Initiative, 2020).

Even companies whose core business is not sustainable can issue green bonds, like the gas and oil company Repsol. What is expected is that, the proceeds should be used to improve the efficiency of the company's fossil combustion activities. However, these bonds were not included in the major green bond indexes. Criticism is that the investments will ultimately extend the life of the equipment, increasing associated emissions. The Climate Bond Initiative does not call the Repsol Green Bond "greenwashing" because investors were adequately informed about its intended use. Nevertheless, it criticizes Repsol for demonstrating through these bonds that they have not fully understood the goal of sustainability (Repsol, n.d.; Climate Bonds Initiative, 2017).

3.3. How Greenwashing Can Be Tackled

Due to the popularity of green bonds, the issue of greenwashing has become more apparent. Measures to tackle greenwashing include independent external audits, green bond taxonomies, stricter environmental disclosure requirements, government regulations and oversight, and phasing out fossil fuels. These measures aim to increase transparency, reduce information asymmetry, and ensure that green bonds truly promote sustainable investments.

A study by Dorfleitner et al. (2022) which examined the impact of the environmental friendliness of bonds on their asset pricing, also published an interesting way to combat greenwashing in its conclusion. The findings of the study reveal that independent external audits are essential for reducing information asymmetry in the green bond market. If published, these would increase investor confidence and reduce the risk of greenwashing. They also call for more binding rules to promote transparency in the industry and easier access to third-party ratings.

Another study by the Leung et al. (2022) which investigated a total of 1,888 green bonds issued by 643 companies, found another effective measure to tackle greenwashing. The study evaluated the effectiveness of green bond taxonomies and environmental disclosure requirements in reducing greenwashing activities. The results indicate that economies with a green bond taxonomy had a 24 percentage point lower probability of greenwashing bonds. Similarly, comprehensive environmental disclosure reduced the overall probability of greenwashing bonds by 21 percentage points compared to economies without disclosure requirements. Therefore, taxonomies for green bonds and stricter environmental disclosure requirements can be useful in reducing greenwashing behavior.

The EU Taxonomy is a well-known example of how greenwashing is attempted to be mitigated in green bonds. The regulation provides a classification system of which activities in a company can be considered sustainable. The taxonomy offers investors and market participants the possibility to identify truly sustainable investments, as it also requires reporting and disclosure of how the proceeds are used for projects. In total, the regulation describes six overall objectives. Thus, in order to be considered sustainable, activities must pursue at least one of the following objectives: climate change mitigation, climate change adaptation, sustainable use and protection of water and marine resources, transition to a circular economy, pollution prevention and control and/or protection and restoration of biodiversity and ecosystem[2].

A study has also examined the behavior of government regulations and the relationship with greenwashing in China. It was found that both government incentives and sanctions for not following the regulations are an efficient way to curb greenwashing. In addition, a lack of government oversight of companies' environmental information leads to a reduction in the seriousness of the company's reports. In addition, the reports of companies, in terms of their greenwashing behavior, should be verified by third-party certifiers. These serve as a source of information for the government as well as the companies themselves (Zhang et al., 2022). The European Parliament published a press release in 2022 with the European Green Bond Standard. This set out the requirements for green bonds in Europe and thus serves as a uniform framework. The standard includes both external oversight of compliance and penalties for non-compliance. The implementation of these is intended to promote the credibility of green bonds and encourage investment in responsible green bonds[3] (European Parliament, 2022).

Another way to stop greenwashing is to phase out fossil fuels. This would encourage the development of renewable energy. In order to promote investments in renewable energies, the provision of financial resources is crucial. This is the only way to ensure the phase-out of fossil fuels (World Economic Forum, 2022; United Nation, 2022). The phase-out would also mean that investors who have bought green bonds from fossil fuel companies would no longer have to worry about them being used to finance non-green projects. The phase-out could also have a positive impact on banks. They also have fossil fuel balance sheets due to their lending to fossil fuel companies. Banks that have adopted the Green Bond Principles continue to have extensive fossil fuel loan portfolios. This is contrary to the goals of green bonds, which could be countered by the introduction of the phase-out (Climate Bonds Initiative, 2016).

---

2 For more detailed information see "*Regulation (EU) 2020/852 of the European Parliament and of the Council of 18 June 2020 on the establishment of a framework to facilitate sustainable investment, and amending Regulation (EU) 2019/2088*", https://eur-lex.europa.eu/legal-content/EN/TXT/?uri=celex%3A32020R0852

3 For more detailed information see "*Proposal for a Regulation of the European Parliament and of the Council on European Green Bonds*". https://eur-lex.europa.eu/legal-content/EN/TXT/?uri=CELEX%3A52021PC0391

4. Conclusion

Climate change caused by human activity is undeniable and has a global impact. To combat climate changes, companies can, among other things, issue green bonds which have demonstrated remarkable potential in mobilizing large-scale capital towards environmentally beneficial projects. These bonds offer a way to raise capital specifically for green projects that contribute to sustainability and climate change mitigation. Moreover, the use of green bonds offers advantages to both issuers and investors. Issuers can reach a broader investor base and improve their sustainability image, while investors have the opportunity to support green projects and earn sustainable financial returns.

However, green bonds also face challenges, particularly related to threat of greenwashing which jeopardizes the credibility of this financial tool and the broader momentum towards sustainable development. Therefore, it is important and essential to ensure that green bonds are subject to strict verification and reporting requirements to prevent greenwashing and ensure transparency which will help leveraging the full potential of green bonds. In other words, to unlock the potential of green bonds and address the challenges they pose, it is required to strengthen verification processes, improve reporting standards, and ensure that green bond issuance is linked to real environmental benefits. By maintaining the integrity and credibility of green bonds we can effectively mobilize capital for sustainable and climate-friendly projects, contributing to a more resilient and low-carbon future for the planet. As the green bond market continues to evolve and grow, the finance world must be in position by increasing its commitment to real sustainable practices. Accordingly, an effective trade-off between financial growth and environmental integrity is not only desirable but required for our shared sustainable future.

References

Asia Development Bank. (2021). Asia Bond Monitor. https://www.adb.org/sites/default/files/publication/752331/asia-bond-monitor-november-2021.pdf.

Baker, M., Bergstresser, D., Serafeim, G., & Wurgler, J. (2022). The pricing and owernership of US green bonds. *Annual Review of Financial Economics*, 14, 415–437. https://doi.org/10.1146/annurev-financial-111620-014802

BNN Bloomberg. (2021). 2022 is a year to call out greenwashing in China. https://www.bnnbloomberg.ca/2022-is-a-year-to-call-out-greenwashing-in-china-1.1698357

Cheong, C., & Choi, J. (2020). Green bonds: A survey. *Journal of Derivatives and Quantitative Studies*, 28(4). http://dx.doi.org/10.1108/JDQS-09-2020-0024

Climate Bonds Initiative (CBI (n.d.a.)), Interactive Data Platform. https://www.climatebonds.net/market/data/ (26.06.2023).

Climate Bonds Initiative (CBI (n.d.b)), Interactive Data Platform. https://www.climatebonds.net/market/data/#use-of-proceeds-charts (14.06.2023).

Climate Bonds Initiative. (2016). Deep-dive: Should the fossil fuel industry, and other non-green companies, be issuing green bonds? https://www.climatebonds.net/2016/06/deep-dive-should-fossil-fuel-industry-and-other-non-green-companies-be-issuing-green-bonds#:~:text=The%20beauty%20of%20green%20bonds%20issued%20by%20the,be%20earmarked%20for%20the%20green%20business%20units%20alone.

Climate Bonds Initiative. (2017). An oil & gas bond we knew would come eventually: Repsol: Good on GBPs, not so sure on green credentials. https://www.climatebonds.net/2017/05/oil-gas-bond-we-knew-would-come-eventually-repsol-good-gbps-not-so-sure-green-credentials

Climate Bonds Initiative. (2020). Green bond endorsed projects catalogue. https://www.climatebonds.net/files/files/China-Green-Bond-Catalogue-2020-Consultation.pdf

Deschryver, P., & de Mariz, F. (2020). What future for the green bond market? How can policymakers, companies, and investors unlock the potential of the green bond market? *Risk and Financial Management*, 13(3), 61, http://https://doi.org/10.3390/jrfm13030061

Dorfleitner, G., Utz, S., & Zhang, R. (2022). The pricing of green bonds: External reviews and the shades of green. *Review of Managerial Science*, 16, 797–834. https://doi.org/10.1007/s11846-021-00458-9

Dutordoir, M., Li, S., & Neto, J. Q. F. (2022). Determinants of firms' choice between green and conventional bonds: Why is the corporate green bond market still so 'Green'? Available at SSRN: https://ssrn.com/abstract=4156431 or http://dx.doi.org/10.2139/ssrn.4156431

European Parliament. (2022). European green bond standard: New measures to reduce green washing, https://www.europarl.europa.eu/news/en/press-room/20220516IPR29640/european-green-bond-standard-new-measures-to-reduce-green-washing

Fatica, S., & Panzica, R. (2021). Green bonds as a tool against climate change? *Business Strategy and the Environment*, 30(5), 2688–2701. https://doi.org/10.1002/bse.2771

Flammer, C. (2021). Corporate green bonds. *Journal of Financial Economics*, 142(2), 499–516. https://doi.org/10.1016/j.jfineco.2021.01.010

Freeburn, L., & Ramsay, I. (2020). Green bond: Legal and policy issues. *Capital Markets Law Journal*, 15(4), 418–442.

Hornby, L. (2017). China leads world on green bonds but the benefits are hazy. https://www.ft.com/content/84ac893a-028e-11e7-aa5b-6bb07f5c8e12

Hyun, S., Park, D., & Tian, S. (2019). Differences between green bonds versus conventional bonds, handbook of green finance – Energy security and sustainable development. .Singapore: Springer.

ICMA-International Capital Market Association. (2021). Green bond principles, voluntary process guidelines for issuing green bonds. https://www.icmagroup.org/assets/documents/Sustainable-finance/2022-updates/Green-Bond-Principles-June-2022-060623.pdf

International Energy Agency. (2009). Cleaner coal in China, https://doi.org/10.1787/9789264048164-en

Jensen, L. (2020). EU climate target plan raising the level of ambition for 2030. European Parliamentary Research Service. https://www.europarl.europa.eu/RegData/etudes/BRIE/2020/659370/EPRS_BRI(2020)659370_EN.pdf#:~:text=On%2011%20December%202019%2C%20the%20Commission%20presented%20a,just%20transition%20for%20the%20regions%20and%20workers%20affected

Jung, J. C., & Sharon, E. (2019). The Volkswagen emissions scandal and its aftermath. *Global Business and Organizational Excellence*, 38(4), 6–15. https://doi.org/10.1002/joe.21930

Leung, V., Wan, W., & Wong, J. (2022). Greenwashing in the corporate green bond markets. Research Department, Hong Kong Monetary Authority. https://www.hkma.gov.hk/media/eng/publication-and-research/research/research-memorandums/2022/RM08-2022.pdf

Löffler, K. U., Petreski, A., & Stephan, A. (2021). Drivers of green bond issuance and new evidence on the "greenium". *Eurasian Economic Review*, 11, 1–24. https://doi.org/10.1007/s40822-020-00165-y

NASA. (2023). The effects of climate change, https://climate.nasa.gov/effects/ (25.05.2023).

National Bank of Belgium. (2020). Are green bonds different from ordinary bonds? A statistical and quantitative point of view. https://www.nbb.be/doc/ts/publications/wp/wp394en.pdf (10.06.2023).

New Climate Institute. (2022). Corporate climate responsibility monitor 2022. Assessing the transparency and integrity of companies' emission reduction and net-zero targets. https://newclimate.org/sites/default/files/2022-06/CorporateClimateResponsibilityMonitor2022.pdf

Repsol. (n.d.). Green bonds for funding sustainable projects. https://www.repsol.com/content/dam/repsol-corporate/en_gb/sala-de-prensa/repsol-news/29/articulos_eng.pdf

Reuters. (2021). Clean coal loans put China`s green dilemma on spot. https://www.reuters.com/breakingviews/clean-coal-loans-put-chinas-green-dilemma-spot-2021-11-18/

Securities and Exchange Commission. (n.d.). What are bonds? https://www.investor.gov/introduction-investing/investing-basics/investment-products/bonds-or-fixed-income-products/bonds (10.06.2023).

UNFCC. (2015). Framework convention on climate change. https://unfccc.int/sites/default/files/resource/docs/2015/cop21/eng/l09r01.pdf

United Nation. (2022). Integrity matters: Net Zero commitments by businesses, financial institution, cities and regions. https://www.un.org/sites/un2.un.org/files/high-level_expert_group_n7b.pdf

World Bank. (2022). The International Bank for Reconstruction and Development (IBRD) Funding Program: Green Bonds. https://treasury.worldbank.org/en/about/unit/treasury/ibrd/ibrd-green-bonds

World Economic Forum. (2021). What are green bonds and why is this market growing so fast? https://www.weforum.org/agenda/2021/10/what-are-green-bonds-climate-change/ (25.05.2023).

World Economic Forum. (2022). 5 ways to tackle greenwashing, according to UN experts. https://www.weforum.org/agenda/2022/11/greenwashing-stop-report-un-experts/

Yeow, K. E., & Ng, S. H. (2021). The impact of green bonds on corporate environmental and financial performance. *Managerial Finance*, 47(10). https://doi.org/10.1108/MF-09-2020-0481

Zerbib, Olivier David. (2016). Is there a green bond premium? The yield differential between green and conventional bonds. Published in the *Journal of Banking and Finance*, 98, 39–60, 2019, as "The effect of pro-environmental preferences on bond prices: Evidence from green bonds". Available at SSRN: https://ssrn.com/abstract=2889690 or http://dx.doi.org/10.2139/ssrn.2889690

Zhang, T., Qin, H., & Xu, W. (2022). Environmental regulation, greenwashing behavior, and green governance of high-pollution enterprises in China. *International Journal of Environmental Research and Public Health*, 19(19). https://doi.org/10.3390/ijerph191912539

Emre ZEHİR

Green Banking: What Is Changing in the Banking Sector?

Abstract: While financial innovations sometimes emerge out of need, sometimes the conditions for innovation to emerge also play a role. In the last decade of the 20th century, new products have been developed for solutions to the problems that emerged with the climate and environmental issues. The financial sector has the leading role in the inter-sectoral cooperation necessary for the products to be inclusive. Financial institutions continue to be the main source for providing the necessary capital to combat the climate crisis and environmental problems. Accordingly, this situation continues to affect the banking sector, which has been sitting at the heart of the financial system, especially in European countries. Although this situation has opened up an area for the banking sector, the risks that may arise from the climate crisis also shape the sector. In this chapter, the positive and negative effects of activities called green banking on the sector will be examined. At the same time, proactive approaches that the banking ecosystem can take against the opportunities and risks that may arise in the future will be discussed. In this scope, Turkish banking sector is examined in terms of being green or not.

Keywords: Green Banking, Turkish Banking Sector, Environmental Risks

1. Introduction

The amount of carbon dioxide (CO_2) equivalent greenhouse gases in the atmosphere has started to increase exponentially after industrial revolution. As a result of rising CO_2 equivalent gases in the atmosphere, global warming is triggered and biosphere integrity is deployed. Thus, greenhouse gases can be seen main driver of the climate crises. In addition to global warming, the loss of biodiversity also affects many issues such as acidification of the oceans, drought, food security. According to the Stockholm Resilience Center (n.d.), as is shown in Figure 1, four of the nine planetary borders have been already exceeded and the remaining five borders will exceed in a short time if the current situation continues.

The goal set by Paris Agreement in 2016 of keeping global warming below 1.5° by 2050 is a desirable situation, but the probability of its realization depends on the speed of steps to be taken. The study conducted by Rockström et al. (2017) demonstrates the urgency of solution regarding climate crises. Under one scenario, where global warming peaks in 2020, the probability of reaching the

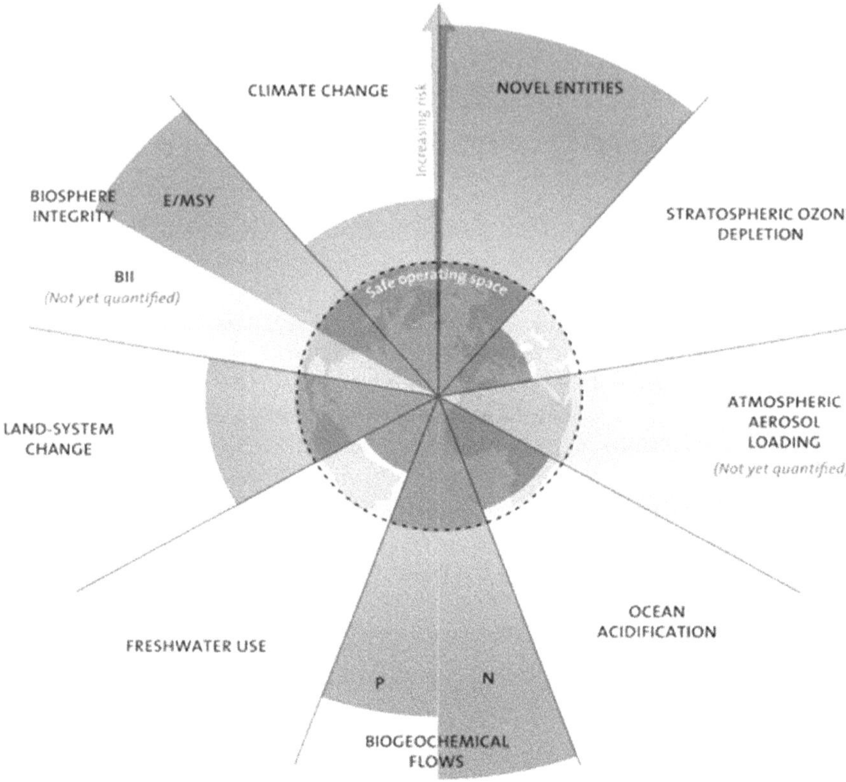

Figure 1: Planetary boundaries
Source: Stockholm Resilience Center (n.d.)

1.5° target in 2100 is 50 %; under another scenario, where global warming is kept at 2° or below, this probability rises to 66 %. In this case, reducing the carbon dioxide equivalent greenhouse gas emissions mostly caused by human activities and reaching the targets require an interdisciplinary collective effort. Although authorities work both individually and collectively to limit global warming and combat its ecological, social and economic consequences, more severe actions should be taken.

Many sectors, especially energy, transportation, industry and construction, use fossil resources to meet their energy needs. The biggest step and hope taken so far in reducing the carbon footprint of products, especially reducing the use of fossil resources and increasing the share of renewable energy sources in energy use. The main objective of the European Green Deal published by the European Union is to reduce fossil fuel consumption and achieve net carbon emissions. However, the energy crisis after the war between Russia and Ukraine enabled fossil resources to continue to be used for a while. This situation suspended the goal of being a carbon neutral continent by 2050, which was targeted by the European green agreement, for a while (European Union, 2022). In such an environment, the speed of the steps to be taken have increased and the necessary financing sources for green transformation have also raised.

The need for innovation in every field for zero-carbon economy transformation, such as in renewable energy production, electric vehicles, environmentally harmless waste, efficient waste management, re-usable products etc., has also emerged in the financial field. The need for financing lower carbon economy, standing at the midpoint of the collaborations required for green transformation and transition to zero-carbon economy, has revealed the concept of green finance. There is no a generally acceptable definition of green finance. However, a definition for green finance can be derived based on the terms of use of green financial instruments, the financing of projects that make a positive contribution to the environment, or the refinancing of projects to reduce the environmental impact of existing projects. In this context, this study defines green finance as financing the new environmentally friendly projects or refinancing the old projects that have a positive impact on the environment, as well as financing people's need for green products.

Indeed, organizations such as the Principles for Responsible Investment, Principles for Sustainable Banking and the Task Force for Climate-Related Financial Disclosures, established under the United Nations Environment Initiative in Finance, have been set up to create a green and sustainable world. In addition, non-profit organizations such as the Climate Bonds Initiative and the International Capital Market Association (ICMA) continue to contribute to the development of green and sustainable finance by developing principles for instruments such as sustainable bonds, green bonds, social bonds and green loans. As a result, the financial innovations needed for the green transformation continue to be provided and developed.

New green products in financial markets have gained momentum since companies from different sectors aim to transform their businesses greener. However, firms in emerging markets have disadvantages when compared with the ones in developed markets due to their inadequate ability to issue securities in international market. Underdeveloped capital markets are a further cause for concern in developing countries. Hence, banking system which stand at the heard of financial markets in developing countries holds an important role for green transition.

The remainder of this study is structured as follows: Section two presents an overview of green banking, section three explains environmental risks for the banking system, section four points out a need for green credit policy in Turkey, and the final section concludes.

2. Green Banking

Green banking is a concept that first emerged in 2009 in Florida, USA (Mathew, 2021). Banking activities where banks make a positive contribution to the environment in their day-to-day operations inside and outside the institution can be referred to as green banking. According to one view, green banks are seen as institutions that aim to make financial profits by considering only environmental factors (Coalition for Green Capital, 2022). However, adapting and putting green financial products into use within the traditional banking system can also be called green banking (Lalon, 2015). For this reason, it will be useful for future discussions to take a look at the existing structure of green banking in the literature. It is stated in the literature that there are certain processes for banks that can be described as green banks. Lalon (2015) listed some of the distinguishing features of green banks as follows:

- Contributing to the environment through automation and digital banking,
- Contributing to safety and security by changing the negative effects of society,
- Prioritizing investments and loans that have a positive impact on the environment,
- Achieving sustainable and green growth in line with industrialization and social goals,
- Creating a friendly environment inside and outside the bank,
- Considering clients as family members, providing advice and monitoring for pollution reduction projects through the use of an Environmental Due Diligence (EDD) checklist, and putting scientific methods into practice,
- Saving money and increasing a country's GDP through cost and energy savings,
- Changing the mental abilities of civil servants and clients according to their green sensitivity,
- Supporting institutions, people and the nation as a whole to live a life of dignity.

Mathew (2021) states that banks have some advantages if they choose to become a green bank in their domestic and international operations. Going green provides banks advantages in areas such as supply chain management, corporate resource management, and customer relationship management. On the other hand, the steps that banks are taking to become a green bank also have advantages for the stability of the financial system. Banks can eliminate the risks that may arise from environmental events. Banks' role in preventing environmental risk contributes to the financial system in terms of stability.

As mentioned above, green banking has practices in developing countries where the banking system plays an important role in the financial system. The initiatives in the field of green banking in these countries also has an important role in the development of practices. In this context, most academic studies on green banking focus on examples such as India, Bangladesh, Malaysia and Pakistan (Mathew, 2021; Sharma and Choubey, 2022; Hossain et al., 2020). Additionally, green banking initiatives are supported by international organizations. For instance, International Finance Corporation (IFC) developed training program in the field of green banking.

Many of the banks in the current banking system consider environmental and social impacts in addition to financial profits in their banking services. In this context, priority is given to financing green projects, especially at the lending stage. For example, banks in Turkey offer products and services that contribute to the green economy for both their corporate and retail clients. In the corporate context, credit facilities are available for green projects. Some examples of green projects are renewable energy projects, waste management projects,

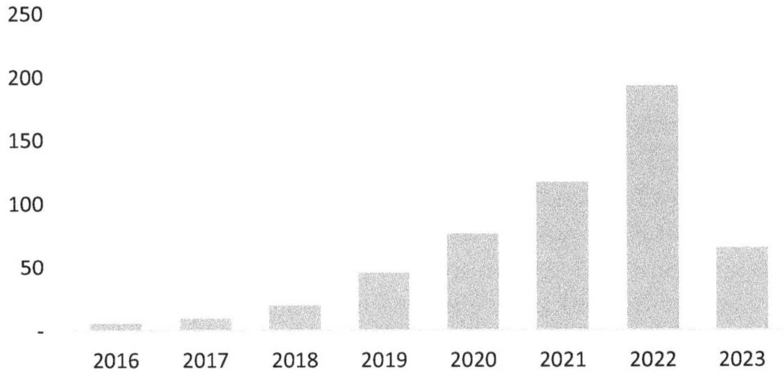

Figure 2: Green loans amount across globe (in billion USD)
Source: Refinitiv

emission reduction investments, etc. In the retail segment, instruments such as loans for financing electric vehicles and green housing loans are part of the banking services. However, there are no regulations for green credit standards in Turkey yet.

The Green Loan Principles (GLP) are regulated by the Loan Markets Association in 2018 (LMA, 2018) can be used to classify credit in green notation for the Turkey in absence of any regulation. GLP, like green bond principles, consists of four main contents. The first content in GLP is the use of proceeds. This is a commitment that the credit provided will be used for green projects. The environmental impacts of the project should be measurable if possible and should provide a net positive environmental contribution. The second component of GLP, on the other hand, is the process of project evaluation. Criteria such as the borrower's clear communication with lenders, the project's environmental sustainability goals, and indication of the appropriate areas of the project should be clearly explained. And the third component of the GLP is revenue management, which states that the credit received is kept in a separate account and used only for projects that have a positive environmental impact until the project is completed. Finally, reporting states the environmental contributions made each year per project, how much of the credit is used and how much of the project is completed by the time the debtors repay their debt. This information should be reported regularly and clearly each year.

Detailed information on green loans is provided by various data providers. Figure 2, for example, shows the relevant statistics from Refinitiv for the period from January 2016 to May 2023. According to Refinitiv, USD 193 billion green loans were used in 2022. As mentioned above, the interest in green financial products is increasing year by year.

3. Effects of Environmental Risks on Banking System

Banks are institutions that use only small amounts of paper, generate less waste and emit few CO2 equivalents into the atmosphere. So it can be said that banks are environmentally friendly institutions in terms of their internal operations. For this reason, it is not possible to say that they have a major impact on climate issues only because of their own internal processes. However, if we look at the projects financed by banks, the environmental impact of these projects is very high (Bingül and Türk, 2019).

Ünüvar and Yeldan (2023) calculated the sectoral share of loans and CO2 equivalent greenhouse gas emissions released by the same sectors for the Turkish banking sector. As can be seen in Table 1, the energy sector has the

Table 1: Share of loans and carbon emissions across sectors in Turkey

Sectoral Activity	Share in Loan Allocation	Share in Carbon Emissions
Manufacturing excluding cement	23.7 %	9.0 %
Construction activity	16.5 %	17.3 %
Financial services	10.7 %	0.3 %
Energy	7.7 %	35.8 %
Transportation and communication	6.6 %	19.0 %
Agriculture	4.2 %	16.5 %
Tourism activity	3.5 %	0.1 %
Mining	1.5 %	0.5 %

Source: Ünüvar and Yeldan (2023)

highest carbon emissions with 35.5 %. The sector that ranks second with a 19 % is the transportation and communication sector, which is highly dependent on fossil resources. Moreover, construction and agriculture sectors also have similar percentage shares in carbon emissions. On the other hand, all remaining sectors have percentage shares less than 10 %. When the share of sectoral loans in total loans is weighted by the amount of carbon emissions, the energy sector becomes the most carbon-intensive sector. If loan progress in the light of green banking principles were applied, sectors with high dependence on fossil resources would be excluded by the banking system. This might force them to work more innovatively and reduce their carbon emissions.

Unmanaged environmental risks threaten the stability of the overall financial system. Thus, green banks play a driving force in the economy through their lending channels. Doing that, banks provide financing for the greener products that contribute to combat effect of climate change and help to reduce the effect and severity of climate events. In this context, environmental risks can be categorized into two categories: physical and transition risks. Figure 3 presents such a classification. Direct losses are also referred to as physical risks, which arise as a result of floods, storms, droughts and other weather events. The frequency and financial impact of such events have increased rapidly today. Transition risks, on the other hand, describe the losses that may occur as a result of climate-related events or environmental regulations. As a matter of fact, although economic units are individually affected from environmental risks, both physical and transition risks, the total impact will be influential on the overall economy and the stability of the financial system. In this context, it is useful to mention how

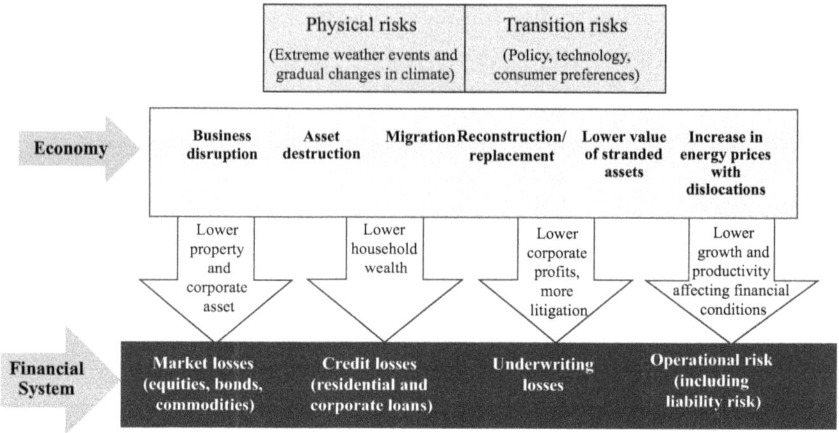

Figure 3: Classification of environmental risk on effecting financial stability
Source: IMF (2019)

environmental financial risks are categorized. It should not be forgotten that the reduction of carbon emissions will contribute to financial stability by reducing the risks arising from climate change.

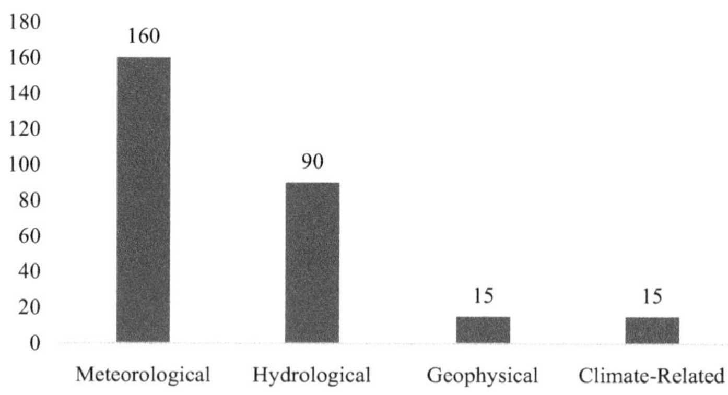

Figure 4: Losses from environmental events (in billion USD)
Source: Munich RE (2023)

The IMF (2019) stated that physical and transition risks may affect the economy through the deterioration of firms' operations, destruction of assets, reconstruction costs, depreciation in asset value, and increases in energy costs. The effects on the economy endanger the stability of the financial system. The main issue that will affect the banking sector is the expected losses on loan repayments. The risks that environmental factors impose on businesses primarily create business-related risks and then impact on the economy and indirectly on financial stability. The financial impact of environmental factors on financial stability is also shown in Figure 4.

The environmental events that took place in 2021 caused total damage of USD 280 billion. Of this damage, 160 billion USD was caused by extreme meteorological events due to climate change. The share of 90 billion USD is caused by hydrological events such as floods, droughts, etc. With 120 billion USD of the property damage incurred in 2021 covered by insurance, 160 billion USD of risks have been transferred to the financial system, while 160 billion USD of risks have been placed on the shoulders of businesses and individuals (Munich RE, 2022). As the frequency of events related to climate change and their severity increase, the portion that will be transferred to the financial system may also increase significantly. However, it should be considered that this amount of 120 billion USD was transferred only to the insurance system (Munich RE, 2022). On the other hand, other losses transferred to the financial system, such as loan repayments or impairment of assets are not considered. For this reason, it is difficult to examine the impact of environmental risks on the banking system as a whole. In this context, green credit policies should be introduced to assess the impact of environmental events on the banking system. However, concrete steps towards green banking policies have not yet been taken in many countries. The Basel Committee, which decides on the identification of risks in banking and the holding of the necessary capital in response to the risks, has not yet developed a precise documentation and calculation method for the assessment of environmental risks within financial risks. However, the Committee states that risks should be treated with a holistic view and within this framework it provides recommendations for the assessment of environmental risks within the category of financial risks. The Committee has published a handbook for banks and supervisors explaining how climate-related risks should be integrated into traditional risks (Basel Committee on Banking Supervision, 2021).

Figure 5 clearly shows how climate risks should be approached. This figure which is published by the Basel Committee, emphasizes that banks should identify risks prior to addressing climate-related risks. How climate-related risks are identified depends on the banks and regulators themselves, as well

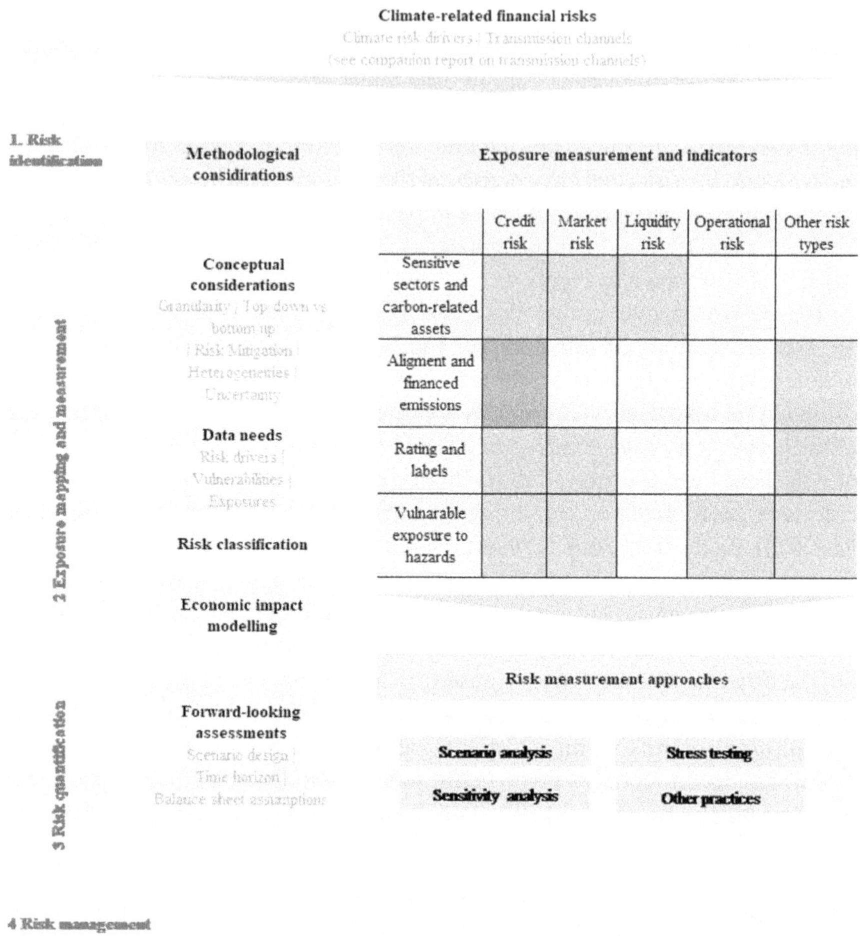

Figure 5: Climate risk assessment framework for banks and supervisors
Source: Basel Committee on Banking Supervision (2021)

as the level of risk to which their clients are exposed. These risks can be both physical and transition related risks. The second stage of the assessment will be determination of the levels of risk exposure and the risk effects. For example, companies in Turkey which operates in the field of cement production around the European Green Deal and exports to the European Union are exposed to transitional risk. The expected risk will be as high as the proportion at which the carbon density of the products they produce exceeds the threshold. This risk will spill over through the companies to the banks and thus through the banks to the banking system. The risk that arises throughout the banking system will spill over into the financial system.

The third part of the climate risk assessment is the quantification of risks. At this stage, some tests can be performed for individual banks and the banking system as a whole. These tests have been defined by the Basel Committee as scenario analysis, stress testing, sensitivity analysis and other applications. For example, the Banking Regulation and Supervision Agency (BRSA) conducted a scenario analysis in its study entitled "*Possible Effects of The European Union's Carbon Border Adjustment Mechanism on the Turkish Banking Sector Credit Portfolio*", in line with the Basel Committee's recommended practice. The report examined the potential impact of the carbon tax that the European Union will impose on companies on the repayment capacity of companies' current loans. The main finding of the report, shown in Table 2, is that the non-performing loan (NPL) ratio in the banking system will increase by 0.09 points.

Mesutoğlu (2022) shows in his study how the above-mentioned risks can have a concrete impact on the banking system, which is why it is necessary to make the banking system greener and expand green banking practices. Both the steps to be taken by the regulators of the banking system and the expansion of green central banking practices are necessary for a green transformation. In another study, Hossain et al. (2020) notes that it will be important for central banks and other regulators to take an active role in greening financial markets. Ünüvar and Yeldan (2023) also emphasized in their work for Turkey that Central Bank of the Republic of Turkey should lead the green transformation. In other words, the acceleration of green banking applications as a result of the increased sensitivity of consumers claimed in the studies will not be sufficient for greening the banks alone. The role of supervisory and regulatory institutions on the financial system will be an important and trigger for green transformation.

4. Need for Green Credit Policy in Turkey

Green bonds and green loans are the most important instruments with which the financial system can contribute to the green transformation. These two green products can have a green label if they comply with international standards. They will play an important role in the fight against climate change, thanks to the monitoring of green-labeled financial resources and the measurement of their effects through continuous reporting. In this context, the existence of

Table 2: Possible effects of European green deal on Turkish banking sector (NPL, %)

Sectors	Current NPL (December 2021) (a)	Estimated (2026 and beyond) (b)	Change in NPL (b-a)
Cement	0.00	1.20	1.20
Electricity	5.02	5.02	0.00
Fertilizer	0.68	0.94	0.26
Iron and Steel	2.13	5.05	2.92
Aluminum	2.17	6.65	4.48
Total (Five Sectors)	**3.83**	**4.77**	**0.94**
Total Loans	**3.16**	**3.25**	**0.09**

Source: Mesutoğlu (2022)

a green credit policy in the banking system is important. According to Wang and Zhia (2016), green credit policies (GCP) combine economic decisions with environmental decisions to achieve optimal outcomes. Moreover, Xing et al. (2020) state that GCP will contribute greatly to sustainable development. In this context, a Gross Domestic Product (GDP) set for Turkey is essential for both the continued functioning of the financial system and the transition to a carbon-neutral economy. However, developing green credit policies requires great effort. This is because the creation of a green taxonomy by regulatory and supervisory institutions and the existence of a green ecosystem are also important.

Financial regulators such as central banks can motivate banks to provide environment-friendly projects with easier access to capital. Emerging market regulators use a combination of regulations, guidelines, taxation, fiscal and non-fiscal incentives. Regulators can also use rewards, which in some cases lead to very positive outcomes. For example, the green credit policy developed in China in 2007 was a joint initiative of the State Environmental Protection Administration (SEPA), the People's Bank of China (PBOC) and the China Banking Regulatory Commission (CBRC). As it can be observed from Chinese example, building a green banking framework for Turkey, requires cooperation between CBRT and BRSA Turkey. Therefore, the GCP required for the development of a green banking system must be a set of measures and not just individual regulations. In addition, a nationwide climate strategy is also needed.

As it is mentioned above, most banks in Turkey offer the necessary products for green transformation. However, the products offered individually are not sufficient to implement both the green transformation and the green banking steps. The mentioned work of BRSA and the calculations of Ünüvar and Yeldan

(2023) show that the steps that need to be taken for green transformation and to maintain financial stability should go beyond these individual efforts.

The relevant literature argues that the absence of GCP contributes to financial stability and promotes the green innovation needed for green transformation. Ding et al. (2022) assert that GCP mechanism stimulate the innovation in heavily polluting firms to curb their carbon emission via technological innovation. It is also important to mention here that the study shows that the mechanism also reduces the credit channels of high polluting substances while improving the sustainability performance of the companies. Similarly, Zhou and Zhang (2023) depict that bank competition in green finance reduces the fund available for the firms and increases financing cost in China. However, reduced financing sources forces firms to be more innovative in greener way. Lampertia et al. (2021) took the GCP discussion one step further and investigated how green financial policies might affect climate-related risks in the presence of them. They stated that only a policy set full of financial restrictions can have negative consequences economically, while a green financial policy supported by a set of climate policies can yield better results.

The review of literature demonstrates that in the conventional economic environment, it is becoming harder to get bank loans in the absence of GCP. Thus, green innovation become necessary for companies who want to get bank loans. It can be stated that firms producing high pollution differentiate in terms of financing cost from the low pollutant ones. Zhang et al. (2022) indicate that high-pollutant firms pay more interest on their debt. Hence, the absence of GCP makes firms to be environmentally friendly. As a part of green banking activity, GCP helps sustainable development while forcing firms to go greener. Hu et al. (2021) investigated how the presence of green credit policies in China affects business innovation in the economy. The main finding of the study indicates that green credit policies show that firms are very successful in green innovation and contribute to green transformation.

For many reasons, Turkey's transition into a green economy will be necessary in the coming periods. The important factors mentioned are: Turkey's declaration of Nationally Determined Contribution (NDC) in response to the Paris Agreement, the European Green Deal that will come into effect in 2026, and climate change. Turkey's NDC pledge to achieve net zero emissions by 2053 is one of the most important factors for the transition to a green economy. In addition, the European Green Deal provides for a carbon tax on exported products if a certain carbon intensity value is exceeded during the production process. In order to be able to sell their products on the European market, Turkey's main trading partner, all sectors need to transition their businesses to a low-carbon economy. As described in the relevant literature, green banking and GCP force industries to become more innovative in order to respond to GCP requirements. In this respect, green banking will be a driving force for the green transition in Turkey.

5. Conclusion

It is well known that measures to combat climate change and reduce its impacts are still insufficient. The targets set in the Paris Agreement to limit global warming to below 2°C are scientifically improbable. This is why the next steps should be carefully implemented in line with the target. It is expected that the steps to be taken in cooperation with the sectors and international cooperation will continue to increase rapidly. In this context, the area in which the financial sector will contribute to the green transformation is referred to as green finance. However, the financial sector not only provides the necessary sources of finance but also has a structure that encourages other sectors to green transformation.

In developing countries, where the banking sector plays a crucial role in the financial system, it also has an important role to play in the green transition. Banks are expected to give importance to green projects and to make their lending policies more environmentally friendly. At the same time, banks are expected to be the driving force behind the green transition. In this context, banks that emphasize environmental sustainability in their lending and financing policies are referred to as green banks. Unfortunately, it is not easy for banks within the conventional banking system to move towards green, as economic sustainability is an essential part of banking. However, many existing banking institutions are integrating green banking products into their services. Currently, 132 banks worldwide, representing 40 % of bank assets, have signed the Net Zero Banking Commitment and are members of the Net Zero Banking Alliance (NZBA), which aims to reduce the carbon footprint of banks' investment and loan portfolios to zero by 2050 (UN Environment Programme, 2023). By doing so, they provide some of the financing needed for the green transition. However, as mentioned above, financing the green transition requires both collective awareness and individual effort. It means that great part of affords have to be taken. It can be said that the financial system is one of the platforms that will be affected by climate-related risks. One of the necessary elements for maintaining financial stability and financing the green transformation is the existence of the GCP. While the GCP penalizes companies that damage the environment when lending, it encourages them to be more innovative on environmental issues.

The aim of this study is to explain how green the Turkish banking system is and how green credit policies are necessary for the green transition. Banks operate in Turkey have many tools to support green transitions. Although Turkish banks offer green banking products in the form of loans, in the absence of a protocol, the banks have not disclosed the size of their green loan portfolio. Even though four Turkish banks are signatories to the NZBA, the rest have not expressed any intention to make this commitment. The banks' individual offerings are not sufficient for green transformation. The lack of GCP and participation in global alliances make green transformation more difficult. It is also important to note that the lack of a policy makes it difficult to track the activities of green banks. Activities such as the green funds that banks finance or provide for large green projects can only be tracked through public disclosures. There is no aggregated data on green banking activities for Turkey. Banks will continue to play an important role in green financial markets and thus play a crucial role in promoting green change in the Turkish economy. In this case, ensuring financial stability and promoting green transformation is the most important issue for green banking. To achieve this, regulatory measures should be taken and policies should be implemented as soon as possible.

References

Basel Committee on Banking Supervision. (2021). *Climate-related financial risks – measurement methodologies.* Bank for International Settlements.

Bingül, B. A., & Türk, A. (2019). Türkiye'de Yeşil Bankacılık. *Finansal Araştırmalar ve Çalışmalar Dergisi.*

Coalition for Green Capital. (2022). *Coalition for Green Capital.* Retrieved from https://coalitionforgreencapital.com/:

Ding, X., Jing, R., Wu, K., Petrovskaya, M., Li, Z., Steblyanskaya, A., . . . Makarov, V. (2022). The impact mechanism of green credit policy on the sustainability performance of heavily polluting enterprises – based on the perspectives of technological innovation level and credit resource allocation. *International Journal of Environmental Research and Public Health.* 19(21).

European Union. (2022). Retrieved from https://commission.europa.eu/strategy-and-policy/priorities-2019-2024/european-green-deal_en

Hossain, M. A., Rahman, M., Hossain, M., & Karim, M. (2020). The effects of green banking practices on financial performance of listed banking companies in Bangladesh. *Canadian Journal of Business and Information Studies.* 2(6), 120–128.

Hu, G., Wang, X., & Wang, Y. (2021). Can the green credit policy stimulate green innovation in heavily polluting enterprises? Evidence from a quasi-natural experiment in China. *Energy Economics*. 98.

IMF. (2019). *Global financial stability report: Lower for longer*. Washington.

Lalon, R. M. (2015). Green banking: Going green. *International Journal of Economics, Finance and Management Sciences*. 3(1), 34–42.

Lampertia, F., Bosetti, V., Roventini, A., & Tavoni, M. (2021). Three green financial policies to address climate risks. *Journal of Financial Stability*. 54.

LMA. (2018). *Green loan principles supporting environmentally sustainable economic activity*.

Mathew, A. (2021). Green banking: An innıvative initiative for sustainable financial development. *EPRA International Journal of Multidisciplinary Research (IJMR)*. 7(12), 50–54.

Mesutoğlu, B. (2022). *Possible effect of the European Union's carbon border adjustment mechanism on the Turkish banking sector credit portfolio*. Banking Regulation and Supervision Agency. Istanbul.

Munich, R. E. (2022). *Munich RE*. Retrieved from www.munichre.com/en/risks/natural-disasters-losses-are-trending-upwards.html

Rockström, J., Gaffney, O., Rogelj, J., Meinshausen, M., Nakicenovic, N., & Schellnhuber, H. (2017). A roadmap for rapid decarbonization. *Science*. 355(6331), 1269–1271.

Sharma, M., & Choubey, A. (2022). Green banking initiatives: A qualitative study on Indian banking sector. *Environment, Development and Sustainability*. 24, 293–319.

Stockholm Resilience Center. (n.d.). Retrieved from https://www.stockholmresilience.org/research/planetary-boundaries.html

UN Environment Programme. (2023). *UN environment programme finance initiative*. Retrieved from Net-Zero Banking Alliance: https://www.unepfi.org/net-zero-banking/

Ünivar, B., & Yeldan, A. E. (2023). Greencentral banking under high inflation-more of a need than an option: An analytical exposition for Turkey. *Development Policy Review (Early view)*.

Wang, Y., & Zhia, Q. (2016). The role of green finance in environmental protection: Two aspects of market mechanism and policies. *Energy Procedia*. 104, 311–316.

Xing, C., Zhang, Y., & Wang, Y. (2020). Do banks value green management in China? The perspective of the green credit policy. *Finance Research Letters*. 35.

Zhang, M., Zhang, X., Song, Y., & Zhu, J. (2022). Exploring the impact of green credit policies on corporate financing costs based on the data of Chinese A-share listed companies from 2008 to 2019. *Journal of Cleaner Production*. 375.

Zhou, B., & Zhang, C. (2023). When green finance meets banking competition: Evidence from hard-to-abate enterprises of China. *Pacific-Basin Finance Journal*. 78.

Kersten KELLERMANN and Elif NUROĞLU

Could Size Ceilings Make the TBTF Regime More Effective?

Abstract: This chapter examines the use of size ceilings for banks as a regulatory tool to enhance the effectiveness of the too big to fail (TBTF) regime. It introduces the concept of systemically important banks (SIBs) and explores the essential features of TBTF regime. The chapter argues that the optimal size of a bank from a business perspective may differ from its socially optimal size. Furthermore, it is argued that due to the challenge posed by a potential bailout, there is a legitimate public interest in the home country of a SIB to prevent the bank from growing beyond a socially acceptable and sustainable size. The chapter also provides a brief discussion of recent events in Switzerland related to the Credit Suisse crisis, where the effectiveness of the TBTF legislation was called into question.

Keywords: Too Big to Fail, Too Big to Save, TBTF Regime, Systemically Important Banks, Bank Regulation

1. Introduction

In September 2009, Adair Turner wrote that one of the most important challenges for global banking regulation and supervision was how to cope with too-big-to-fail (TBTF) systemically important banks (SIBs). Claudia Buch (2020), Vice-President of the Deutsche Bundesbank, recalls in 2020 the situation where systemically important banks "... *were weakly capitalized, resolution regimes for banks were missing, and taxpayers' money was often used to bail out banks.*" Reporting a evaluation of the TBTF reforms by the Financial Stability Board (FSB, 2010), she comes to the conclusion that the reforms appear to be working. Higher capital requirements, enhanced supervision, and new regimes for the recovery and resolution of banks have achieved their objectives. Buch (2020) summarizes that authorities now have a much wider range of options to deal with banks in distress. The TBTF reforms brought benefits to society and are seen as credible by market participants. However, the report states that the resolution of SIBs is a complex process, and obstacles to resolvability remain (FSB, 2020).

Following the financial crisis of 2007/2008, the Swiss legislator promulgated special rules for the stabilization and restructuring of SIBs. Efforts have been made to enhance resolution frameworks for SIBs. These frameworks aim to provide a mechanism for the orderly resolution of failing banks, minimizing the systemic impact and reducing the need for taxpayer-funded bailouts. During the crisis of 2008, the Swiss systemically important bank UBS had to be bailed out using taxpayers' money. The UBS rescue plan provided for the transfer of CHF 45.9 billion of the bank's illiquid assets to a stabilization fund controlled by the Swiss National Bank (SNB). The federal government strengthened UBS's capital base with CHF 6 billion. Yet, when Credit Suisse recently found itself in an acute crisis of confidence, the TBTF law proved to be ineffective. Clients and investors lost confidence in Credit Suisse, triggering a veritable run on the bank, which posed an immediate threat to the bank's liquidity situation. During a press conference on April 5th, 2023, in Bern, the Swiss Finance Minister Karin Keller-Sutter summarized the debacle in simple terms: "*Now we have a case where this 'Too Big to Fail' legislation does not properly reflect the situation. The tools can hardly be applied.*" Her conclusion is that if the 'Too Big to Fail' rules had actually been applied to Credit Suisse, it would have almost certainly triggered a financial crisis.

The crises led to a takeover of Credit Suisse by UBS, supported by a public liquidity backstop. The Swiss Federal Department of Finance (2023a) evaluates the merger very optimistically by stating, "*... it will strengthen confidence in the financial system and create stability for the international financial system, thereby averting serious consequences for the Swiss economy.*" At the same time, the merger will keep the cost for the state and taxpayers as low as possible. When two SIBs merge, resulting in the creation of a mega-bank in a relatively small economy like Switzerland, while at the same time not ruling out the possibility that the TBTF legislation may prove inapplicable in times of crisis, there is a need for a new assessment and critical reflection. This is the challenge that the present chapter undertakes.

The present paper is structured as follows: Section 2 provides some introductory remarks on the nature of systemically important banks (SIBs). The failure of a SIB can significantly impact the monetary, fiscal and macroeconomic stability of an economy in different ways. It can have far-reaching implications not only for the domestic economy but inversely affect the global finical system. Section 3 introduces the TBTF regime. Section 3.1 illustrates that when large banks are protected from market exit through a TBTF regime, the market is no longer able to fulfill its disciplining function. TBTF thus undermines the foundations of a competitive system. Section 3.2 demonstrates how TBTF regimes legitimize themselves despite their shortcomings by preventing the high costs associated with the bankruptcy of SIBs. Section 3.3 compares the costs of bank failure to the costs of the TBTF regime. The TBTF regime potentially imposes high fiscal and macroeconomic costs when rescue measures are applied. This clearly shows that

TBTF regimes are a burden to society, albeit a bearable one. Section 4 reveals that banks can potentially expand to dimensions that exceed the bailout capacity of the state. The TBTF problem then evolves into a too big to save (TBTS) problem. TBTS highlights the challenges faced by policymakers in finding viable solutions to prevent the failure of a SIB. Section 5 raises the question of whether size ceilings for banks can be a solution to the TBTF problem. Finally, the paper briefly addresses the recent events in Switzerland concerning Credit Suisse. Section 6 concludes.

2. Systemically Important Banks

Goodhart (2014) and Goodhart et al. (2006) emphasized that the specific structure and dynamics of the financial sector can generate inherent instability and vulnerability. The financial system is characterized by the endogenous nature of risk. The impact of maturity transformation and high leverage faced by banks magnifies shocks, making banks vulnerable to insolvency[1] and illiquidity[2]. The distress of a single bank can significantly disrupt the functioning of the financial system and cause widespread economic damage. Likewise, changes in the real economy can influence financial conditions, asset valuations, and risk perceptions. The interplay between the financial sector and the real economy leads to feedback effects in the sense that financial variables affect investment decisions, consumption patterns, and overall economic activity. The crisis of 2008 taught us that the collapses of a few large and systemically important banks can impose high costs on the global financial system.

The IMF, BIS, and FSB (2009) listed the size of a bank as the number one factor of systemic relevance. However, the precondition for systemic relevance is a kind of 'qualified' size. The FSB assesses banks for their systemic importance based on a set of indicators and methodology established by the Basel Committee on Banking Supervision (BCBS). The methodology

1 A financial institute is solvent where it meets the applicable capital adequacy requirements. A serious problem of insolvency arises when a valuation of assets at liquidation values casts doubts on the coverage of creditor claims (SFBC, 2008). Heller and Kuhn (2009) point out that in a crisis situation, it is often difficult to distinguish between solvency and liquidity problems.

2 According to the SFBC (2008), a serious liquidity problem arises where a bank is no longer in a position to meet its payment obligations; existing liquidity no longer covers obligations that are payable (or will soon be payable) and the bank is unable to procure liquid assets under market conditions. A bank may be solvent yet still be illiquid.

considers various factors to determine a bank's systemic importance, including size, interconnectedness, global activity, complexity, and substitutability (BIS, 2020). SIBs have substantial interconnections with other financial institutions, so their failure can have cascading effects throughout the financial system, triggering a domino effect that leads to the failure of other institutions and potentially causing a financial crisis. To prevent contagion, public authorities may be compelled to provide financial support or bailouts to SIBs to prevent their failure and mitigate the systemic risks they pose. In the end, SIBs can become so large and interconnected that policymakers perceive them as being too important to allow them to fail, earning them the notorious label of being "too big to fail."

The specific methodologies and criteria used to identify SIBs may vary across jurisdictions, as they are ultimately determined by national or regional authorities. The FSB (2020) distinguishes Globally Systemically Important Banks (G-SIBs) and Domestically Systemically Important Banks (D-SIBs). G-SIBs are banks that are deemed to have a global impact on the stability of the financial system. They are subject to additional regulatory requirements and heightened supervisory oversight due to their potential impact on the global financial system. The FSB uses threshold scores to determine which banks are designated as G-SIBs. It provides guidance and promotes coordination among relevant national authorities to ensure consistent approaches to the identification and supervision of systemically important banks (G-SIBs). The FSB designates a list of G-SIBs that is regularly updated, reflecting changes in the risk profiles and systemic importance of banks. The publication of the G-SIB list provides transparency about the banks that are considered systemically important and subject to additional regulatory requirements.

D-SIBs are banks that are deemed to have a significant impact on the stability of their domestic financial systems. The identification and characterization of D-SIBs are primarily the responsibility of national or regional authorities. Different countries may have their own methodologies and criteria for assessing domestic systemic importance, such as the size of the bank relative to the domestic economy, interconnectedness with other financial institutions, importance for providing critical services, and the potential for contagion within the domestic financial system. The FSB encourages its member jurisdictions to identify and designate D-SIBs to ensure appropriate regulatory and supervisory measures are in place to mitigate systemic risks at the national level. Each bank is assigned a score based on these factors, and the higher the score, the greater the bank's systemic importance.

3. What Characterizes the TBTF Regime?

The term TBTF was originally coined in the USA in the 1980s and later famously used by American Congressman McKinney at a hearing in connection with the Continental Illinois crisis (COP, 2009). It stands for "*too important to the stability of the financial system on account of its size for the institution to be allowed to fail into insolvency by the government.*" The TBTF problem provokes a TBTF regime where authorities put a set of policies, regulations, and practices in place to address the systemic risks posed by SIBs. The primary objective of this regime is to safeguard financial stability by mitigating systemic risks that arise from the interconnectedness of banks with other financial entities, their size, and their critical role in the functioning of the economy (Kellermann, 2011).

According to Stern and Feldman (2004), a TBTF regime is a policy environment in which uninsured creditors expect the government to protect them from prospective losses from the failure of a big bank. A TBTF regime is thus characterized by the following three attributes: Firstly, the institution at risk of illiquidity and insolvency is assessed as TBTF. These institutions will generally be SIBs. SIBs are typically identified based on criteria set by regulatory authorities and are subject to enhanced regulation and supervision to mitigate the risks they pose.[3]

Secondly, there are regulation, supervision, and protection measures: Various measures are implemented by national authorities to increase the resilience of SIBs, such as stricter capital and liquidity requirements, enhanced risk management practices, and stress testing. The goal is to reduce the likelihood of SIBs failing. The measures are intended to prevent the collapse of the institution. However, there are also resolution frameworks in TBTF regimes. Resolution frameworks refer to the established mechanisms and procedures put in place to manage the potential failure of SIBs without causing severe disruptions to the overall financial system and economy. It consists of a resolution authority, bail-in mechanisms, and so-called "living wills." The living will provide information on the SIB, enabling the resolution authority to resolve the bank in an orderly

---

3 SIFI (Systemically Important Financial Institution) is a broader term that encompasses not only banks but also other types of financial institutions, such as insurance companies, investment banks, and other non-bank financial entities. SIFI designation is applied to institutions that, if they were to experience financial distress or failure, could significantly disrupt the stability of the financial system. Like SIBs, SIFIs are subject to heightened regulatory oversight and may be subject to additional regulatory requirements.

manner (BIS, 2023; FINMA 2020). However, the feasibility and effectiveness of a resolution mechanism for SIBs remain a controversial topic. The concept of systemic importance and the resolution of banks seem challenging to align, which makes the idea of a resolution mechanism for SIBs not really convincing. SIBs are highly complex institutions with interconnections in various areas of the financial system. An orderly and effective resolution of such banks is extremely difficult. Unwinding a SIB in distress will most certainly destabilize other institutions and markets. The risk of bank runs or panic selling will always loom.

Thirdly, there are the parties that are affected or benefit directly from state bailouts: SIBs potentially benefit from the TBTF regime and bailouts, particularly the creditors, shareholders, employees, and the management boards of TBTF institutions. Bailing out large institutions can create moral hazard with respect to decision-makers. The moral hazard problem has received a great deal of attention in the literature (Cordella and Yeyati, 2003). By knowing that they will probably be bailed out in case of trouble, a TBTF regime may encourage investors, owners, and managers to take risks. It thus potentially weakens market discipline.

3.1 Avoiding Market Exit

The ultimate aim of a TBTF regime is to prevent SIBs from experiencing a market exit and avoid systemic consequences. The TBTF regime must thus be justified based on the high social costs associated with the market exit of SIBs. These costs make it socially unacceptable for a bank to exit the market in case of failure. However, free market exit is vital for the efficient functioning of the market. It is a fundamental aspect of the freedom to compete and participate in economic activities. In the case that a conventional company is unable to meet its financial obligations and becomes insolvent, it undergoes a bankruptcy process, which involves the orderly resolution of its affairs and a forced market exit. In this case, the company leaves the market without significant barriers or constraints.

According to Schumpeter (1911), market exit is an important aspect of the process of creative destruction, fostering innovation, productivity, and overall economic growth. When unsuccessful firms exit the market, resources are freed up and can be reallocated to a more productive use. By ruling out market exit, the TBTF regime undermines this important function of market economies. The TBTF regime restricts the reallocation of resources from poorly managed banks to more prudently managed banks. Hildebrand (2009) expresses this dilemma as follows: "If we are committed to a market-based system, the financial system of the future must expose financial institutions of all sizes and structures to the ultimate test of the marketplace. The very definition of a market economy is that it must allow for failure as a sanction for excessive risk-taking or managerial incompetence. In the event that large, systemically relevant financial firms face the threat of failure in the next crisis, the financial system of the future must allow for their orderly resolution. Such a system needs to ensure that the failure of a large bank does not have serious negative consequences for the provision of financial services to the real economy."

3.2 Social Costs of a Bank Failure

In the context of a TBTF regime, policymakers and regulators assess the social costs associated with the failure of a SIB. They evaluate whether the social costs of allowing a bank to fail are acceptable. If these costs reach a socially unacceptable threshold, a bank bailout should be implemented. The social costs of the failure and consequently the market exit of a bank comprise internal and external costs (Kellermann, 2010). Internal costs include the common costs associated with the firm's bankruptcy, which are borne by the owners, creditors, depositors, and employees of the bank. External costs are passed on to society. The failure of banks can disrupt the financial system and generate costs for other financial institutions through contagion. From a macroeconomic perspective, bank failures can lead to recessions, higher unemployment rates, and reduced economic growth. Bankruptcies can result in layoffs, leading to increased demands for unemployment benefits and retraining programs for employees. A credit crunch can place a massive strain on growth. Central banks often find it challenging to implement and execute monetary policy during financial crises, which can lead to difficulties in controlling inflation, managing interest rates, and maintaining overall financial stability. Furthermore, disruptions to the payment system can have adverse effects on the real economy (Swiss Federal Council, 2008).

In the fiscal context, a further category of costs arises. The government's ability to collect tax revenues, meet budgetary targets, and implement fiscal policies can be severely impaired. Indirectly, fiscal costs arise due to growing needs for state expenditure on socio-political measures. This potential burden on the public budget generates fiscal repercussions. Governments may also be forced to intervene with emergency measures, such as providing liquidity support to firms. These support measures can strain public finances, increase government debt, and potentially limit the government's ability to pursue its fiscal objectives.

3. 3 Policy Measures to Prevent a Bank Failure

The TBTF regime aims to prevent bank failure or avoid the described high costs associated with the failure of a SIB. Stern and Feldmann (2004), distinguish three policy measures as central feature of a TBTF regime: *Firstly*, measures taken by the central bank in providing liquidity to banks and maintaining financial stability. One of the primary functions of a central bank is to act as the *lender of last resort* (Heller and Kuhn, 2009). Central banks also use open market operations to inject liquidity into the banking system, they can adjust reserve requirements and maintain a discount window, which is a facility where banks can borrow directly from the central bank in times of need. Central banks also provide standing facilities, such as the overnight lending facility or the deposit facility. They further may offer longer-term loans or special liquidity programs to support banks facing sector-specific challenges or liquidity shortages due to external shocks. The goal of these liquidity-providing measures is to maintain the stability and smooth functioning of the financial system.

Secondly, governments can provide financial support to troubled banks by injecting capital directly into the institution. This can be done through the purchase of preferred shares, common equity, or other financial instruments. The governments′ aim is to bolster the bank's capital base and to increase its solvency to restore confidence in the institution.

Thirdly, governments may further provide guarantees on a bank's assets, such as loans or securities to stabilize the bank's balance sheet and prevent a sudden withdrawal of funds by depositors. In extreme cases, governments may even temporarily nationalize a troubled bank to protect depositors, and prevent a complete collapse. Once the bank's condition improves, it may be reprivatized or restructured.

4. Approaching the Threshold of "Too big to save"

In this chapter, we discuss the issue of TBTF in light of recent events: In May 2023, a bank of gigantic proportions emerged in Switzerland after the merger of UBS and Credit Suisse (CS). The fusion, driven jointly by the SNB, and Financial Market Supervisory Authority (FINMA), creates a significant concentration risk for the Swiss economy. For Switzerland the TBTF problem thus has intensified. If the new UBS were to encounter a crisis, Switzerland would most likely face massive macroeconomic and fiscal imbalances. Thus, the question arises whether the new megabank is sustainable for Switzerland and the Swiss safety net. Would

Switzerland be capable of rescuing the new behemoth in case of emergency or could it be that the new Megabank has become too big to save?

The term "too big to save" or "too big to rescue" suggests that even though financial institutions may be considered too big to fail, their size and complexity make them difficult or costly to rescue or bail out in times of financial distress. The concept of TBTS is related to the idea that certain institutions or entities can become so large, complex, or interconnected that it becomes extremely challenging or impractical for governments or regulators to effectively rescue or bail them out in the event of a crisis or financial distress (Pozen, 2010). In this case, size and complexity of an institution exceed the capacity of the government to intervene and provide financial assistance. The banks stress can then cause significant problems for its host country and even challenge its monetary and fiscal autonomy (Figure 1).

4.1 Too Big to Save and Country Size

Different challenges may potentially restrict the ability of governments to provide adequate support or bailout packages to institutions of significant size and complexity. Let's briefly summarize the main challenges: Firstly, the legal frameworks governing bailouts can pose obstacles to rescuing SIBs. These frameworks may have limitations or conditions that make it difficult for governments to intervene effectively. Secondly, political considerations and public opinion can reduce the willingness of governments to intervene in the rescue of SIBs. The fear of public backlash or the perception of rewarding risky behavior can create hesitancy in providing support. Furthermore, governments may be reluctant to intervene due to concerns about encouraging moral hazard behavior. The existence of TBTF regimes can make SIBs more prone to taking on excessive leverage and engaging in risky activities. To avoid moral hazard, governments try to limit their support to banks. However, the problem of TBTS is particularly valid for small countries or those with deteriorating public finances. Small countries with large banks are particularly vulnerable because their relatively limited financial resources may prevent them from providing adequate support or bailout packages to institutions of significant size and complexity (Demirguc-Kunt and Huizinga, 2010).

An illustrative case is Iceland's banking crisis, which exemplifies a situation where the authorities considered the banks too big to save. The crisis, occurring in 2009, was a complex event with multiple contributing factors. The three largest banks in Iceland, Glitnir, Landsbanki, and Kaupthing, had grown rapidly and accumulated significant debt, leaving them highly vulnerable to the global financial turmoil. The size and interconnectedness of these banks played a role in the challenges faced during the crisis, alongside factors such as excessive risk-taking, regulatory weaknesses, and external shocks (Baudino et al., 2020). The Icelandic government faced significant challenges in rescuing these banks due to their size and the magnitude of their financial difficulties. Eventually, the decision was made not to bail out the banks, leading to their collapse. The authorities believed that the banks had become too big and too intertwined with the rest of the economy, posing a risk to the country's financial stability. Concerns about burdening taxpayers and the risk of moral hazard influenced the decision to opt for alternative measures such as capital controls, currency devaluation, and prioritizing domestic depositors over foreign creditors. This approach differed from the traditional bailout strategies employed by other countries during the global financial crisis (Boyes, 2009).

The Icelandic case clearly illustrates how the insolvency of a systemically relevant bank can jeopardize a country's fiscal autonomy and its currency. Iceland sought financial assistance from the IMF and implemented realignment measures under the terms of a standby arrangement with the IMF (IMF, 2008). The OECD (2009) recommended that if Iceland were to become an EU member, it should join the euro area to benefit from the economic advantages, including the credibility of the European Central Bank and lower risk premiums. In conclusion, the challenges faced in providing support or bailout packages to large and complex institutions highlight the need for careful consideration of alternative approaches and regulatory tools to effectively address the TBTF problem.

4.2 Too Big to Save and Market Discipline

From a theoretical perspective, large banks should suffer from being located in a small country or a country that runs large government deficits. Both limit the location's capacity to insure the bank against insolvency. Governments may be forced to resolve bank failures in a way that implies large losses to bank creditors. In this case banks may gain shareholder value by downsizing or splitting up. In downsizing banks reduce risks for themselves and stay able to rely on the financial safety net. Thus, one would expect banks in small countries to face market pressure to downsize until they escape the TBTS status. However, Demirguc-Kunt and Huizinga (2010) find that banks – independent of their specific location – grow beyond the size that maximizes their implicit subsidy from the financial safety net. The research suggests, that relying on the disciplining forces of the market seems to be the wrong way to solve the TBTS.

Rather, the TBTS problem highlights the importance of appropriate regulatory tools. Adequate policies that address the risks posed by excessively large and interconnected institutions need to be developed and implemented in time.

The TBTS problem emphasizes the need to rethink the TBTF regime. The dilemma facing policy makers is that if ongoing reforms do not credibly eliminate the 'too big to fail' problem the 'too big to save' problem may become the cause of an inability to deal effectively with the resolution of SIBs in an upcoming crisis. In case of emergency, to orchestrate a rescue without creating further instability or contagion effects can become overwhelming for authorities. Vanberg (2009) therefore proposes that state liability guarantees for G-SIBs as part of a TBTF regime be transferred to supranational bodies. FINMA CEO Urban Angehrn states in July 2023: "*The events surrounding Credit Suisse show how important it is to make concrete preparations for crises. This meant that the authorities had options on the table with the restructuring plan and with the emergency plan that simply did not exist ten years ago. At the same time, it is clear that there are important lessons to be learned from the Credit Suisse crisis for future crisis preparations.*"

5. Size Ceilings as Regulatory Tools

In general, economists take one of the following three positions regarding the TBTF problem: Each of these approaches can be assigned a specific regulatory strategy (Fisher, 2010). *Too big to fail is too big to exist*: The TBTF characteristic should not be allowed for any financial institution. This can be achieved either by developing specific resolution procedures for systemically important banks (FINMA, 2009; FSA, 2009; Kunz, 2010) or through size limitations. Advocates of this position as Fisher (2010), Hoenig et al. (2009), Johnson and Kwak (2010), and Reich (2010) argue for direct or indirect size limitations on SIBs. *Too big to fail is here to stay*: Some economists, such as Krugman (2009), believe that the TBTF problem cannot ultimately be addressed through size limitations. Classic market discipline or "autopilot" as Krugman calls it cannot be implemented even if banks are limited in size due to the specific network character of the banking system. It generally has to be accepted that certain institutions are TBTF. Regulatory efforts must thus focus on reducing the probability of impending insolvency for banks. Possible regulatory instruments for this purpose include stricter capital and liquidity requirements, increased transparency in financial markets, and improved and internationally coordinated supervision (BCBS, 2009). The third position some economists take is "*TBTF pays*". They emphasize the macroeconomic benefits of large banks and the danger of overregulation (Dimon, 2009; Rajan, 2010). In good times, these benefits are gladly enjoyed by national economies. Big banks are considered a source of wealth and prosperity. However, these benefits do not come without risks. The empirical literature provides numerous studies that demonstrate risk transfer between the state and the banking sector. Using Data on CDS on bank and government bonds interlinkages become visible (Claessens et al., 2010; Völz and Wedow, 2009).

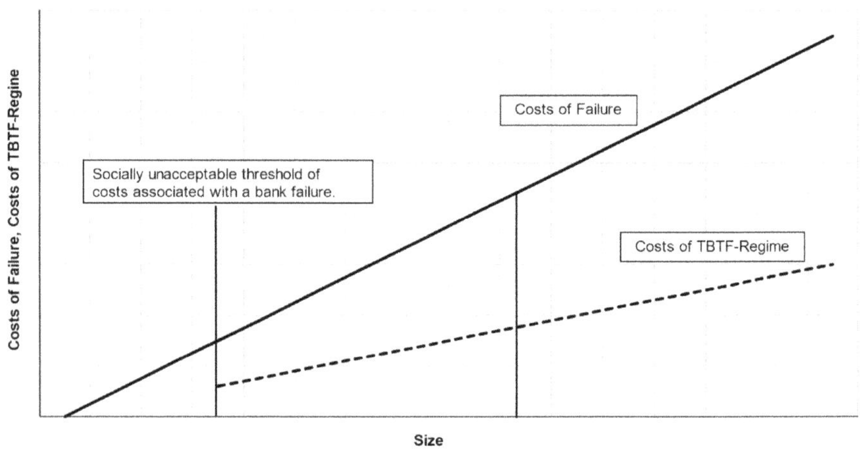

Figure 1: Costs of failure and costs of TBTF-regime

Each of the three positions has its justification and deserves to be considered in the policy debate. The problem becomes more straightforward when assuming systemically important banks that have reached a size which stretches the rescue capacities of its host country to the limits. If the TBTF problem evolves into the TBTS issue, the policy interest should be to reduce bank size. Regulation should aim on constraining the size or scale of banks below the TBTS-threshold, where governments' abilities to stabilize the banking system cannot be doubted.

Direct and indirect measures are suggested (Hoenig et al., 2009): *Indirect size limitations* aim to amplify business-related disadvantages of larger sizes. This can be achieved through progressively size-dependent capital and liquidity requirements. It is also conceivable to impose special taxes on large banks. Indirect size limitations thus leverage the steering function of taxes and regulatory costs (Acharya et al., 2010). Explicitly removing liability limitations for owners and managers of banks can also create incentives for size reduction. *Direct size limitations* directly intervene in the decision-making space of an enterprise. The TBTS problem suggests the implementation of ceilings or maximum threshold on the size of a bank. This can be done through the implementation of "Limits of Scope," such as the Volcker Rule, the Glass-Steagall Act, etc., and through the implementation of "Limits of Scope".

Nevertheless, size limitations are generally regarded as the last resort of financial market regulation. Currently, they do not play a major role in the debate on financial market regulations (King, 2009). In the past decade, there have been only a few attempts to implement bank size limitations. Following the financial crisis of 2008, Iceland implemented restrictions on bank size and activities to reduce systemic risks. In 2013 the US senators Warren and John McCain proposed the "21st Century Glass-Steagall Act", a bill aimed to restrict the size and activities of financial institutions to avoid risks associated with "too big to fail" institutions. Switzerland held a referendum in 2018 on the "Vollgeld" initiative, which proposed limiting bank size and aimed to limit the ability of commercial banks to create money through lending. However, the initiative was rejected by a majority of voters.

5.1 Optimal Bank Size from Business versus Societal Perspective

In the ordoliberal tradition of economic governance, there is no doubt that the optimal size of a company from a business perspective can differ from the economically optimal operating size. In a market economy, the size of a company should primarily be determined by business factors, such as its specific business model. However, if the home country bears the risk of a bailout there is a legitimate public interest in preventing the bank from growing beyond a socially acceptable and sustainable size. This can lead to a discrepancy between private and public interests, forming a welfare-economic justification to curb the growth incentives of private enterprises. Often risks are linked to explicit or implicit government guarantees. Explicit liability guarantees, are jeopardize the sustainability of public finances and macroeconomic stability in times of crisis. Government guarantees can be interpreted as subsidies. By implementing appropriate size limitations, a misallocation induced growth incentives resulting from explicit or implicit government guarantees can be corrected. From the perspective of potential creditors, SIBs benefit from the TBTF regime, as it indirectly insures the bank against the consequences of entrepreneurial risks. The subsidy nature of the TBTF regime creates growth incentives for banks and exacerbates the problem of SIBs (Brewer and Jagtiani, 2009). The growth incentive is based on the expected government assistance in times of crisis and exists regardless of whether the bank actually receives a bailout. The mere expectation of government assistance distorts the behavior of banks and their creditors (O'Hara and Shaw, 1990). Additionally, government guarantees not only affect the risks of the favored banks but also influence the risk choices of their competitors (Cordella and Yeyati, 2003; Hakenes and Schnabel, 2010; Gropp et al., 2010). The TBTF regime creates allocative distortions throughout the financial system, extending beyond the realm of TBTF banks. Particularly for small economies with significant financial industries, the question of size limitations on SIBs is relevant. This applies to both G-SIBs and D-SIBs. as well as implicit government guarantees, known as state liability.

5.2 How to Determine Size Ceilings

The question is how to determine the threshold beyond which a bank is not allowed to expand. It is reasonable to discuss these issues based on theoretical approaches in institutional economics (Erlei et al., 2007). When determining size ceilings, factors such as the national social risk preference or the national ability to externalize the risks of a bank collapse into the international arena should be considered. Two criteria can be used to determine the socially acceptable size of a financial institution:

Externalization of risks and the systemic risk induced by SIBs: According to Richardson et al. (2010), SIBs represent the most pressing systemic risk. This applies not only to small economies but also to the United States, where banks with a balance sheet total of $100 billion are already considered systemically relevant. Size limitations could prevent banks from becoming a systemic risk due to their size. Size ceilings prevent externalization of risks induced by the TBTF regime. They should depend on a bank´s systemic relevance.

Sustainability and bailout capacities (TBTS): Through explicit or implicit government guarantees, the state assumes obligations that can exceed its fiscal and macroeconomic bailout capacities. Prominent examples are Iceland and Ireland, two countries that faced significant difficulties during the financial crisis. The maximum bailout costs that can be sustained in times of crisis could provide guidance for potential size limitations. Banks should not be allowed to grow beyond the TBTS threshold (Figure 1).

From an empirical perspective, there is little evidence, that speaks against size limitations. Clark (1988), finds no size advantages beyond a deposit volume of only $100 million. Hughes and Mester (2008) also find little empirical evidence of size advantages. At the same time, they provide evidence that TBTF guarantees generate growth incentives to banks. The Geneva Report (Ferguson et al., 2007) shows that in the past, consolidations in the banking sector did not lead to efficiency gains. Only TBTF subsidies prevented efficiency losses from bank mergers (Johnson and Kwak, 2010). Haldane (2010) asserts that in large banks with balance sheet totals exceeding $100 billion, no size advantage can be observed.

6. Discussion and Conclusions

According to the Swiss Federal Department of Finance (2023b) bankruptcy of Credit Suisse would have had drastic consequences for the Swiss economy. In April 2023 the Swiss economy just run the risk of grinding to a halt. The bankruptcy of CS could have resulted in a situation, were small and medium enterprises (SMEs) and households throughout Switzerland had found it almost impossible to function economically. The acquisition of Credit Suisse by UBS prevented the disaster, albeit at high costs for Swiss taxpayers. Disappointingly, Switzerland's TBTF legislation proved useless in a critical moment: a blunt weapon in the fight against a fire-breathing dragon.

Against this background, the article critically examined the fundamentals of the TBTF regime. It demonstrates that when large banks are protected from insolvency by a TBTF regime, the market can no longer fulfill its disciplining function. TBTF undermines the foundations of the competitive system and market discipline. At the same time, the TBTF regime implies high risks for society and carries the danger of unforeseen costs caused by a bailout. In Switzerland, the acquisition of Credit Suisse by UBS and thus the merger of two G-SIBs creates a mega-bank with a balance sheet total approaching 200 % of Swiss GDP. The article raises the question, whether this new UBS is "Too Big to Save". A bank that has reaches a size that exceeds the state's capacity for rescue in times of crisis jeopardizes the fiscal and macroeconomic autonomy of the country where the bank is headquartered. The article advocates for the adoption of size ceilings for banks as a crucial regulatory tool to significantly enhance the effectiveness of the TBTF regime.

References

Acharya, V. V., Cooley, T. F., Richardson, M. P., & Walter, I. (2010). *Regulation Wall Street. The Dodd-Frank Act and the New Architecture of Global Finance.* New Jersey: John Wiley.

Baudino, P., Sturluson, J. T., & Svoronos, J.-P. (2020). *The Banking Crisis in Iceland*, FSI Crisis Management Series No 1, Bank of International Settlement (BIZ), Basel March 2020.

BCBS – Basel Committee on Banking Supervision. (2009). *Consultative Proposals to Strengthen the Resilience of the Banking Sector*, 12/17/2009, Basel.

BIS - Bank for International Settlements (2020). Containment measures policy interventions. Annual Economic Report, June 2020.

BIS - Bank for International Settlements (2023). Promoting global monetary and financial stability. Annual Economic Report, June 2023.

Boyes, R. (2009). *Meltdown Iceland: Lessons on the World Financial Crisis from a Small Bankrupt.*USA: Bloomsbury.

Brewer, E., & Jagtiani, J. (2009). How Much Did Banks Bay to Become Too-Big-to-Fail and to Become Systemically Important?. *Federal Reserve Bank of Philadelphia, Working Papers*, 09–34.

Buch, C. (2020). *Too-Big-to-Fail Evaluation,* Remarks by Prof. Claudia Buch, Vice-President of the Deutsche Bundesbank, from FSB press briefing, Frankfurt am Main, 26 June 2020.

Claessens, S., Herring, R. J., Schoenmaker, D., & Summe, K. A. (2010). *A Safer World Financial System. Improving the Resolution of Systemic Institutions*, Geneva Reports on the World Economy 12.

Clark, J. A. (1988). Economies of Scale and Scope at Depository Financial Institutions: A Review of the Literature. *Economic Review*, September/ October, 16–33.

COP – Congressional Oversight Panel. (2009). *Assessing Treasury's Strategy: Six Months of TARP, April oversight report,* April 7, 2009.

Cordella, T., & Yeyati, E. L. (2003). Bank Bailouts: Moral Hazard vs. Value Effect. *Journal of Financial Intermediation, 12*, 300–330.

Demirguc-Kunt, A., & Huizinga, H. (2010). Are Banks Too Big to Fail or Too Big to Save? International Evidence from Equity Prices and CDS Spreads, *World Bank Policy Research Working Paper.*

Dimon, J. (2009). No More 'too big to fail', *The Washington Post*, November 13, 2009.

Erlei, M., Leschke, M., & Sauerland, D. (2007). *Neue Institutionsökonomik* (2nd Ed.). Stuttgart: Schäffer Poeschel Verlag.

Ferguson, R. W., Portes, R., Hartmann, P., & Panetta, F. (2007). International Financial Stability, *Geneva Reports on the World Economy No. 9*, International Center for Monetary and Banking Studies, CEPR, London.

FINMA – Swiss Financial Market Supervisory Authority. (2009). *Finanzmarktkrise und Finanzmarktaufsicht*, Bern.

FINMA - Swiss Financial Market Sıpervisory Authority (2020). Financial market supervision against the backdrop of the pandemic, Annual Report.

Fisher, R. W. (2010). Financial Reform or Financial Dementia? Remarks at the SW Graduate School of Banking 53rd Annual Keynote Address and Banquet, Dallas, Texas, June 3, 2010. http://www.ffiec.gov/nicpubweb/nicweb/nichome.aspx

FSA – Financial Services Authority. (2009). *A Regulatory Response to the Global Banking Crisis: Systemically Important Banks and Assessing the Cumulative Impact*, Turner Review Conference Discussion Paper, 09/04.

FSB – Financial Stability Board. (2010). *FSB Welcomes US Proposals for Reducing Moral Hazard Risky*, Press release, January 22, 2010. http://www.financialstabilityboard.org/press/pr_100122.pdf

FSB – Financial Stability Board. (2020). *Evaluation of the Effects of Too-Big-to-Fail Reforms*, Consultation Report, 28 June 2020.

Goodhart, C. (2014). The Parlous State of Macroeconomics and the Optimal Financial Structure. *International Review of Financial Analysis, 36*, 78–83.

Goodhart, C. A. E., Sunirand, P., & Tsomocos, D. P. (2006). A Model to Analyse Financial Fragility. *Economic Theory, 27*, 107–142.

Gropp, R., Hakenes, H., & Schnabel, I. (2010). *Competition, Risk-Shifting and Public Bail-out Policies*, Working Paper Series of the Max Planck Institute for Research on Collective Goods, May 2010.

Hakenes, H., & Schnabel, I. (2010). Banks without Parachutes: Competitive Effects of Government Bail-out Policies. *Journal of Financial Stability*, 6(3), 156–168.

Haldane, A. G. (2010). *The $100billion Question*. Comments delivered at the Institute of Regulation & Risk, Hong Kong, 30 March 2010.

Heller, D., & Kuhn, H. (2009). Die Nationalbank als Lender of Last Resort, Schweizer Nationalbank (ed.), *Die Schweizerische Nationalbank 1907–2007* (S. 433–439), Zürich: Verlag Neue Zürcher Zeitung.

Hildebrand, P. M. (2009). *Policy Implications of the Financial Crisis*, Swiss National Bank, Speech on the Conference 'From Fragility to Stability', University of Geneva, 18 November 2009.

Hoenig, T. M., Morris, C. S., & Spong, K. (2009). *Resolution for Financial Companies That Pose Systemic Risk to the Financial System and Overall Economy*, Federal Reserve Bank of Kansas City, revised version, December 2009.

Hughes, J. P. H., & Mester, L. (2008). *Efficiency in Banking: Theory, Practice and Evidence*, Research Department Federal Reserve Bank of Philadelphia, January 2008.

IMF – International Monetary Fund. (2008). *Executive Board Approves US $ 2.1 Billion Stand-By Arrangement for Iceland*, Press Release No.08/296, November 19, 2008.

IMF, BIS and FSB. (2009). *Report to G20 Finance Ministers and Governors: Guidance to Assess the Systemic Importance of Financial Institutions, Markets and Instruments: Initial Considerations*, Prepared by Staff of the International Monetary Fund and the Bank for International Settlements, and the Secretariat of the Financial Stability Board, October 2009.

Johnson, S., & Kwak, J. (2010). *13 Banks – The Wall Street Takeover and the Next Financial Meltdown.* New York: Pantheon Books.

Kellermann, K. (2010). Strategie für eine optimale Finanzmarktaufsicht, *Die Volkswirtschaft, Magazin für Wirt-schaftspolitik*, Eidgenössisches Volkswirtschaftsdepartement und Staatssekretariat für Wirtschaft (ed.), Nr. 4, 8–11, Bern.

Kellermann, K. (2011). Too Big to Fail: A Thorn in the Side of Free Markets. *Empirica – Journal of European Economics, 38*, 331–349.

King, M. (2009). *Speech by Mervyn King*, Governor of the Bank of England, to Scottish business organizations, Edinburgh, Tuesday 20 October 2009.

Krugman, P. (2009). Banking on the Brink. *The New York Times,* February 23, 2009.

Kunz, P. (2010). *TBTF – Überlegungen zur "Too Big To Fail"-Problematik*, Jusletter vom 17. Mai 2010.

OECD. (2009). *OECD Economic Surveys: Island*, September 2009, Paris.

O'Hara, M., & Shaw, W. (1990). Deposit Insurance and Wealth Effects: The Value of Being "Too Big to Fail". *Journal of Finance, 45*(5), 1587–1600.

Pozen, R. (2010). *Too Big To Save – How to Fix the US Financial System.* New Jersey: John Wiley & Sons, Inc.

Rajan, R. G. (2010). *Fault Lines: How Hidden Fractures Still Threaten the World Economy.* Princeton: Princeton University Press.

Reich, R. (2010). *Break Up the Banks*, April 5, 2010, http://robertreich.org

Richardson, M., Smith, R. C., & Walter, V. (2010). Large banks and the Volcker rule. In: V. V. Acharya, T. F. Cooley, M. P. Richardson, & I. Walter (eds.), *Regulation Wall Street: The Dodd-Frank Act and the New Architecture of Global Finance*, Chapter 7 (pp. 181–212). New Jersey: John Wiley.

Schumpeter, J. (1911). *Theorie der wirtschaftlichen Entwicklung: eine Untersuchung über Unternehmergewinn, Kapital, Kredit, Zins und den Konjunkturzyklus.* Leipzig: Duncker & Humblot.

SFBC – Swiss Federal Banking Commission. (2008). *Bankeninsolvenz. Situation in der Schweiz und auf internationaler Ebene*, Januar 2008.

Stern, G. H., & Feldman, R. J. (2004). *Too Big to Fail: The Hazards of Bank Bailouts.* Washington, D.C.: The Brookings Institution.

Swiss Federal Council. (2008). *Botschaft des Schweizer Bundesrates zu einem Massnahmenpaket zur Stärkung des schweizerischen Finanzsystems*, 5. November 2008, Bern.

Swiss Federal Department of Finance. (2023a). FAQ Credit Suisse EFD, June 9, 2023.

Swiss Federal Department of Finance. (2023b). Faktenblatt des Eidgenössischen Finanzdepartement EFD, April 5, 2023.

Vanberg, V. J. (2009). Wettbewerb und Regelordnung. In: N. Goldschmidt & M. Wohlgemuth (eds.), *Untersuchungen zur Ordnungstheorie und Ordnungspolitik 55*. Walter Eucken Institut, Tübingen: Mohr Siebeck Verlag.

Völz, M., & Wedow, M. (2009). Does Banks' Size Distort Market Prices? Evidence for Too-Big-to-Fail in the CDS Market, *Deutsche Bundesbank Discussion Paper Series 2: Banking and Financial Studies*, No. 06/2009.

Onursal YAZAR and Aslı AYBARS

Fiduciary Duty and ESG Investing

Abstract: Sustainable finance covers the broad area of financial activities that integrate environmental, social, and governance related factors in financial decision-making. ESG investing, as a subset of sustainable finance, includes these factors in investment decision processes. Aim of this chapter is to summarize selected studies related to ESG investing and responsibilities of fiduciaries who have duty to act solely in the interest of beneficiaries. A detailed description of fiduciary duty is provided and potentially conflicting aspects of ESG investing and fiduciary duty owed by investment managers are evaluated. After revealing a brief history of ESG investing, the chapter summarizes recent studies about the impact of ESG investing on both corporate financial performance and investment performance. Although there are increasing number of studies concluding with positive or at least neutral relationship between ESG and performance, ESG investing still does not guarantee better performance. Thus, investment managers still have to prioritize their fiduciary duty and they should refrain from sacrificing some portion of expected return for ESG purposes when managing client portfolios.

Keywords: Sustainable Finance, Fiduciary Duty, ESG Investing, Duty of Loyalty, Prudent Investor

1. Introduction

Sustainability is the general word that may stand for the ability of all economic agents to maintain and improve their economic strength in the long run without underestimating the importance of environmental and social impacts. These economic agents may be individuals, companies, non-profit organizations, municipalities, states, and whole society in broadest terms. When the environment is considered, which is the habitat of all these units, sustainability can be interpreted as conducting economic and social activities in such a way that minimize negative effects on nature and natural resources.

Sustainable finance evolved as a solution to business related sustainability problems in the society and the environment. Firms and projects that contribute to the improvement in sustainability issues are generally provided financing at lower costs by lenders and investors through sustainable finance. When we speak of investors as providing financing for sustainability, we move into the area of ESG investing. ESG investing is simply taking environmental, social and governance factors into consideration in the investment decision-making processes. As awareness on these factors increase in the society, expectations from investment managers to allocate more funding into ESG investments grow. Investment managers on the other hand, are ethically and legally bound by a duty to act in the best interest of the investors. This is where the discussion starts: Is ESG investing in the best interest of the investors?

In this chapter, the debate of whether ESG investing is deteriorating investment performance or not is examined from the perspective of fiduciaries. 'Fiduciary duty' is a common term in several disciplines and stands for "responsibility of someone to whom one trusts or relies upon". Just like a doctor has to exercise utmost care for his/her patients or a lawyer has to act in the best interest of the clients, fiduciary duty requires an investment manager to manage a client's assets with ultimate care, diligence and prudence. Therefore, an investment manager has two objectives: satisfying modern expectation of contributing to sustainability through selection of industries or securities in their investment decisions and fulfilling their fiduciary duties. Whether the dual goals can be achieved at the same time or are they contradictory to each other is the key question which we try to find an answer.

In the next section, a brief evolution of investing is given with a special focus on ESG investing which is an inevitable product of sustainable finance. Also investment management as a profession and a financial service provided by a firm is described in the same section. In the following section, description of fiduciary duty and its application in investment management are given in detail. In Section 4, potential conflicts between fiduciary duty and ESG investing are discussed. The relation between ESG investing and investment performance is tried to be analyzed from evidences found in various studies in Section 5 before the final remarks in Section 6.

2. Investing

Investing or the allocation of resources with the expectation of future benefits, has a long and varied history dating back to ancient civilizations and continuing in the Middle Ages among European merchants. Creation of joint stock companies allowed investors to own shares in a company and share its profits. In the 17th century, the first examples of modern stock markets such as the Amsterdam Stock Exchange and London Stock Exchange were established.

The modern economy kept growing and new industries were developed through the 18th and 19th centuries with the period being named as Industrial Revolution. New investment opportunities arose as investors began to finance the construction of railroads, factories, and other infrastructure with their excess savings.

In 1900s, the growth of modern finance and technology resulted in the emergence of collective investment pools such as mutual, pension and hedge funds and non-public investment alternatives mainly in the form of private equity. In the recent decades, the rise of computer technology also resulted in growth of algorithmic trading and other forms of high-frequency trading.

Overall, the history of investing is a rich and complex subject, with numerous influences and developments shaping the field over time. The literature on investing reflects this complexity, offering a wide range of perspectives and approaches to investing. In the next subsection, a brief definition and history of ESG (Environmental, Social, and Governance) investing, which is in the agenda of individual and institutional investors as an investing theme for more than half century with an increasing pace lately, can be found.

2.1 ESG Investing

Sustainable finance and ESG investing are closely connected, as sustainable finance encompasses a broader range of financial activities that integrate ESG factors into financial decision-making; whereas similarly ESG investing stands for including the same three factors in investment decision process alongside financial factors. The term "ESG investing" is nowadays more widely used while the terms "sustainable investing" and "socially responsible investing" can also be used interchangeably with slight variations in what they exactly represent.

According to Morgan Stanley Capital Index (MSCI), provider of ESG indexes and ESG ratings, "ESG investing began in the 1960s as socially responsible investing, with investors excluding stocks or entire industries from their portfolios based on business activities such as tobacco production or involvement in the South African apartheid[1] regime[2]." SRI expanded globally in 1980s and 1990s with the launch of ethical and socially responsible investment funds.

"The United Nations Principles for Responsible Investment (PRI) is established in 2006 as an investor initiative in partnership with UNEP Finance Initiative and UN Global Compact, providing a framework for investors with six Principles for the integration of ESG factors into investment decisions".[3]

1 See https://au.int/en/auhrm-project-focus-area-apartheid for further information on The Apartheid.

2 https://www.msci.com/esg-101-what-is-esg/evolution-of-esg-investing

3 See https://www.unpri.org/about-us/about-the-pri for detailed information on UNPRI and its six Principals.

With efforts of PRI and increasing demand from investors, who prefer to align their investments with their personal values, ESG investing became more main stream in 2000s and 2010s. The number of ESG funds and assets under management (AUM) increased significantly as institutional investors and asset managers incorporated ESG factors into their investment processes.

ESG investing accelerated its growth in popularity in the last decade, with more investors seeking to achieve financial returns and making positive impact on environmental and social matters at the same time as a consequence of their investments. According to the PwC's 2022 report named "Exponential Expectations for ESG" total global ESG AUM has increased from USD 2.2tn in 2015 to USD 18.4tn in 2021 and is expected to grow to USD 33.9tn by 2026 in base case scenario.[4] Europe is the leading region in terms of ESG AUM both historically and in future expectations. Approximately 70 % of global ESG AUM belongs to Europe, whereas North America has as share of only 25 %. However, the growth trend is similar in both regions, making the pair keep dominating global ESG investing for years to come.

2.2 Investment Management

In their renowned textbook named as "Investments", Bodie et al. (2014) define portfolio management as "process of combining securities in a portfolio tailored to the investor's preferences and needs, monitoring that portfolio, and evaluating its performance." Investment management, which could be used interchangeably with portfolio management, can also be defined as "the professional management of various securities and assets, typically within the context of a portfolio, to meet specified investment goals for the benefit of the investors." Both activities require expertise in financial analysis, market research, portfolio construction, risk management, and performance evaluation to optimize risk and return in accordance with investor needs and preferences.

It's important to note that investment management can be carried out by various entities, including asset management firms, investment advisors, pension funds, endowments, and individual portfolio managers. Therefore, an investment manager or a portfolio manager can either be an individual, whose profession is to manage other's portfolio, or an investment management firm, which recruits individual portfolio managers to give a similar service of investment management for investors.

---

4 https://www.pwc.com/gx/en/financial-services/assets/pdf/pwc-awm-revolution-2022.pdf

In the same book, Bodie et al. (2014) make a simple but very important statement about regulations: "Only professional and institutional investors are constrained by regulations." Let's rephrase this statement as "Non-professional and individual investors[5] are not constrained by regulations." Obviously this is not fully true as all investors have to follow certain rules while trading in securities exchanges. For example trading with material non-public information and market manipulation are both illegal in many countries and unethical according to "CFA Institute's Code of Ethics and Standards of Professional Conduct".[6] What we are trying to demonstrate is that individual investors are free in their security selection for investment purposes. Nobody can blame, no court can judge or no ethical code and standard can label an individual investor as unethical for investing in a security that turns out to be a totally wrong investment decision or a very risky one.

To revisit the original statement of Bodie et al. (2014); regulations, legal and ethical constraints become applicable only when the task of management of assets moves from investors as principals to investment managers as their agents. To better understand this concept, Jensen and Meckling (1976) describe agency relationship as a "contract under which one or more persons (the principal(s)) engage another person (the agent) to perform some service on their behalf which involves delegating some decision making authority to the agent." According to the study, if interests of the agents (investment managers) are not aligned with the principals' (investors'), they will be inclined to conduct contrary to their fiduciary duty owed to investors. These conflicts of interest may be due to various causes from compensation structures to stock ownership, board membership to referral arrangement and etc.

At this point where we introduce principal and agent problem in asset management, which deteriorates fiduciary duty, let's discuss the concept of fiduciary duty and its application in investment management in detail.

3. Fiduciary Duty

Before expecting investment managers to be considerate of sustainability issues in their investment decisions, one needs to understand their primary responsibility

5 For the purpose of discussion on above paragraph, the term "individual investor" should be interpreted either as a person or an entity that invest for own account rather than for others.

6 https://www.cfainstitute.org/-/media/documents/code/code-ethics-standards/code-of-ethics-standards-professional-conduct.pdf

towards clients which is named as fiduciary duty. In the following sub-sections, we will give the general definition of fiduciary duty and what it stands for in investment management together with fundamental fiduciary duties which are duty of loyalty, care and prudence.

3.1 Definition of Fiduciary Duty

The word "fiduciary" in English stems from the Latin word "fiducia" having the meanings trust, confidence, reliance, and assurance.[7] The latter word "duty" can simply be replaced by responsibility and in general terms, the whole phrase of "fiduciary duty" can be explained as "responsibility of someone to whom one trusts or relies upon". It can be inferred from above definition that the term "fiduciary duty" requires two parties; one having the responsibility of acting in such a way that someone entrusted would act and the other one expects the former to act trustfully. The fiduciary who is the party with the responsibility, duty or obligation is required to act in other party's best interests, usually known as the beneficiary, even if doing so may conflict with the fiduciary's own interests. The concept of fiduciary duty has its roots in the Roman law and "Fiduciary Law" continues to be a branch of law referring to the legal principles and rules that govern the relationship between a fiduciary and their clients or beneficiaries. Therefore, we must conclude that fiduciary duty is both an ethical responsibility and legal obligation to act in the best interests of the clients or beneficiaries, with the highest level of loyalty, honesty, and care.

A fiduciary relationship can be established in various ways, depending on the context and the parties involved. In general, a fiduciary relationship arises when a person or entity (the fiduciary) agrees to act in the best interests of another person or entity (the beneficiary) and assumes a position of trust and confidence with respect to the beneficiary. For example, a client may hire a financial adviser and sign an agreement that sets out the fiduciary duties and obligations of the adviser. In some cases, the law may impose fiduciary obligations on certain parties by virtue of their relationship with others. For example, a pension fund manager has a fiduciary obligation to act in the best interests of the beneficiaries of the pension fund, the pensioners. A fiduciary relationship can also be established by the conduct of the parties. For example, a doctor who provides medical advice to a patient may be considered a fiduciary if they assume a position of trust and confidence with respect to the patient.

---

7 http://www.perseus.tufts.edu/hopper/resolveform?type=exact&lookup=fiducia&lang=la

It's important to note that not all business relationships give rise to fiduciary obligations. In general, a fiduciary relationship requires a higher degree of trust and confidence than a standard business or professional relationship, and imposes a higher standard of care and loyalty on the fiduciary. Fiduciaries who breach their obligations of acting in the best interest of the beneficiary can be held liable for damages and may face legal sanctions.

There are several common components or check points for the establishment of a fiduciary relationship:

- One party (beneficiary) gives the responsibility of acting to his/her best interest in a specific matter to the other party (the fiduciary),
- One party (the fiduciary) accepts the responsibility given by the other party (the beneficiary),
- The fiduciary has superior knowledge and skills over matters within the scope of the relationship,
- The fiduciary has discretion over the decisions to be made in the name of the beneficiary about the subject matter.

Whether a relationship is a fiduciary one or not can be judged case by case although there will always be vague situations where it is difficult to arrive at a clear conclusion. When disagreements arise, fiduciary law and judges will be in charge if parties go to the court; however, checking for the four prerequisites above will help the professionals and their clients to understand about the type of relationship they are entering into.

3.2 Fiduciary Duty in Investment Management

Fiduciary duty in investment management refers to the legal and ethical obligation of investment managers to act in the best interests of their clients, putting their clients' interests ahead of their own. This duty is particularly important because investment managers are often responsible for managing large sums of money on behalf of clients, who may not have the expertise or knowledge to make investment decisions themselves.

One of the fundamental assumptions of economic theory is that every entrepreneur seeks to maximize their profits.[8] This assumption is contradictory to the expected conduct from a fiduciary in investment management. As the beneficiary, you trust that the fiduciary is acting solely in your best interest. Contractually, legally and due to the very nature of investment management

8 See De Scitovszky (1943) and Kopltn (1963) for discussions on this assumption.

conduct, you expect that your investment manager to whom you give the discretion to manage your wealth invests your dollars on a reasonable basis, with utmost care and after a thorough, diligent, and independent analysis just like a prudent investor would do. However, the same fiduciary who has the liability to act in your best interest is also a member of the same modern finance industry where profit maximization is one of the most repeated mottos. There are many profitable ways or potential distractions for investment managers not to act in beneficiaries' best interest, such as higher brokerage fees from excessive trading, trading for one's self before pending client trade, misrepresentation of performance, and etc.

The importance of fiduciary duty in investment management cannot be overstated. Investors rely on investment managers to make decisions about how to manage their money and grow their wealth. If investment managers fail to act in their clients' best interests, they may make decisions that benefit themselves at the expense of their clients, leading to poor investment performance and financial losses.

The fiduciary duty provides a legal framework to hold investment managers accountable for their actions and ensures that investors have recourse if they are harmed by an investment manager's actions. This duty also helps to promote trust and integrity in the investment management sector, which is critical for maintaining a healthy and efficient financial market.

There are two ways that investment managers oversee assets of investors discretionally. First option is directly managing portfolios of clients in segregated accounts. Under this scenario, portfolio managers set professional business relationships with their clients based on trust, honesty, and good faith to achieve their financial objectives. They are expected to know their clients and invest in accordance with their investment goals, risk tolerances and financial, legal, tax related and other restrictions and concerns. The portfolio manager's responsibility is to oversee the client assets by making investment decisions on behalf of the client, monitoring the portfolio's performance, and making adjustments as needed. The client, on the other hand, is responsible for providing the portfolio manager with information about his/her investment goals, risk tolerance, and other relevant factors that may impact the investment strategy. This relationship between a portfolio manager and the client is a fiduciary relationship where the portfolio manager as fiduciary has a legal obligation that requires him/her to act in the best interests of the client and to put client's interests ahead of his/her own. This duty requires the portfolio manager to exercise highest degree of care, loyalty, and prudence in managing the portfolio. As a fiduciary, the portfolio manager must avoid conflicts of interest and disclose any conflicts that cannot be avoided. This includes disclosing any fees or compensation they receive that could potentially influence their investment decisions. Additionally, the portfolio manager must provide the client with full and fair disclosure of all material facts related to the investment strategy, including risks and potential benefits.

Second choice is to manage investors' assets through pooled funds according to their mandates disclosed in fund prospectuses, where all legal and institutional information about the fund, its investment strategy, allowable securities, potential risks, management fee and other charges and purchasing and redemption rules are written. In general, funds are incorporated in one form or the other as legal entities according to laws and regulations of the jurisdiction of incorporation. Mutual funds, pension funds or trusts are all structures of pooled funds which may be used interchangeably for the purpose of explaining fiduciary duty in investment management.

A mutual fund is a type of investment product in which investors participate by purchasing its shares and become shareholders. Collected cash is invested in equities, bonds, and other financial instruments to form a diversified portfolio with an expected return and certain level of risk. Similar to a company, a mutual fund has shareholders who are its investors, a board of directors responsible for the fund's oversight and overall management, a portfolio manager who manages the fund's portfolio in accordance with its investment objectives specified in the fund prospectus. Fund administrator is responsible for operational functions, whereas custodian is a bank or trust company responsible for safe-keeping of securities in fund's portfolio. Although it may have differences depending on in which country the fund is incorporated, common purpose is to ensure that the fund is managed in the best interests of its shareholders and operates in compliance with applicable laws and regulations minimizing conflict of interests.

Similar to the fiduciary duty of an investment manager to clients, in the mutual fund structure, the fiduciary duty of an investment manager is owed to the fund beneficiaries or shareholders as they ultimately own the assets in fund's portfolio. In the following section, we will discuss main responsibilities of fiduciaries.

3.3 Fundamental Fiduciary Duties in Investment Management

Fiduciary duties of investment managers can be classified under several titles. Different regulators and professional associations may label them in various ways but the main duty is same among all: to act in beneficiary's best interest.[9]

---

9 See Interpretation by Securities and Exchange Commission of US https://www.sec.gov/rules/interp/2019/ia-5248.pdf

As described in U.S. Department of Labor's website[10], "The Employee Retirement Income Security Act of 1974 (ERISA) is a US federal law which sets standards for retirement and health plans in private sector to provide protection for pension plan participants". ERISA, not only imposes fiduciary duty on investment managers with discretion and authority but also on plan administrators, and investment advisers as well. The same act states that fiduciaries have four duties: (1) the duty of loyalty to plan participants; (2) the duty to act prudently in investments; (3) the duty of diversification to minimize the risk of big losses; and (4) a duty to follow rules on applicable plan documents.

On the enforcement front, fiduciaries who fail to abide by these principles may bear personal liability to cover losses of investors and courts may take any necessary action against fiduciaries to cover losses when there is breach of fiduciary duty.

On the ethical and self-regulation front, CFA Institute (2024), with more than 190,000 members globally who adheres to the widely accepted CFA Institute Code of Ethics and Standards of Professional Conduct (Code and Standards) counts loyalty, prudence and care among fiduciary duties owed to clients.

3.3.1 Duty of Loyalty

The duty of loyalty is a key component of fiduciary duty, and it requires fiduciaries to put their clients' or beneficiaries' interests before their own and avoid any conflicts of interest that may arise. In practical terms, this means that fiduciaries must act with honesty, transparency, and fairness in all of their dealings with their clients or beneficiaries. They must prioritize their clients' or beneficiaries' interests over their own financial gain and avoid any actions or decisions that could harm their clients or beneficiaries.

According to Code and Standards, conflicts between investment professionals and clients may arise from various sources including aggressive or short-term focused compensation schemes in investment management firms, personal trades and security ownerships, board memberships, interdepartmental investment banking relations and brokerage fees. The best practice for the fulfillment of duty of loyalty is to avoid conflicts. However, it is not possible to avoid all possible conflicts in a non-ideal world. Therefore investments managers, as professionals or as firms, should disclose all unavoidable conflicts of interests and let the investors decide on the objectivity of the investment manager.

---

10 https://www.dol.gov/general/topic/retirement/erisa

To illustrate, a financial adviser should prioritize his/her duty of loyalty to the client and make recommendations that are in the client's best interest, even if it means recommending lower-fee investments that may result in lower commissions for the adviser. Similarly, a trustee who has a fiduciary duty to the beneficiaries of a trust must manage the trust assets in a way that maximizes the beneficiaries' interests, even if it means foregoing personal gain.

3.3.2 Duty of Care and Prudence

In Valsan and Yahya (2013), the duty of care is discussed in the context of portfolio management. The authors emphasize that portfolio managers have a fiduciary duty to act in the best interests of their clients, and this duty requires them to exercise care, skill, and diligence in managing client assets. The article highlights the importance of investment analysis, portfolio monitoring, and risk management in fulfilling the duty of care. Portfolio managers are expected to conduct thorough research and analysis before making investment decisions, monitor portfolios regularly to ensure that investments remain aligned with client objectives and risk tolerances, and take steps to manage risks appropriately. The authors also discuss the importance of disclosure and transparency in fulfilling the duty of care. Portfolio managers are expected to provide clients with clear and accurate information about investment performance, fees and expenses, and any conflicts of interest that could impact their decision-making.

The American Law Institute (1959)[11], commonly referred as "Prudent Man" Rule, defines the duty of the fiduciaries to beneficiaries as: "...to make such investments and only such investments as a prudent man would make of his own property having in view the preservation of the estate and the amount and regularity of the income to be derived...". Duty of care is explained as not making an investment unless thorough research is conducted related to the safety of the investment. To do this, a prudent man collects all available information, takes advice, if necessary, from other professionals or experts but finally decide with his own judgment. Furthermore, according to the Prudent Man Rule, an investment manager is expected to use the skills of an ordinary intelligence man. If the investment manager has a greater degree of skill than this, he or she can be held liable for a loss due to not using such skill.

11 See FDIC's web site or find the original statement in references https://www.fdic.gov/regulations/examinations/trustmanual/appendix_c/appendix_c.html#_toc497113665

4. Fiduciary Duty and ESG Investing

ESG investing is the investment front of sustainable finance and can be undertaken by investors themselves as principals or investment managers as agents of investors. The responsibilities of investment managers are even stricter than other agents in classical principal and agent relationships. Investment managers have the utmost duty to solely look out for their beneficiaries' benefits. In the following parts, we explain how ESG investing may contradict fiduciary duty of an investment manager and under which condition an investment manager can fully integrate ESG factors into investment decisions without breaching fiduciary duty.

4.1 Conflicting Ideals: Profit Maximization vs. Financing Sustainability

Friedman (1970) strongly argues that social responsibility can't be the responsibility of a business, as only human beings can take responsibilities and that the sole responsibility of a firm's executives should be to maximize profits and increase shareholder wealth. The study which is also known as Friedman doctrine, states that executives themselves may feel responsibility on social issues and they are free to pursue these responsibilities as principals of themselves. When they allocate sources to social responsibilities on behalf of their firms beyond levels that would increase shareholder value, they will breach their duty of profit maximization to shareholders.

As to move to the investment front, Schanzenbach and Sitkoff (2020) defines what is called fiduciary duty in the law as a sacred trust in investing other people's money. They add that there is increasing pressure on trustees, the investment managers, to include three ESG factors in investment decisions. However, this sacred trust, by law, requires that trustees seek only the interests of the beneficiaries.

The article describes two types of ESG investing: "collateral benefits ESG" and "risk-return ESG." Collateral benefits ESG is ESG investing for ethical and moral purposes or for the benefit of a third party, while risk-return ESG is ESG investing with the purpose of improvement in risk-adjusted returns. According to the study, sole sense of ethics of investment manager related to ESG matters or to obtain collateral benefits to third parties won't satisfy the duty of loyalty of the fiduciary. In addition, the study compares prohibitory "sole interest rule" in ERISA and regulatory "best interest rule" under corporate law. Latter leaves room for having some unavoidable conflicts of interest between the fiduciary and the beneficiary, whereas former requires exclusive benefit of the beneficiary and allows no unauthorized conflict. Accordingly, a fund manager who is influenced by self or third party's interest, is breaching his/her duty of loyalty. This approach doesn't leave any flexibility for a trustee to consider for ESG factors unless the beneficiary has such concern and lists ESG screening as part of the investment mandate.

Schanzenbach and Sitkoff (2020) concludes as, risk-return ESG investing, is allowable by a fund manager on the same conditions as any other active investing strategy – no more and no less. Next, the duty of loyalty prohibits collateral benefits ESG as a mandatory rule under ERISA and as a default rule in charities and personal trusts. Accordingly, if an investment manager reasonably arrives at the conclusion that depending on ESG factors will provide benefits on risk and return, and is exclusively motivated by this outcome, the manager shouldn't hesitate in using them. It is added that there are precedents where United States Supreme Court decided as whenever a pension trustee acts with other than financial benefits to the beneficiary, he/she breaches his/her duty of loyalty to the pensioners.

4.2 Investor's Consent on ESG Investing

Before trying to find evidence from prior studies whether ESG investing improves risk adjusted returns, let's define an exemption under which ESG investing would be permissible even in the absence of Schanzenbach and Sitkoff's (2020) two conditions. It's applicable for almost all sorts of duties to clients and that is in the case investor as principal consents for ESG investing, even in cases where return expectations of ESG investing is less than non-ESG investing for a given level of risk.

This consent should be included in writing in the agreement between the investment manager and the investor, and/or in the Investment Policy Statement (IPS). According to CFA Institute, the IPS is a tailor-made document which is uniquely prepared for the preferences, expectations, and circumstances of each investor.[12] With this definition, we can call the choice of ESG investing a preference. Fiduciary duty in investment management dictates that there can't be such a thing as preference of the investment manager other than choosing securities that meet risk-return objectives of the investor. However, as principal, the investor has the right of having investment preferences. For example, investment preference of an investor could be interest-free investing known as

12 "https://www.cfainstitute.org/-/media/documents/article/position-paper/investment-policy-statement-individual-investors.pdf"

Islamic Finance, investing in certain niche sectors such as electric car producers, investing in certain preferred countries for personal reasons, or ESG investing in our case.

In the absence of such a consent or willingness by the investor, the investment manager should make sure that there exist potential financial benefits to beneficiaries as a result of each ESG investment decision, at least in jurisdictions such as US or at least until the day the discussion of ESG investing and fulfilling fiduciary duty is finalized in favor of ESG investing being in alignment with fiduciary duties.

5. ESG Investing and Performance

There are two dimensions of ESG investing and performance that need to be examined. The first one is the link between ESG performance of a firm which can be measured by ESG scores and its financial performance. And the second one is the impact of integrating ESG factors in decision making process in security selection and portfolio performance. Both relationships are investigated extensively in numerous studies some of which are summarized in the following two sub-sections.

5.1 ESG and Corporate Financial Performance

Friede et al. (2015) reviewed 60 studies on the relationship between ESG and financial performance of corporations combining 2,200 unique studies from 1970 to 2015. They found evidence for the business case for ESG investing. It is explained that the opposite investor perception may be biased due to findings of portfolio studies that show a neutral or mixed ESG and financial performance relation on average, which are not necessarily negative. They add however that around 150 of these studies are covered by various systematic risks in portfolios and implementation costs and more than 2,100 firm-focused studies suggest a positive relation between ESG and financial performance.

They continue that ESG outperformance opportunities hold true for many markets, specifically for North America, Emerging Markets, and in non-equity asset classes. Their results offer that since the mid-1990s there have been stable positive correlation patterns in main studies regarding the ESG–Corporate Financial Performance (CFP) over time. The study concludes that long-term responsible investing is important for all sorts of investors to fulfill their fiduciary duties and align interests with the broader society. This requires a detailed understanding of the ways of integrating ESG factors into investment processes.

In another study which investigates a similar evidence for years between 2015 and 2020, Whelan et al. (2021) aggregated more than 1,000 studies and came up with six conclusions: ESG related financial performance improves over longer terms, ESG integration as an investment strategy performs better than negative screening approaches, ESG investing provides protection on the downside, particularly during a social or economic crisis, corporate level sustainability initiatives drive better financial performance due to more innovation and better risk management, planning for low carbon improves financial performance and lastly ESG disclosure on itself doesn't improve financial performance. According to the study, based on 245 studies between 2016 and 2020, positive and/or neutral results for investing in sustainability dominate negative ones as very few studies concluded that there exists a negative correlation between financial performance and ESG.

Velte (2017) evaluated the impact of overall ESG performance and component-wise ESG performance of selected firms in Germany on their financial performance from 2010 to 2014. They measured financial performance with ROA (return on assets) and Tobin's Q ratio[13] (ratio of market value to book value of equity and liabilities). The study concludes that ESG performance and separately environmental, social and governance score performances have positive effect on ROA, where governance score performance has the strongest impact. On the Tobin's Q front, which better reflects the market performance of a firm, there isn't any significant impact of ESG performance.

Huang (2021) reviews and summarizes 21 selected studies between 1980 and 2019 and concludes that there is a positive and significant relation between ESG performance and CFP, particularly on the environmental front. However this relationship yields only 2 % difference in explained variance in CFP, which is economically modest according to Huang who suggests that firms' main motivation for ESG activity can't be only financial performance.

General conclusion in above studies which review thousands of individual studies in different years and markets are far from suggesting that ESG investing deteriorates CFP. Most of the conclusions imply positive or at least neutral relation between those two. Therefore, from the perspective of this chapter, the empirical evidence of positive linkage between ESG performance and corporate financial performance is supportive for an investment manager who integrates ESG factors into investment decision making without breaching his/her fiduciary duty.

---

13 See Tobin (1969) for Tobin's Q ratio.

5.2 ESG and Investment Performance

Fiduciary duty permits ESG investing with the conditions that risk-return metrics of the investment portfolio improve and investment is not undertaken with the sole purpose of collateral benefits. Evidence of return improving characteristic of ESG investing for a given risk level is demonstrated in this part, as well as findings to the contrary.

Fish et al. (2019) used a methodology of weighted portfolio returns according to ESG scores of US and European companies from 2008 to 2018 where companies with higher ESG scores had higher weights in the portfolio. They used two optimization techniques: classical Mean Variance optimization and Hierarchical Risk Parity. Although there were slight differences in the portfolio performances depending on the optimization technique, only negligible differences existed between unadjusted and ESG-score weighted returns. The study concludes as investors do not need to sacrifice from portfolio performance when being considerate on ESG factors in investment management.

Bermejo Climent et al. (2021) demonstrates the impact of ESG disclosure on corporate equity performance in Europe using data on end-year balance-sheet information and monthly total returns for the 2005–2019 period for all European companies and Bloomberg's ESG data. The study shows evidence that ESG disclosure as a whole result in improved portfolio return. When broken into its components, environmental and governance related disclosures have positive impact on portfolio returns, with the latter having strongest impact. On the contrary, social disclosures result in negative impact on portfolio return and positive effect on portfolio volatility.

Cesarone et al. (2022) included an additional ESG constraint in mean-variance optimization model on top of classical risk and return targets analyzing empirical evidences between 2006 and 2020. They divided time horizon into two in order to take into account regime shifts in terms of ESG such as the one around 2015 when Paris agreement was signed. They found evidence that on the more recent period, higher ESG targets resulted in higher portfolio performance in the US markets. Even in the last year of the data when COVID-19 pandemic was in existence, positive effect of ESG criteria on performance was observed. In European markets however, including ESG as a factor in the model did not have effect on portfolio performance.

In their two-stage mean-variance optimization methodology, Prol and Kim (2022) create stock tranches according to ESG scores and obtain efficient portfolios with maximum excess return per unit of volatility (Sharpe ratios) for equities trading in NYSE for the years between 2018 and 2019. They find that more sustainable portfolios, particularly those in the top ESG deciles, perform worse than less sustainable ones and have lower Sharpe ratios. The study attaches this finding to the lower diversification possibilities in ESG return profiles and they note the limited time span of the study.

Zehir and Aybars (2020) analyze the performance of eight portfolios constructed with high ESG-score stocks in Europe and Turkey between 2004 and 2018. They check the effect of each E, S, and G factors on performance both separately and together as a whole by constructing top and bottom portfolios where related ESG scores of stocks within the portfolios are highest and lowest respectively. Although the study finds out that top ESG-score and top Governance-score portfolios underperform their relevant bottom portfolios according to certain metrics and under different models, the overall conclusion is that there is no significant impact of ESG investing on portfolio performance for the given period and region.

Aggliardi et al. (2023) examine financial performance of S&P 500 companies from 2003 to 2022 and seek evidence for its relation with environmental pillar of ESG. They form four clusters from A to D, A having the highest E (environmental) scores and classify each firm into one single cluster throughout the time span depending on the highest frequency in which a firm belongs to. Those firms of which E-score changes frequently from one year to another are bundled under a fifth cluster named T representing environmentally dynamic firms. Empirical evidence shows that firms with low environmental scores perform better financially while higher scored firms are less risky and more resilient. Assets with a dynamic environmental profile, those in cluster T, outperform on average in terms of return and risk.

In summary, conclusions from studies on ESG and investment performance are more mixed compared to the ones on ESG and corporate financial performance. E, S and G components of ESG have different effects on investment performance and overall risk metrics of the portfolios. Therefore, empirical evidences from studies mentioned in this sub-section are far from offering an end to the discussion on fiduciary duty and ESG investing particularly on the investment performance front.

6. Conclusion and Final Remarks

In this chapter, an important sub-division of sustainable finance, ESG Investing is discussed with a perspective of investment managers' fiduciary duty. As emphasized in detail, fiduciary duty is the responsibility of trustees to solely act in the best interest of trust beneficiaries while managing their assets. There are two separate ideals that investment managers try to achieve: investing with consideration of environmental, social, and governance related matters for the ultimate benefit of society, while increasing portfolio return for a given risk level as part of their fiduciary duty to beneficiaries.

In order to investigate whether these two ideals can be achieved simultaneously, we have provided a recent literature review regarding the relationship between ESG investing and performance with specific focus on both corporate financial and investment performance. Although there are studies that provide evidence both in favor of and in contradiction to ESG Investing's positive impact on performance, we can infer that general prejudice that ESG investments worsen return compared to non-ESG investments is not necessarily true.

As stakeholders', particularly consumers' and investors' preference shift towards more environment friendly products and services, socially considerate companies with fair and transparent business and governance practices; more companies change their way of doing business and implement sound ESG strategies. Whether those strategies are sincere efforts for the benefit of our planet and society or remain just as tactical moves to meet demand from clients would be a further study topic. In any event, the pool of investable companies with ESG scores, and with high ESG scores, is widening every year. Therefore, the recent evidence of positive or at least neutral relationship between ESG investing and performance may be explained by the increasing percentage of firms with ESG scores within corporate world. Accordingly, the life of an investment manager who is trying to fulfill his/her fiduciary duty and satisfy ESG expectations at the same time will be getting less complicated as number of potential investable firms in ESG front that can offer similar or better returns than non-ESG counterparties increase.

As evidence also shows, ESG investing is still not the guarantee for better performance. There are still plenty of studies concluding that some ESG factors when included in investment strategies in some markets and time periods have negative impact on performance. Thus, investment managers still have to prioritize their fiduciary duty over the sole purpose of ESG investing and they should refrain from sacrificing some portion of expected return when managing client portfolios with three ESG factors in mind.

As a last word, the involvement of ESG factors in investment decisions seems to gain additional weight in the near future as natural resources get scarcer, social problems such as work-force inequality and uneven income distribution increase and demand for transparency grows. Therefore, we believe that fiduciary duty and ESG investing debate will remain unresolved and studies in this topic will grow in number in the coming years.

References

Agliardi, E., Alexopoulos, T., & Karvelas, K. (2023). The environmental pillar of ESG and financial performance: A portfolio analysis. *Energy Economics, 120*, 106598.

Bermejo Climent, R., Garrigues, I. F. F., Paraskevopoulos, I., & Santos, A. (2021). ESG disclosure and portfolio performance. *Risks*, *9*(10), 172.

Bodie, Z., Kane, A., & Marcus, A. J. (2014). *Investments* (10th ed.). McGraw-Hill Education.

Cesarone, F., Martino, M. L., & Carleo, A. (2022). Does ESG impact really enhance portfolio profitability?. *Sustainability*, *14*(4), 2050.

CFA Institute. (2024). Code of ethics and standards of professional conduct. https://www.cfainstitute.org/-/media/documents/code/code-ethics-standards/code-of-ethics-standards-professional-conduct.pdf

De Scitovszky, T. (1943). A note on profit maximisation and its implications. *The Review of Economic Studies*, *11*(1), 57–60.

Fish, A. J. M., Kim, D. H., & Venkatraman, S. (2019). The ESG sacrifice. Available at SSRN 3488475.

Friede, G., Busch, T., & Bassen, A. (2015). ESG and financial performance: Aggregated evidence from more than 2000 empirical studies. *Journal of Sustainable Finance & Investment*, *5*(4), 210–233.

Friedman, M. (1970). A Friedman doctrine: The social responsibility of business is to increase its profits. *The New York Times Magazine*, *13*(1970), 32–33.

Huang, D. Z. (2021). Environmental, social and governance (ESG) activity and firm performance: A review and consolidation. *Accounting & Finance*, *61*(1), 335–360.

Jensen, M. C., & Meckling, W. H. (1976). Theory of the firm: Managerial behavior, agency costs and ownership structure. *Journal of Financial Economics, 3*(4), 305–360.

Kopltn, H. T. (1963). The profit maximization assumption. *Oxford Economic Papers*, *15*(2), 130–139.

Prol, J. L., & Kim, K. (2022). Risk-return performance of optimized ESG equity portfolios in the NYSE. *Finance Research Letters*, *50*, 103312.

Schanzenbach, M. M., & Sitkoff, R. H. (2020). Reconciling fiduciary duty and social conscience: The law and economics of ESG investing by a trustee. *Stan. L. Rev.*, *72*, 381.

The American Law Institute. (1959). *Restatement (second) of trusts: Prudent man rule.*

Tobin, J. (1969). A general equilibrium approach to monetary theory. *Journal of Money, Credit and Banking*, *1*(1), 15–29.

Valsan, R. D., & Yahya, M. A. (2013). Fiduciary duties and responsibilities of portfolio managers. *Portfolio Theory and Management, 165–182.*

Velte, P. (2017). Does ESG performance have an impact on financial performance? Evidence from Germany. *Journal of Global Responsibility*, 8(2).

Whelan, T., Atz, U., Van Holt, T., & Clark, C. (2021). ESG and financial performance: Uncovering the relationship by aggregating evidence from 1,000 plus studies published between 2015–2020. New York: *NYU STERN Center for sustainable business.*

https://www.stern.nyu.edu/sites/default/files/assets/documents/ESG%20Paper%20Aug%202021.pdf

Zehir, E., & Aybars, A. (2020). Is there any effect of ESG scores on portfolio performance? Evidence from Europe and Turkey. *Journal of Capital Markets Studies*, *4*(2), 129–143.

Çağrı AKSOY HAZIR

Sustainability Reporting Practice of Listed Companies in Turkey: Are They Hard or Soft Sustainability Disclosurers?

Abstract: Sustainability reporting is an essential vehicle for stakeholders to better understand the companies' long-term value drivers and their contribution to sustainable development. Although sustainability reporting gives companies the chance to present their commitment to sustainability, governments' choices in this area vary. Many countries have adopted mandatory sustainability reporting, while many other countries have taken a voluntary approach to sustainability disclosure. Turkey is one of those countries that does not have a legal requirement for sustainability disclosure and has adopted a voluntary approach to sustainability disclosure. Most of the listed companies in Turkey focus on sustainability disclosure in their annual reports, considering only the environmental aspects. Notwithstanding the availability of the reporting framework of Global Reporting Initiative (GRI), some companies use the GRI framework to enhance their accountability to stakeholders on sustainability issues. The lack of legal regulation in sustainability reporting causes inconsistencies in reporting practices. Ong et al. (2016) developed a GRI-based disclosure index with the goal of evaluating the sustainability reporting practices of listed companies in Turkey by incorporating the core principles of Clarkson et al. (2008)'s hard and soft disclosure items from the environmental disclosure index. With the help of content analysis, the level and quality of sustainability disclosure made by listed companies in Turkey will be evaluated in this chapter and its genuine impact on sustainability in Turkey will be revealed.

Keywords: Sustainability Reporting, Hard and Soft Disclosures, GRI, Turkey, Total Sustainability Disclosure Score

1. Introduction

During the past decades, sustainable development has been an increasing concern for governments, policymakers, and companies. The growing pressure to strengthen the paths towards sustainable development encouraged companies to include environmental and social concerns in their business operations, to increase their transparency, and to enhance their accountability to their stakeholders. Sustainability reporting is an effective instrument that offers stakeholders information about the companies' environmental and social impacts. Sustainability reporting provides stakeholders with insights into sustainability-related activities and is one of the most relevant channels for managers to be legitimated in the field of sustainability and to enrich companies' accountability about environmental and social impacts (Orazalin and Mahmood, 2020; Romero et al., 2019; Stolowy and Paugam, 2023). It is also one of the mechanisms to contribute to the achievement of the sustainable development goals of the UN (Tumwebaze et al., 2022).

Sustainability reporting is used by companies to improve corporate financial stability (Orazalin, 2019), ensure the improvement of corporate image (Imran Khan et al., 2019), meet the accountability expectations and obligations of the stakeholders (Greiling et al., 2015). de Villiers and Sharma (2020) define sustainability reporting as a platform for the provision of information on economic, environmental, and social performance to various stakeholders. It becomes a common reporting practice to secure legitimacy from the company's stakeholders. Unfortunately, sustainability reporting practices are translucent and do not enable the reader to attain a comprehensive picture of a company's environmental and social performance (Mamun, 2022). A variety of reporting frameworks, such as Global Reporting Initiative (GRI), International Integrated Reporting Council (IIRC) and Sustainability Accounting Standards Board (SASB – now absorbed by ISSB), or Corporate Sustainability Reporting Directive (CSRD in Europe) have emerged from international organizations to provide guidance for businesses to report their activities and impacts on environmental and social issues (Afolabi et al., 2023; Papa et al., 2022; Stolowy and Paugam, 2023). Some jurisdictions mandate sustainability reporting or disclosure, including the USA, New Zealand (de Villiers et al., 2022), the UK, and India, where mandatory sustainability reporting exists for certain sustainable activities (Bhatia and Tuli, 2018a). The EU has also introduced a requirement for European companies to disclose information on the environment, society and governance in their annual reports or to publish sustainability reports (de Villiers et al., 2022; Papa et al., 2022).

In most countries, the adoption of sustainability reporting practices is still voluntary. Despite the absence of enforceable legal frameworks, reporting practices in those countries have evolved from conventional financial reports and are now supported with environmental and social information. (Hahn and Kühnen, 2013). Turkey is an example of one of those countries. In Turkey, listed companies should declare the compliance with sustainability principles (SPK, n.d.)[1]. Jurisdictions in Turkey allow companies to choose among various sustainability reporting frameworks, and the existence of numerous concepts

---

1 https://spk.gov.tr/surdurulebilirlik

causes diversity in sustainability reporting practices and incompleteness of the reported information. Sustainability reporting practice in Turkey differs among companies, and the level of sustainability information across listed companies against the GRI indicators is unknown. The regulators have not changed the circumstances for the companies. From the previous literature, it is not clear what kind of sustainability information disclosed at what level.

A better understanding of how businesses affect environmental and social concerns has been made possible by the establishment of the GRI guidelines as a standard set in sustainability reporting (de Villiers et al., 2022). Numerous earlier studies have shown that GRI is widely used by businesses worldwide (Afolabi et al., 2023). It improves the transparency level and quality of sustainability reporting (Machado et al., 2021) and enables companies to disclose quantitative and qualitative sustainability information (Mamun, 2022).

In this context, this study aims to shed light on the sustainability reporting practice in Turkey using a sustainability disclosure index that was developed to measure economic, environmental, and social performance of sustainability by focusing on the core principles of hard and soft disclosure items of Clarkson et al. (2008) from the GRI-based environmental disclosure index. To achieve this aim, a research methodology based on a content analysis of the disclosures on sustainability in integrated reports or stand-alone sustainability reports was designed, and the sustainability reporting practices of listed companies in Turkey were compared and assessed with key indicators outlined in the GRI (2021) reporting standards. To examine the nature and extent of voluntary sustainability reporting in Turkey, this study analyzes sustainability reporting practices in the context of an emerging market. This study also contributes to the development of a new assessment tool for the practice of sustainability reporting by utilizing a GRI-based disclosure index that considers all aspects of sustainability. Moreover, it aims to compare the degree of sustainability reporting in Turkey and to better understand sustainability reporting practices. It is also the first study that examines both hard and soft disclosure levels in Turkish sustainability reporting.

The remaining research is set up as follows: the theoretical underpinnings of sustainability reporting together with the relevant literature are outlined in Section 2, which also evaluates the most pertinent research on actual sustainability reporting practices. The research methodology and findings regarding the degree of sustainability disclosure are presented in Sections 3 and 4, respectively. The main findings of the study will be reported in Section 5 along with a discussion of the consequences.

2. Sustainability Reporting and Literature Review

The issue of sustainability reporting as gained relevance among academicians, practitioners, and policymakers over the years. Sustainability reporting is a tool through which companies promote accountability and integrate financial and non-financial performance. It generates a favorable transparency climate, which is demanded and expected from all stakeholders, and is also a mean to increase efficiency, accountability, and effectiveness in the business environment (Bhatia and Tuli, 2018b). It is believed that transparency and accountability can add value to sustainable development, and sustainability reporting can be a resource (Stefanescu, 2022).

To explore the notion and relevance of sustainability reporting, many theoretical frameworks were developed. The main theories to inform the study of the sustainability reporting in non-financial disclosure are Legitimacy Theory (Suchman, 1995) and Stakeholder Theory (Freeman, 1984). On the other hand, other theories with a specific reference to agency, signaling, or social movement have been used to explain the materiality and importance of sustainability reporting (Di Leo et al., 2023). Stakeholder Theory asserts that companies need to manage positive relationships through sustainability reporting to satisfy stakeholders' information needs (Freeman, 1984). According to Schmelzer (2013) companies' reputation and performance, also sustainability activities can help companies in gaining the support of stakeholders and contributing back to society, which yields numerous benefits such as competitive advantage and lower risks. From the perspective of Stakeholder Theory, sustainability reporting might become a strategic tool to manage stakeholder engagement (Romero et al., 2019) and voluntary sustainability reporting is an effective tool that benefits a broad range of stakeholders in the economic, environmental, and social fields (Ismail Khan et al., 2023).

Another noticeable theory to explain sustainability reporting is Legitimacy Theory. According to Suchman (1995), a broad perception or assumption that the entity's actions are appropriate in a social system of standards, values, and beliefs can be created by gaining legitimacy. To legitimize companies' activities, sustainability reporting can be used as a tool to shape the public's view favorable and avoid adverse media reportage (Cowan and Deegan, 2011). According to Gray et al. (1995), companies can operate within a value system equivalent to society's value system. sustainability reports might be used to legitimize business activities and indicate that the reporting company is operating within the acceptable norms and values of society (Orazalin and Mahmood, 2020). In other words, from the Legitimacy Theory perspective, companies are required to satisfy social expectations beyond legal requirements, and they should concentrate on the disclosure of higher levels of sustainability information (Carroll, 1991).

In the context of those theories, sustainability information is voluntarily or mandatory disclosed. The lack of a general, internationally accepted definition of non-financial information causes a debate on the choice between mandatory and voluntary sustainability reporting. Economic, environmental, and social information under the term sustainable information is usually disclosed by companies voluntarily through integrated reports, stand-alone sustainability reports, and within annual reports (Romero et al., 2019). There is a considerable amount of research about the extent of sustainability reporting practices by companies in various sectors and in various countries. Sustainability disclosure, which is defined as the practice of measuring and disclosing the triple bottom line, enables companies to identify areas of strong and lagging economic, environmental, and social activities (Stacchezzini et al., 2016)

Earlier studies have revealed variations in the sustainability reporting practices of companies. Guthrie and Farneti (2008) explored the sustainability reports (based on GRI guidelines) of Australian companies and found that the disclosure rate of GRI indicators was only 32 %. Huang and Wang (2010) evaluated the trend in sustainability reporting practices among Chinese companies. Findings revealed that the Chinese companies focused on social issues with 96 %. Cowan and Deegan (2011) investigated the strategic legitimizing nature of voluntary emissions reporting by Australian companies and found that companies disclosed minimum information with inadequate care for environmental and social risks. Chen et al. (2015) carried out a structured content analysis of 75 global manufacturing companies' GRI-based sustainability reports and found that companies mainly preferred to disclose social issues, such as employment, human rights, corruption, and product responsibility. Zahid and Ghazali (2015) analyzed Malaysian companies' sustainability reporting practices, and the disclosure of social indicators by Malaysian companies was found to be higher than that of environmental and economic indicators. Dissanayake et al. (2016) explored the reporting practices of listed companies in Sri Lanka. The results revealed that most companies concentrated on social issues and mostly ignored environmental issues. Ehnert et al. (2016) found that Forbes top 250 companies disclosed the categories; labor and economics, more than the categories; human rights and product responsibility. Bhatia and Tuli (2018b) tried to explain the extent of sustainability reporting practices in the USA and UK. They compared the disclosure scores of USA and UK companies. The findings showed that disclosure scores of US companies are higher than those of UK companies for all categories: economic, environmental, and social. They also explained that the level of sustainability reports is quite low, both in the USA and the UK. In another study of Bhatia and Tuli (2018a), sustainability reporting practices of developing countries (Brazil, Russia, India, China and South Africa as BRICS) and developed countries (USA and UK) were compared. Their results revealed that companies in developing countries have higher disclosure scores as compared to companies in developed countries. In developing countries, the economic category is heading, and the laggard category is social. On the other hand, in developed countries, companies' disclosures on environmental and economic indicators are greater than those on social indicators. Jadhav et al. (2020) assessed the sustainability reporting practices of Australian logistic companies using content analysis, and the results indicated that energy and emissions, health and safety, employment, and diversity were the most reported ones. Mamun (2022) reported that disclosures in the economic and labor practices category were greater than those in product responsibility and human rights categories. Ismail Khan et al. (2023) examined the sustainability reporting practices in Pakistan using content analysis and found that companies in Pakistan reported economic performance indicators more than environmental and social performance indicators.

In this study, sustainability disclosures of listed firms in Borsa Istanbul will be evaluated using the revised sustainability disclosure index of Clarkson et al. (2008). They developed a content analysis index, which was based on GRI reporting guidelines and suitable for companies' environmental reports, that aimed to measure the extent of a company's environmental disclosure in their reports. The aim of Clarkson et al. (2008) was to develop an environmental scoring index, and they used 95 weighted items, which followed the reporting requirements of GRI reporting guidelines. They defined 79 items as "hard disclosure items" and 16 items as "soft disclosure items". Hard disclosure items cover information that focuses on goals and measures that cannot be replicated by companies with low environmental performance. On the other hand, soft disclosure items cover information that presents a general claim and is not easily verifiable (Papa et al., 2022). Clarkson et al. (2013) argued that this scoring index captures the multiple dimensions that reflect a company's current environmental strategy and commitment. To assess the extent to which US companies implement environmental disclosure, Clarkson et al. (2008) developed this index and reported that companies with good environmental performance are more. The scores of companies with strong environmental performance are below what the GRI reporting guidelines suggested should be expected. In the study of Clarkson et al. (2011), the environmental information voluntarily disclosed by Australian companies were related with their environmental performance. The results indicated that the environmental disclosure scores of Australian companies improved between 2002 and 2006. The highest disclosure score obtained exceeded slightly more than 50 % of the maximum available score. Clarkson et al. (2013) discussed whether environmental disclosure is progressively informative relative to environmental performance indicators. They showed that voluntary environmental disclosures provide valuation relevant information. They reported that the extent of hard disclosure items increased between 2003 and 2006.

Ong et al. (2016) revised the index of Clarkson et al. (2008) by integrating the social and economic dimensions of GRI G3.1 guidelines and used this index to assess the sustainability reporting practices of Australian companies. They distinguished between hard and soft disclosures made by the company on sustainability and came to the conclusion that Australian companies made more soft disclosures than hard disclosures. The index of Clarkson et al. (2008) was utilized by Luque-Vílchez et al. (2019) to assess the quality of environmental reporting, and they linked the results to the directors of the reporters' dedication to their own company and the environment. The results of the study demonstrated a favorable correlation between the level of environmental disclosure and the personal values of pro-environmental managers. Papa et al. (2022) compared the pre- and post-EU Directive environmental disclosures of 16 Italian companies and also used the index of Clarkson et al. (2008). They confirmed that soft disclosure items are more prevalent in sustainability reports than hard disclosure items for the period between 2016 and 2018. They found that soft disclosure items increased more than hard disclosure items. In this respect, the aim of this study is to assess the sustainability reporting practices of listed companies in Turkey using a new content analysis-based sustainability disclosure index.

3. Methodology and Sample Data

The sample size of the study consists of 100 companies taken from Turkey's respective index, namely BIST 100. Companies with the same year end period (31.12.2021) that voluntarily disclose stand-alone sustainability reports or integrated reports are included in this study. The final sample consists of 62 companies; 40 of those companies had stand-alone sustainability reports, and 22 of those companies had integrated reports. If a company has only an annual report and sustainability information is not available, it is classified as a silent company. 38 companies in the BIST 100 index are silent. The stand-alone sustainability reports and integrated reports are obtained from companies' websites.

To measure the level of sustainability reporting practice, content analysis is performed on the disclosed reports. As a data collection technique, content analysis is appropriate for codifying qualitative information and deriving quantitative information for further evaluation (Cohen et al., 2012). The qualitative information collected by applying the content analysis using a newly developed sustainability disclosure index, which was first developed as an environmental disclosure index by Clarkson et al. (2008) based on GRI reporting guidelines and is extended with the new published GRI (2021) Reporting Standards. The index of Clarkson et al. (2008) is suitable for this study, because it considers only voluntary reporting and facilitates analysis of both the level and the nature of the reporting (Clarkson et al., 2011). This index consists of seven categories: four categories of them represent hard disclosure items namely "governance structure and management system", "credibility", "environmental performance indicators" and "environmental spending" and remaining three categories represent soft disclosure items, namely "vision and strategy claims", "environmental profile" and "environmental initiatives". Ong et al. (2016) revised this index and integrated the economic and social dimensions of sustainability

Table 1: Categories of sustainability disclosure index

Category		Items	Max. Score
Hard Disclosure Items (A1–A4)			
A1	Governance Structure-Management System	12	12
A2	Credibility	4	4
A3	Economic Performance	17	102
	Environmental Performance	31	186
	Social Performance	37	222
A4	Sustainability Spending	2	2
Soft Disclosure Items			
A5	Vision and Strategy	7	7
A6	Sustainability Initiatives	3	3
A7	Disclosure on Management Approach-Economic	7	7
	Disclosure on Management Approach-Environmental	7	7
	Disclosure on Management Approach-Social	17	17
Total		144	569

using GRI G3.1 reporting guidelines. In this study, Ong et al. (2016)'s index, was revised using the new published GRI (2021) Reporting Standards. There are three main sections in the latest version of the GRI: Universal GRI Standards, Sector Specific Standards and Topic Specific Standards. The foundations standards (GRI 1), general disclosure standards (GRI 2), and management approach standards (GRI 3) of the Universal GRI Standards offer high-level reporting on company information. Topic Specific Standards offer recommendations for reporting on social, environmental, and economic sustainability (GRI 401–418), as well as the environment (GRI 201–207). All three performance indicators; economic, environmental, and social in the new GRI (2021) are included in this sustainability disclosure index. Category A1 and A2 have also been harmonized with the Universal GRI Standards. Table 1 summarizes the categories with their maximum scores.

Category A1 focuses on the governance structure and management systems with respect to sustainable development, and category A2 emphasizes the credibility of corporate disclosure on sustainability. The extent to which companies disclose specific economic, environmental, and social performance indicators is assessed in category A3. Category A4 concentrates on the company's disclosure of dollar savings (in this study, TL savings) from existing sustainability programs and their efforts (Clarkson et al., 2008). Soft disclosure items from A5 to A7, which are not easy to verify and which could be provided by all companies regardless of their sustainability performance, assess the disclosure of corporate vision and strategy, the corporate sustainability profile, and the disclosure of sustainability initiatives that can be implemented without necessarily committing to sustainable development (Clarkson et al., 2011). For the categories A1, A2, A4, A5, A6 and A7, the presence of the item is scored as 1, and the absence of the item is scored as 0. Category A3 carries the most weight of all categories, because it contains hard data that convinces stakeholders about sustainability performance (Clarkson et al., 2008). The scoring scale for A3 items is from 0 to 6. One point is granted, when

- indicator is reported.
- indicator is reported with respect to peers/competitors or industry.
- indicator is reported with respect to prior periods.
- indicator is reported with respect to targets.
- indicator measure is reported as absolute and standardized.
- indicator is reported at disaggregated level. (i.e. business unit, geographic segment)

4. Results

The average scores for total sustainability disclosure of selected companies from the BIST 100 index are depicted in Table 2.

Table 2: Sustainability disclosure scores of the sample

Scores	Mean Score of Total Sust. Disc. Score	Max. Score	Min. Score
Sust. Disc. Scores of sustainability reports	204	318	13
Sust. Disc. Scores of integrated reports	117	326	8
Sust. Disc. Scores of All Reports	145	326	17

The results show that, regardless of whether companies have published stand-alone sustainability reports or integrated reports, they contribute to the overall assessment of sustainability information to varying degrees. The average total sustainability disclosure score of the sample is 145, which is well below the maximum total sustainability disclosure score. The sustainability disclosure scores of selected companies vary from 17 to 326. The sustainability disclosure score of companies, that published stand-alone sustainability reports is better than that of companies, that published integrated reports. When comparing the total sustainability disclosure scores of reporting groups, Table 2 shows that the company, that published the integrated report, has the highest score of 326. However, the integrated reporting group also has the lowest disclosure score of 8.

The average scores of the hard and soft disclosure items for BIST 100 companies are presented in Table 3.

It is apparent that the average scores of hard disclosure items and soft disclosure items are below the maximum available scores. The average percentage score of hard disclosure items is 23 % and the mean percentage score of soft disclosure items is 59 %. It is evident that BIST 100 companies disclosed soft disclosure items more than hard disclosure items. The hard and soft disclosure item-based analysis shows that companies in Turkey preferred to disclose hard environmental disclosure items. Hence, as per the mean percentage score of hard disclosure items, economic performance indicators have the lowest scores, respectively. As seen from Table 3, it is interesting that, there were also companies, that did not disclose any of the hard or soft economic performance indicators. Additionally, the soft disclosure item-based scores demonstrate that businesses reported more soft disclosures in the environmental sustainability aspect compared to the economic and social sustainability aspects.

Table 3: Mean scores of hard and soft disclosure items

Scores	Mean Sample Score	Min. Sample Score	Max. Sample Score	Max. Index Score	Mean as % of Max. Index Score
Hard Disc. Items	121	10	290	528	23 %
Hard Eco. Disc. Items	*12*	*0*	*41*	*102*	*12 %*
Hard Env. Disc. Items	*56*	*3*	*144*	*186*	*30 %*
Hard Soc. Disc. Items	*38*	*2*	*96*	*222*	*17 %*
Soft Discl. Items	24	7	39	41	59 %
Soft Eco. Disc. Items	*4*	*0*	*7*	*7*	*50 %*
Soft Env. Disc. Items	*5*	*3*	*7*	*7*	*76 %*
Soft Soc. Disc. Items	*9*	*2*	*15*	*17*	*50 %*

To further assess the sustainability disclosure practice in Turkey, the sustainability disclosure scores of companies are analyzed category-wise. Table 4 indicates the mean disclosure scores and percentage disclosure scores of the analyzed companies.

Table 4: Category-wise sustainability disclosure scores

Scores	Mean Sample Score	Min. Sample Score	Max. Sample Score	Max. Index Score	Mean as % of Max. Index Score
A1	10	3	12	12	85 %
A2	3	1	4	4	79 %
A3	106	5	272	510	21 %
A4	1	0	2	2	41 %
A5	6	1	7	7	82 %
A6	1	0	3	3	37 %
A7	17	5	29	31	56 %

As presented in Table 4, the mean percentage of sustainability disclosure scores in category A1 is 85 %. The majority of the companies disclosed their governance structure, high governance body membership, stakeholder engagement policy, and sustainable development strategy. The credibility of the companies' disclosure in their stand-alone sustainability reports or integrated reports is also high. The mean percentage disclosure score for category A2 is 79 %. It is clear that companies provided the least data in category A3, which assesses the degree of performance in the economic, environmental, and social areas. The mean percentage score of A3 is 21 %. The mean percentage disclosure scores in sub-categories of A3 vary from 0 % to 40 %.

In the economic sub-category, indirect economic impacts and economic performance are the highest disclosed aspects, with an average disclosure score of 32 % and 20 %, respectively. Tax policy and anti-corruption are the least disclosed aspects of economic performance indicators. When comparing the mean percentage disclosure scores of environmental sub-categories, companies disclosed the most information on effluents and waste, energy, and emissions. The least disclosed aspects in the environmental sub-category are supplier assessment and biodiversity, with an average percentage disclosure score of 13 % and 15 %, respectively. In social sub-category, employment with 39 %, training with 36 %, occupation and gender diversity with 35 %, are the highest disclosed aspects. However, non-discrimination, rights of indigenous people, and security practices are the least disclosed aspects in stand-alone sustainability reports and integrated reports.

Category A4, which reflects sustainability spending, has a mean percentage score of 41 %. The mean percentage scores of the soft disclosure categories for A5, A6 and A7 are 82, 37 and 56 %, respectively. The consistent results persist across two categories, A1 and A5, which focus on disclosures related to a company's governance structure, management system, vision, and strategy.

5. Conclusion

This study aimed to examine sustainability reporting practice in Turkey by focusing on economic, environmental, and social sustainability. An extended GRI based sustainability disclosure index was developed to provide new insights into the measurement of sustainability practice. The economic, environmental, and social aspects of the recently released GRI (2021) Standards are included in the new index because GRI is the common reporting language in sustainability reporting practices. This study aimed to assess the companies' levels of hard and soft disclosure. The findings have shown that the level of sustainability disclosure is quite low in Turkey. This study has found that listed companies in Turkey prefer reporting soft disclosure items rather than hard disclosure items in their stand-alone sustainability reports or integrated reports. With regard to hard disclosure items, the companies are more focused on environmental performance indicators than economic and social indicators. Companies also reported the least information in the economic performance aspect. The mean of hard and soft economic disclosure items is low since the new sustainability disclosure index included only the economic indicators relevant to sustainability and the normal financial reporting indicators were not awarded any score. Overall, the findings have revealed that the categories; "governance structure and management systems" and "vision and strategy" have reached the highest mean percentage of disclosure scores. The sample companies hardly presented quantitative information in economic, environmental, and social aspects. The content analysis also indicated that indirect economic aspects, economic performance related to sustainability, effluents and waste, energy, emissions, employment, and training were the indicators most reported on, whereas tax policy, anti-corruption, supplier assessment, biodiversity, non-discrimination, and the rights of indigenous people were the indicators least reported on.

This study contributes to the ongoing discussion on the practice of sustainability reporting. The study examines the three dimensions of sustainability reporting practices and advanced the literature by integrating a newly developed GRI based sustainability disclosure index. It also makes a relevant contribution by focusing on sustainability reporting practice in the context of an emerging market. The prevalence of soft disclosure items over hard disclosure items should provide guidance to policymakers making rules governing the mandatory adoption of sustainability reporting. Managers should move beyond compliance with regulations, and awareness and commitment to sustainability performance should be improved by management. Since this study analyzes a data set with a limited number of companies, the results cannot be compared directly to prior studies. However, this study provides preliminary evidence on the sustainability reporting practice in Turkey. Furthermore, future studies can focus on larger sample sizes through investigating all listed companies in Turkey. Additionally, a longitudinal study can provide more evidence to examine the changes in sustainability reporting practice over time. Cross country studies can also be conducted for a comparative analysis.

References

Afolabi, H., Ram, R., & Rimmel, G. (2023). Influence and behaviour of the new standard setters in the sustainability reporting arena: Implications for the Global Reporting Initiative's current position. *Sustainability Accounting, Management and Policy Journal*. https://doi.org/10.1108/SAMPJ-01-2022-0052

Bhatia, A., & Tuli, S. (2018a). Sustainability reporting: An empirical evaluation of emerging and developed economies. *Journal of Global Responsibility*, *9*(2), 207–234. https://doi.org/10.1108/JGR-01-2018-0003

Bhatia, A., & Tuli, S. (2018b). Sustainability reporting practices in US and UK: An empirical comparison. *International Journal of Law and Management*, *60*(4), 1034–1056. https://doi.org/10.1108/IJLMA-04-2017-0102

Carroll, A.B. (1991). The pyramid of corporate social responsibility: Toward the moral management of organizational stakeholders. *Business Horizons*, *34* (4), 39–48.

Chen, L., Feldmann, A., & Tang, O. (2015). The relationship between disclosures of corporate social performance and financial performance: Evidences from GRI reports in manufacturing industry. *International Journal of Production Economics*, *170*, 445–456. https://doi.org/10.1016/j.ijpe.2015.04.004

Clarkson, P. M., Fang, X., Li, Y., & Richardson, G. (2013). The relevance of environmental disclosures: Are such disclosures incrementally informative? *Journal of Accounting and Public Policy*, *32*(5), 410–431. https://doi.org/10.1016/j.jaccpubpol.2013.06.008

Clarkson, P. M., Li, Y., Richardson, G. D., & Vasvari, F. P. (2008). Revisiting the relation between environmental performance and environmental disclosure: An empirical analysis. *Accounting, Organizations and Society*, *33*(4–5), 303–327. https://doi.org/10.1016/j.aos.2007.05.003

Clarkson, P. M., Overell, M. B., & Chapple, L. (2011). Environmental reporting and its relation to corporate environmental performance. *Abacus*, *47*(1), 27–60. https://doi.org/10.1111/j.1467-6281.2011.00330.x

Cohen, J. R., Holder-Webb, L. L., Nath, L., & Wood, D. (2012). Corporate reporting of nonfinancial leading indicators of economic performance and sustainability. *Accounting Horizons*, *26*(1), 65–90. https://doi.org/10.2308/acch-50073

Cowan, S., & Deegan, C. (2011). Corporate disclosure reactions to Australia's first national emission reporting scheme. *Accounting and Finance*, *51*(2), 409–436. https://doi.org/10.1111/j.1467-629X.2010.00361.x

de Villiers, C., La Torre, M., & Molinari, M. (2022). The Global Reporting Initiative's (GRI) past, present and future: Critical reflections and a research agenda on sustainability reporting (standard-setting). *Pacific Accounting Review*, *34*(5), 728–747. https://doi.org/10.1108/PAR-02-2022-0034

de Villiers, C., & Sharma, U. (2020). A critical reflection on the future of financial, intellectual capital, sustainability and integrated reporting. *Critical Perspectives on Accounting*, *70*, 101999. https://doi.org/10.1016/j.cpa.2017.05.003

Di Leo, A., Sfodera, F., Cucari, N., Mattia, G., & Dezi, L. (2023). Sustainability reporting practices: An explorative analysis of luxury fashion brands. *Management Decision*. https://doi.org/10.1108/MD-02-2022-0142

Dissanayake, D., Tilt, C., & Xydias-Lobo, M. (2016). Sustainability reporting by publicly listed companies in Sri Lanka. *Journal of Cleaner Production, 129*, 169–182. https://doi.org/10.1016/j.jclepro.2016.04.086

Ehnert, I., Parsa, S., Roper, I., Wagner, M., & Muller-Camen, M. (2016). Reporting on sustainability and HRM: A comparative study of sustainability reporting practices by the world's largest companies. *International Journal of Human Resource Management, 27*(1), 88–108. https://doi.org/10.1080/09585192.2015.1024157

Freeman, R. E. (1984). *Stakeholder theory of the modern corporation strategic management: A stakeholder approach*. Cambridge: Cambridge University Press.

Gray, R., Kouhy, R., & Lavers, S. (1995). Corporate social and environmental reporting A review of the literature and a longitudinal study of UK disclosure. *Accounting, Auditing & Accountability Journal, 8*(2), 47–77. https://doi.org/10.1108/09513579510146996

Greiling, D., Traxler, A. A., & Stötzer, S. (2015). Sustainability reporting in the Austrian, German and Swiss public sector. *International Journal of Public Sector Management, 28*(4–5), 404–428. https://doi.org/10.1108/IJPSM-04-2015-0064

GRI. (2021). Global Reporting Initiative reporting standards.

Guthrie, J., & Farneti, F. (2008). GRI sustainability reporting by australian public sector organizations. *Public Money and Management, 28*(6), 361–366. https://doi.org/10.1111/j.1467-9302.2008.00670.x

Hahn, R., & Kühnen, M. (2013). Determinants of sustainability reporting: A review of results, trends, theory, and opportunities in an expanding field of research. *Journal of Cleaner Production, 59*, 5–21. https://doi.org/10.1016/j.jclepro.2013.07.005

Huang, T., & Wang, A. (2010). Sustainability reports in China: Content analysis. *2010 International Conference on Future Information Technology and Management Engineering, FITME 2010, 2*(07), 154–158. https://doi.org/10.1109/FITME.2010.5654711

Jadhav, A., Rahman, S., & Ahsan, K. (2020). Sustainability practices disclosure of top logistics firms in Australia. *International Journal of Logistics Management, 33*(5), 244–277. https://doi.org/10.1108/IJLM-09-2021-0452

Khan, I., Fujimoto, Y., Uddin, M. J., & Afridi, M. A. (2023). Evaluating sustainability reporting on GRI standards in developing countries: A case of Pakistan. *International Journal of Law and Management*, *65*(3), 189–208. https://doi.org/10.1108/IJLMA-01-2022-0016

Khan, I., Khan, I., & Senturk, I. (2019). Board diversity and quality of CSR disclosure: Evidence from Pakistan. *Corporate Governance (Bingley)*, *19*(6), 1187–1203. https://doi.org/10.1108/CG-12-2018-0371

Luque-Vílchez, M., Mesa-Pérez, E., Husillos, J., & Larrinaga, C. (2019). The influence of pro-environmental managers' personal values on environmental disclosure: The mediating role of the environmental organizational structure. *Sustainability Accounting, Management and Policy Journal*, *10*(1), 41–61. https://doi.org/10.1108/SAMPJ-01-2018-0016

Machado, B. A. A., Dias, L. C. P., & Fonseca, A. (2021). Transparency of materiality analysis in GRI-based sustainability reports. *Corporate Social Responsibility and Environmental Management*, *28*(2), 570–580. https://doi.org/10.1002/csr.2066

Mamun, M. (2022). Sustainability reporting of major electricity retailers in line with GRI: Australia evidence. *Journal of Accounting and Organizational Change*. https://doi.org/10.1108/JAOC-01-2022-0005

Ong, T., Trireksani, T., & Djajadikerta, H. G. (2016). Hard and soft sustainability disclosures: Australia's resources industry. *Accounting Research Journal*, *29*(2), 198–217. https://doi.org/10.1108/ARJ-03-2015-0030

Orazalin, N. (2019). Corporate governance and corporate social responsibility (CSR) disclosure in an emerging economy: Evidence from commercial banks of Kazakhstan. *Corporate Governance (Bingley)*, *19*(3), 490–507. https://doi.org/10.1108/CG-09-2018-0290

Orazalin, N., & Mahmood, M. (2020). Determinants of GRI-based sustainability reporting: Evidence from an emerging economy. *Journal of Accounting in Emerging Economies*, *10*(1), 140–164. https://doi.org/10.1108/JAEE-12-2018-0137

Papa, M., Carrassi, M., Muserra, A. L., & Wieczorek-Kosmala, M. (2022). The impact of the EU nonfinancial information directive on environmental disclosure: Evidence from Italian environmentally sensitive industries. *Meditari Accountancy Research*, *30*(7), 87–120. https://doi.org/10.1108/MEDAR-03-2021-1247

Romero, S., Ruiz, S., & Fernandez-Feijoo, B. (2019). Sustainability reporting and stakeholder engagement in spain: Different instruments, different quality. *Business Strategy and the Environment*, *28*(1), 221–232. https://doi.org/10.1002/bse.2251

Schmelzer, P. (2013). Value relevance of corporate social responsibility reports. *Erasmus Universiteit Rotterdam*, Master's Thesis.

Stacchezzini, R., Melloni, G., & Lai, A. (2016). Sustainability management and reporting: The role of integrated reporting for communicating corporate sustainability management. *Journal of Cleaner Production*, *136*, 102–110. https://doi.org/10.1016/j.jclepro.2016.01.109

Stefanescu, C. A. (2022). Linking sustainability reporting frameworks and sustainable development goals. *Accounting Research Journal*, *35*(4), 508–525. https://doi.org/10.1108/ARJ-07-2020-0196

Stolowy, H., & Paugam, L. (2023). Sustainability reporting: Is convergence possible? *Accounting in Europe*, 1–27. https://doi.org/10.1080/17449480.2023.2189016

Suchman, M. C. (1995). Managing legitimacy: Strategic and institutional approaches author (s): Mark C. Suchman source : *The Academy of Management Review*, *20*(3) (Jul., 1995), 571–610. Published by : Academy of Management Stable URL: https://www.jstor.org. *The Academy of Management Review*, *20*(3), 571–610.

Tumwebaze, Z., Bananuka, J., Kaawaase, T. K., Bonareri, C. T., & Mutesasira, F. (2022). Audit committee effectiveness, internal audit function and sustainability reporting practices. *Asian Journal of Accounting Research*, *7*(2), 163–181. https://doi.org/10.1108/AJAR-03-2021-0036

Zahid, M., & Ghazali, Z. (2015). Corporate sustainability practices among Malaysian REITs and property listed companies. *World Journal of Science, Technology and Sustainable Development*, *12*(2), 100–118. https://doi.org/10.1108/wjstsd-02-2015-0008

Sezer KÜLAH

A Case Study on Sustainability Reporting Assurance

Abstract: An assurance service is a professional, impartial service that improves the quality of information for decision makers. Such services are useful since assurance providers must be independent and deliver information without bias. External auditing of sustainability reports is expected to be one of the most significant sustainability reporting improvements in the future. The issue over sustainability reporting appears to be expanding globally, with firms increasingly reporting on their overall performance and effect. In recent years, there has been a considerable growth in the need for fast, accurate, and relevant sustainability information. Investors, regulators, and evaluators are increasingly demanding assurance that sustainability disclosures are made using appropriate processes and controls, and that the information provided is accurate and reliable. The number of sustainability reports guaranteed by a third party is rising nowadays. Businesses must demonstrate the importance of sustainability reporting to their stakeholders, strengthen internal controls and reporting systems related to sustainability reporting, raise board-level awareness of the importance of sustainability information, and promote better decision-making based on higher quality sustainability information. Organizations utilize sustainability reporting and assurance of sustainability reports to provide accountability to their stakeholders. According to certain surveys, corporations in developed nations that operate in sectors that are paying much more attention on sustainability are more probably to release a sustainability assurance report. The purpose of this study is to provide information using a specific firm as a case study and to highlight how businesses approach sustainability performance in general, as well as how it is represented in sustainability reports. This case focuses on a prominent worldwide home appliance company, namely Arçelik, and its sustainability reporting assurance methods. It investigates Arçelik's sustainability reporting method, the installation of assurance measures, and the results of these efforts. The research also delves into Arçelik's issues in guaranteeing the legitimacy and openness of its sustainability reporting. This study gives insights into the significance and impact of sustainability reporting assurance in the home appliances market by evaluating the case of Arçelik.

Keywords: Sustainability Reporting, Assurance Services, Case Study

1. Introduction

An assurance service is a professional, impartial service that promotes the quality of information for the users of such statements in order to help them in their process of decision making. Decision makers seek assurance services to assist them enhance the dependability and relevance of the information that informs their decisions. Independent Auditors, Certified Public Accountants, and other professions may provide assurance services. Furthermore, the production of sustainability reports has expanded dramatically during the previous two decades. Although it is currently a voluntary practice in most countries, 96 % of the world's 250 largest global companies prepare sustainability reports (Threlfall et al., 2020). First of all, the process, which started on a voluntary basis, has become mandatory in many countries with the effect it has created over time. While there are studies on assurance services for many years, assurance services in sustainability reports are quite new, and it is expected to contribute to the literature with this study. The number of companies that publish some form of sustainability report around the world continues to increase. Little is known about whether assurance improves quality for these reports and whether the assurance services provided by accounting firms increase this quality more than the assurance services of non-accounting firms. (Chen et al., 2019).

In addition, sustainability reports are an important tool used to monitor and report an organization's sustainability performance. These reports gather, evaluate, and disseminate information and statistics on organizations' environmental, social, and governance performance. The accuracy and dependability of sustainability reports are crucial for both companies and those who use them. As a result, sustainability reports are frequently subjected to assurance audits. An assurance audit is a procedure used to confirm the correctness and dependability of a company's financial records. An audit of sustainability reports, on the other hand, varies from an audit of financial reports since sustainability reports are based on non-financial data. For assurance audits of sustainability reports, an independent audit firm is frequently utilized. The audit organization assesses the sustainability report's correctness, dependability, and breadth. The audit organization also assesses the report's conformity with international standards as well as the accuracy of the methodologies employed by the company to gauge its sustainability performance. As a consequence of the assurance audit, the audit company generates an assurance letter or report certifying the report's correctness and dependability. This report informs parties that use the sustainability report on the report's dependability. Therefore, the assurance audit of sustainability reports increases the report's ability to demonstrate the sustainability performance of the organization and provides a reliable source for the parties that will use the report.

With a global perspective, the debate over sustainability reporting is expanding, and firms are increasingly reporting on their overall performance and effect. Previously it was optional but such reporting and assurance are now increasingly obligatory by regulations. Investors and other decision makers require a broader knowledge base to support capital allocation and other choices and they want the information given to be trustworthy. Moreover, as reporting changes, so does the necessity for assurance promises for such as extended forms of reporting (IAASB, 2022). Recently, investors, regulators and other stakeholders have begun to look beyond traditional financial information from companies in their decision-making processes. In response, companies have begun to provide a range of non-financial information. Despite the significant growth in sustainability reporting practices and the growing interest of regulators in these reports, the quality of the information disclosed remains a major concern (Lobo et al., 2022). In addition, the demand for timely, accurate and relevant sustainability information has increased significantly in recent years. In order for sustainability reporting to meet the needs of stakeholders in the public interest, the infrastructure supporting sustainability reporting and assurance needs to be supported by high standards of ethical behavior and independence, along with a robust system of quality management, oversight and enforcement (IESBA, 2022). In addition, two new issues related with sustainability reporting about non-financial information are usually categorized as integrated reporting which is very popular in recent years and information disclosures on sustainability (Reimsbach et al., 2018).

Securing sustainability information has positively affected professional investors' assessments of a firm's sustainability performance, resulting in greater weighting of this information and leading to higher investment judgments (Reimsbach et al., 2018). Studies show that 53 % of 2021 sustainability reports include at least some degree of external assurance. However, as with sustainability reports, no globally approved structure or process for external verification of sustainability information exists. This is expected to change, given the growing interest among investors and other stakeholders in the dependability of sustainability data (Filosa et al., 2021).

Mark A. Weinberger, former Global President and CEO of Earnst and Young audit firm, one of the four major auditing firms, is concerned with assurance auditing in sustainability reports. Investors, regulators and evaluators stated that they want assurance that sustainability disclosures are made through appropriate processes and controls. Moreover, the information provided is accurate and reliable, and as a result, assurance standards will likely evolve towards more rigorous scrutiny of information and assertion that it is free from material misstatement. With many boards and executives putting sustainability on their agenda, external assurance of sustainability information will quickly become an essential component of a company's sustainability reporting journey (Filosa et al., 2021).

Influenced by the ongoing debate on corporate responsibility, an increasing number of companies are publishing what are known as sustainability reports. That is to say, voluntary assurance is expected to be increased in the near future. While the proportion of assurance reports is substantial, this type of assurance market needs too much time to develop (Ruhnke and Gabriel, 2013). Globally, companies are increasingly publishing non-financial sustainability reports. Some of these reports are provided independently and the assurance givers are sometimes members of the audit profession and sometimes they may be from different professions (Simnett et al., 2009).

The rest of the chapter is structured as follows. The assurance of sustainability reports is documented in Section 2. Section 3 introduces sustainability reporting in the household appliance industry and provides a framework for assurance. The case study of Arçelik is explained in Section 4 and the last section contains a discussion and concluding remarks.

2. Assurance on Sustainability Reports

Assurance should be provided by independent third parties and several standards must be satisfied in order to provide trustworthiness over such reports. Therefore, it ensures that the information reported is correct (Emerick, 2022). In other words, decision making process is of vital importance at this stage and such reports promotes the information quality on this process. Such services are valuable because assurance providers must be independent and present impartially with regard to the information reviewed. Individuals are responsible for making these business-related decisions and such decisions need assurance services that will pave the way for increasing the 'reliability and relevance of the information' they use in the decision making process. Assurance services are generally offered by Certified Public Accountants and Independent Auditors. For example, various non-governmental organizations, such as consumer associations, perform tests of products that consumers frequently use, and prepare reports on how these products comply with generally accepted standards and present them to information users. The relevant reports are very useful for consumers to make reasonable decisions in their purchasing processes. In addition, due to their independence from manufacturers, many consumers rely on the reports of relevant organizations. They have been providing assurance services for financial statements for many years (Arens et al., 2020). Similarly, notaries provide assurance services by participating in various promotional activities as observers. In addition, various certification procedures made by certified public accountants can also be evaluated within this scope. Certification

Table 1: AA1000 accountability standard

Standard	Definitions
Inclusivity	People should have a say in decisions that affect them.
Materiality	Decision makers must identify and be clear about the sustainability issues that are important.
Responsiveness	Organizations should act transparently on material sustainability issues and related impacts.
Effect	Organizations must monitor, measure and be responsible for how their actions affect their broader ecosystems.

Source: Accountability (2020)

services can generally be classified into the following categories. These can be listed as audit of financial statements, internal control audit, review, audit of information systems and other certification services (Arens et al., 2020).

When a company decides to make a report on sustainability reporting, board of directors should decide what kind of actions be evaluated in terms of economics, environmental and social issues and what metrics should be applied to acquire related data. Epstein (2008) addresses a number of implementation and measurement challenges with corporate sustainability reporting. The overarching challenge is the difficulty of "implementing the proper systems to pursue sustainability and to evaluate the impacts of sustainability on financial performance and the tradeoffs that must ultimately be made" (Yuthas and Epstein, 2012). These trade-offs include optimizing the business bottom line while balancing the expenses of corporate sustainability management. The corporate sustainability model of Epstein (2008) which is illustrated on Table 1 below provides an efficient framework for adopting sustainability reporting.

There are also ongoing issues related with the reliability of the assurance engagement in sustainability reports. One solution offered to help improve this low reliability has been the introduction of external verification, known as sustainability assurance. The decision to provide a report is seen as a section for reporting on sustainability disclosures and is therefore covered here. It is suggested that assurance may be motivated by a combination of strategic and/or holistic accountability reasons, as both perspectives would benefit from increased perceptions of reliability of reported information.

In the audit of financial statements and reporting, a regulated audit function is used to provide some assurance that the financial information provided by the entity offers a true and fair view of its operations and financial condition. Nearly two thirds of the multinational companies in the Global 250 list submitted an assurance statement in their 2020 sustainability reports, thus pointing to the increase in assurance audits in sustainability reports (Threlfall et al., 2020). Assurance services in sustainability reports can be provided by multinational audit firms, consulting companies and various non-governmental organizations. In the 1990s, there was no framework or more generally a standard that assurance providers could refer to, so there was no integrity in practice. After the 2000s, with the spread of sustainability reports, assurance auditing in sustainability reports started to gain importance and a need for determining a common standard came to the fore.

Generally, there are two types of assurance engagements. Firstly, assurance services regarding the financial statements based on the audit of the financial statements, and secondly, assurance services provided within the framework of consultancy services. Based on all these emerging needs, assurance standards have been established by the International Federation of Accountants (IFAC). ISAE 3000 International Assurance Standard is recognized as one of the most important of these. In addition, the "AA1000AS" standard, which was prepared by a UK-based consultancy firm called "Accountability" by taking the opinions of many stakeholders, can be given as an example (Accountability, 2020). ISAE3000, published by IFAC (2023), is more closely related to financial accounting and auditing practices. It would be useful to open a parenthesis to IFAC. In short, IFAC is an international organization that publishes generally accepted accounting and auditing standards all over the world. Returning to the relevant standard again, ISAE3000 was first published in 2003 and made available to stakeholders. It received its first update in 2013. Although the ISAE3000 standard is not directly related to sustainability reports, it is also referenced in assurance services in sustainability reports. The AA1000AS, on the other hand, is very different from the ISAE3000 standard in that it assesses its quality and adherence to key concepts such as inclusivity, materiality, responsiveness and impact (Laine et al., 2022).

Figure 1 above shows a way to provide information on how organizations address their sustainability performance and how it is presented in their sustainability reports. The components in the Figure 1 can be explained as follows; first component which is brand value is an element that increases company value by providing accurate and reliable information to all stakeholders. Second component which is risk management can be explained as integrates social and environmental issues with the company's risk management processes. Moreover, third component which is strategic alignment can be explained as establishment of the assurance between business strategies and sustainability activities of the enterprise by effectively communicating with the board of directors. Furthermore,

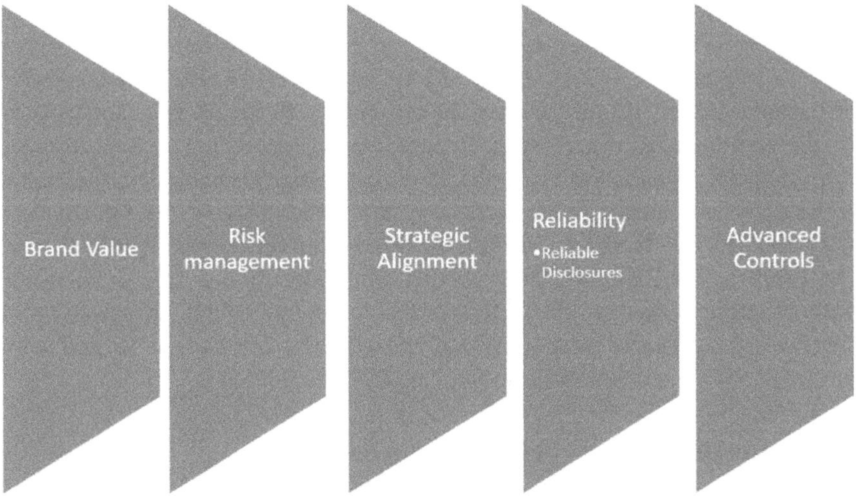

Figure 1: Importance of assurance audit in sustainability reports
Source: PWC Sustainability Report (2021)

fourth component which is reliability can be explained as they provide integrity and reliability by providing independent external assurance in related reports. Last but not least reliable disclosures can be explained as gaining the trust of the manager and the board of directors in terms of reliability and sustainability information within the scope of sustainability in the footnotes of the related reports, and they guide the enterprise in achieving its determined goals.

Some recent studies analyze the extent to which companies report their sustainability disclosures and obtain assurance, which assurance standards are used, and which companies provide assurance services in sustainability assurance. The Trends and Analysis Report for 2019–2021 is the third annual benchmarking study of global practices in sustainability disclosures and assurance. Comparison of global practices shows that although the reporting frequency of relevant analysis information is very high and the frequency of assurance is increasing, for the third year in a row, there continues to be a significant difference between reporting and assurance rates. 95 % of the companies surveyed report some level of sustainability information. 64 % of companies reporting sustainability information provide some level of assurance on this information. 57 % of these assurance activities were performed by audit or audited firms. There is also an increasing trend in ESG reporting in Turkey, with the rate of sustainability disclosures increasing from 72 % in 2019 to 88 % in 2021. Similarly, an increase was observed in assurance reports. Assured ESG information increased from 33 % in 2019 to 52 % in 2021 (IFAC and AICPA and CIMA, 2023). The majority of the assurance reports are limited, the assurance only relates to certain aspects of the sustainability report, such as emissions (Fermin, 2022). Assurance of non-financial information disclosed by an organization enables organizations to establish confidence in the accuracy and authenticity of the information they disclose. The nature and extent of assurance received may vary, and who the company's stakeholders are; whether the company has special financing authorizations related to ESG; whether the company is public or private; it is determined by factors such as which industry the company is in and how advanced the company is in ESG reporting (KPMG, 2021).

3. Assurance Framework and Approach

Before looking at the sustainability reports of Arçelik, consider the bigger picture of sustainability reporting in the home appliances industry. As it is checked, the sustainability report of Arçelik is as similar as its competitors at global level such as Electrolux, Haier, Whirlpool or Samsung. Businesses have always been focused with their bottom lines, or monetary earnings. More and more businesses are beginning to consider sustainability. The Triple Bottom Line Theory extends the standard framework by including two more performance areas: a company's social and environmental consequences. These three bottom lines are known as the three P's: people, planet, and profit (Jindrichovská, Kubíčková and Mocanu, 2020). Providing assurance on these reports is an important contributor to this process (Hodge et al., 2009). As a result, sustainability reporting and securing sustainability reports are used by organizations to provide accountability to their stakeholders (Junior et al., 2014). Companies operating in countries with a more developed legal system and cultural development, particularly in sectors concerned with sustainability, are more likely to issue a statement of assurance. In addition, a study answers the issue of which institutional component is responsible for the adoption of voluntary assurance using a two-stage logit model. It has been demonstrated, in particular, that the normative element has the greatest explanatory power in the assurance demand, followed by coercive pressure (Martínez-Ferrero and García-Sánchez, 2017).

With a greater focus on sustainability and increasing demands for corporate accountability, many companies now report to their stakeholders not only their financial results, but also their sustainability performance on social, environmental and governance issues (Marx and van Dyk, 2011). Publishing non-financial information is a trend that has been seen in listed companies in recent years. Based on this fact, the need arises to ensure the reliability of the published information by verifying it by an independent professional (Miralles Quirós et al., 2021).

Assurance services are requested by organizations for a number of reasons. Some of the internal and external benefits of assurance are obvious, and they frequently strive to increase trust and confidence in governance, management, and stakeholder interactions. Among the assurance benefits stated in many publications are ideas such as enhanced recognition, trust, and reliability. An assured report instills higher trust in the disclosures of an organization's stakeholders. Among other things, it demonstrates the seriousness with which the reporter approaches sustainability reporting. When making investment and rating choices; investors, rating agencies, and other experts are increasingly searching for guarantees such as decreased risk and enhanced value. Reporters and report consumers continue to be concerned about data quality. It is not commonplace for major corporations to rearrange their sustainability reporting in this environment. According to a 2011 survey conducted by KPMG, one of the four leading audit firms, one-third of the top 250 worldwide organizations rearranged non-financial information.

A variety of regulations, indices, and surveys acknowledge the significance of assurance in decreasing data quality concerns. Disclosures that are perceived to be solid and dependable are more likely to be relied on, boosting the value of reporting. Sustainability concerns are being brought up to the board of directors due to the growing interest in sustainability disclosures and their relevance in enhancing business strategy, performance, and reputation.

In terms of stronger internal reporting and management systems, disclosures and data deemed reliable and credible are more likely to be employed in internal decision-making processes. Internal reporting systems and controls that are robust play a key role in controlling the performance and implications of sustainability. External assurance can assist on the assessment and soundness of internal systems and processes for increasing stakeholder communication and offer changes. A reporter's examination of stakeholder engagement methods may be included in assurance processes. Some organizations base their continuing engagement with stakeholders on their reporting methods and/or sustainability reporting. Both of these can aid in the promotion of mutual understanding and communication (Global Reporting Initiative – GRI, 2013).

4. Assurance Process at Arçelik

The longitudinal case study of Sustainability Reporting of Arçelik was subjected to content analysis. A study by Guthrie and Abeyseker (2006) addressed content analysis as a strategy for data collection that develops a procedure for making accurate inferences from text that entails categorizing qualitative and quantitative data into previously defined categories in order to draw patterns. Moreover, according to Steenkamp and Northcott (2007) mechanistic approach, the higher the amount of data, the greater the relevance of a certain issue. Content analysis records items using a unit of analysis, which relates to words, phrases, paragraphs, and sections of pages on the topic. The second method is a mechanistic approach that gives an in depth study. It attempts to comprehend the substance and concept of what is being studied by examining the narrative's

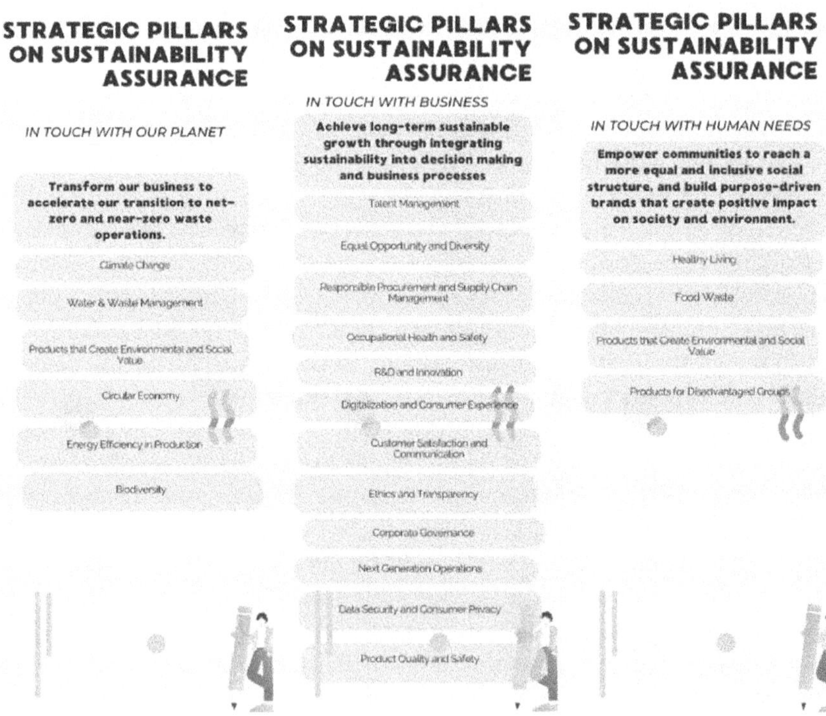

Figure 2: Strategic pillars on sustainability assurance
Source: The sustainability report of Arçelik (2021)

quality, richness, or qualitative content (Unerman, 2000). At this study, mainly sustainability reports are referenced. Since it is not an obligatory requirement to publish sustainability reports, it would be very difficult to make comparative study so that the issue has evaluated as a case study.

Arçelik has 12 brands which are listed as Arçelik, Beko, Grundig, Blomberg, ElektraBregenz, Arctic, Leisure, Flavel, Defy, Altus, Dawlance, and Voltas Beko, and subsidiaries in 51 countries, and 28 production sites in nine countries. In 2021, Arçelik, Turkey's largest white goods maker and Europe's second-largest white goods business by market share, had a combined sale of more than EUR 6.5 billion. Arçelik is Turkey's research and development leader, with 69.5 % of its revenue originating from international markets. To date, the business has filed over 3,000 worldwide patent applications, owing to the efforts of over 2,000 researchers working in 16 research and development and Design Centers in Turkey and 13 research and development offices in nine countries. The company is the only Turkish business in the top 200 list of Companies with the Most International Patent Applications in the Last Ten Years, according to World Intellectual Property Organization statistics (Arçelik Sustainability Report of 2021). For illustration purposes, Arçelik's sustainability goals are grouped into three categories in Figure 2, relating to the planet, people and business.

The absence of a specific legislation on assurance services and the qualifications required of assurance service providers for sustainability reporting have led to the emergence of different types of assurance services. While assurance services are generally performed by accounting firms, they may also be offered by other companies (Manetti and Toccafondi, 2012). Worldwide, these services are offered by Deloitte, EY, KPMG and PWC, which are broadly defined as the big four (Sìmnett et al., 2009). In addition, there are opinions that social workers and environmental experts provide better assurance services (Cohen and Simnett, 2015; Rao, 2012). Assurance services provided by the four major audit firms are considered more reliable around the world (Perego, 2009). Perego and Kolk (2012) evaluated the assurance services of different stakeholders such as accounting firms, consulting firms, certification bodies and academic institutions and determined that audit firms were more preferred. Assurance types are divided into two as assurance services regarding financial statements based on auditing of financial statements and secondly assurance services provided within the framework of consultancy services. The fourteenth Sustainability Report of Arçelik details the company's sustainability strategy, goals, and progress in the environmental, social, and governance issues shortly ESG areas, as well as financial performance highlights. The business strategy of Arçelik is based on long-term growth and wealth building. Such a sustainability report demonstrates how Arçelik integrates sustainability into its core business and fulfills its short-, medium-, and long-term goals, as well as how the company generates value for its stakeholders through the use of In Touch Technology (Arçelik Sustainability Report of 2021).

During the period of study, the social and environmental indicators contained in the report relate to more than 75 % of revenues and business operations. Koç Holding has signed Stakeholder Capitalism Metrics shortly SCM, and Arçelik, as a Koç Group entity, incorporates Stakeholder Capitalism Metrics into its reporting to investors and other stakeholders. The business model of Arçelik was developed in compliance with The International Integrated Reporting Framework shortly IIRC. Reporting Matters, a member of the World Business Council for Sustainable Development (WBCSD), examined and graded Arçelik's 2020 Sustainability Report for the first time. The year of 2021 report has been enhanced as a result of the feedback received. Arçelik joined the United Nations Global Compact in 2021 and became an Early Adopter, publishing Communication on Progress Towards the Ten Principles of the UN Global Compact using a new digital reporting method. Arçelik's sustainability report was developed in accordance with the Global Reporting Initiative requirements which can be explained as comprehensive option and the Sustainability Accounting Standards Board (SASB). Arçelik's performance in connection to international frameworks such as the United Nations Global Compact (UNGC), the UN Sustainable Development Goals (SDGs), and the Women's Empowerment Principles (WEPs) is also included in their reports. Arçelik is a Taskforce on Climate Related Financial Disclosures signatory, and the study contains a comprehensive risk and opportunity analysis on climate-related financial disclosures (Arçelik Sustainability Report, 2020).

Arçelik aims to reinvent itself and its sector and turn into a reliable source of lifestyle solutions for the digital home. Their goal is summarized as a flexible innovator who puts the customer at the center of every choice while preserving the competitiveness. With this goal it is expected to become one of the world's finest places to work while also generating sustainable value through a successful business. Arçelik has fought for more than a half-century to be a sector leader as a notable corporation with a sustainable, enjoyable, and lucrative work environment. The company has promoted gender equality and diversity in the workplace to create a more neutral and inclusive atmosphere, as well as establishing a future oriented culture, talent, and organizational management. It is thought that the depletion of natural resources and the battle against climate change should be everyone's priority, from the public to the business sector, in the quest of a sustainable environment. They have invested in regenerative business models to support the transition to an emission free economy, and we seek to incorporate a circular economy model into the company strategy and operations. Additionally, the company enhances water management to save freshwater for future generations since water stress is one of the critical challenges for the sustainability on environmental issues. The business model in which the company operating is continually evolving, posing both possibilities and problems due to the significant impact of global trends. Moreover, the company places a high priority on adding value to the supply chain management since the COVID-19 epidemic causes huge deteriorations in the process. They design the operations keeping in mind the vulnerable supply chain, shifting customer preferences, and a digitalized environment. In order to adapt to these shifting consumer behaviors, the quality and safety of the products have been improved. Consumer behavior has changed, with a greater emphasis being placed on personal wellbeing. As a result, the company takes action to support people's wellbeing and ensure healthy lifestyles. Furthermore, the company has given digital transformation and innovation first priority in order to fulfill the expectations of the digitally transformed world. While creating significant, long-term value for the entire community, they continue to emphasize integrating purposeful innovation into products, finding innovative approaches to reduce environmental impacts, and leading customers, workers and communities, which are significant steps towards sustainability goals (Arçelik Sustainability Report of 2021).

5. Conclusion

Sustainability reporting is an effort to provide transparent and comprehensive information about a company's economic, social and environmental impacts. These reports are an important source of information for investors, suppliers, customers, the public and other stakeholders. Moreover, they are used to measure the performance of companies on sustainability. The accuracy and reliability of sustainability reports is extremely important for the reputation of companies and the trust of stakeholders. For this reason, sustainability reports are often subject to an independent audit. An assurance audit of sustainability reports is an audit conducted by an independent audit firm that aims to verify that the content of the report is presented in an accurate, comprehensive and appropriate manner. This audit evaluates compliance with reporting standards, accuracy, comprehensiveness and timely presentation of data. Assurance auditing of sustainability reports increases the accuracy and reliability of the report and gives the company's stakeholders more confidence in the reporting.

This audit plays an important role in evaluating the sustainability performance of companies and shows the companies' commitment to sustainability and their performance.

Research on the assurance of sustainability reports is just emerging and more work is needed to explore and examine the practice of assurance (Alsahali and Malagueño, 2022). Another conclusion reached in academic studies is that, first, assurance practitioners need to radically change their practices and professional requirements to increase their reliability and usefulness (Boiral and Heras-Saizarbitoria, 2020). Finally, the complex and multifaceted skills required to run sustainability assurance soundly and the absence of recognized and important training programs in this field are major barriers to the professionalization of assurance providers (Boiral et al., 2019). However, since there is no compelling international regulation regarding sustainability reporting and assurance regarding sustainability reports, managers voluntarily decide whether to employ independent third parties to provide assurance on their companies' sustainability reports. In addition, for companies where sustainability reports are secured by an independent third party, the choice of the assurance provider can (Braam and Peeters, 2018) vary considerably in scope, ranging from assurance over the entire report to assurance over a specific portion of the report, and the level of assurance, ranging from reasonable assurance to limited assurance.

There have been researches that suggest that obtaining sustainability reports boosts their credibility in the eyes of investors, reducing information asymmetries assessed by buying and selling discrepancies. There are studies that quantify the assurance of sustainability reports based on content analysis of assurance statements, in which assurance providers define the assurance process's architecture. The results of a matched sample of over 600 European enterprises with and without assurance reporting sustainability reports suggest that high-quality assurance process design minimizes the extent of information asymmetry. A high degree of assurance in an assurance process eliminates information asymmetry, but a moderate level of assurance in an assurance process is insufficient. The assurance provider's examination of numerical data details minimizes information asymmetry even more. Some studies have found that analytical testing of aggregated indicators, the definition of the assurance provider's competencies, and the definition of sustainability assurance-specific work steps all contribute to reducing information asymmetries in countries without sustainability reporting regulations (Fuhrmann et al., 2017). It can be supported that the opinion that the assurance services envisaged in the studies on sustainability reports will strengthen access to finance can be expressed. As in other areas where assurance services are provided, the biggest obstacle in sustainability reports is the cost issue. Considering the long-term benefits of the related reports to society and economies, it is thought that the impact of this problem will be limited.

This case study looks at the sustainability reporting assurance procedures of Arçelik, a well-known global household appliance manufacturer. It examines Arçelik's approach to sustainability reporting, the implementation of assurance measures and the results of these initiatives. The study also looks at the difficulties in sustainability reporting. All in all, the study analyzes Arçelik as a case study to provide insights into the value and impact of sustainability reporting in the household appliance sector.

References

Accountability. (2020). Guidance on applying the AA1000AS, https://www.accountability.org/

Alsahali, K.F., & Malagueño, R. (2022). An empirical study of sustainability reporting assurance: Current trends and new insights. *Journal of Accounting & Organizational Change*, 18 (5), 617–642. https://doi.org/10.1108/JAOC-05-2020-0060

Arçelik Sustainability report of 2020. https://www.arcelikglobal.com/media/6347/sustainability_report_2020.pdf

Arçelik Sustainability report of 2021. https://www.arcelikglobal.com/media/6938/arcelik21_sustainability_report.pdf

Arens, A.A., Elder, R.J., & Beasley, M.S. (2020). Auditing and assurance services.

Boiral, O., & Heras-Saizarbitoria, I. (2020). Sustainability reporting assurance: Creating stakeholder accountability through hyperreality? *Journal of Cleaner Production*, 243, 118596. https://doi.org/10.1016/j.jclepro.2019.118596

Boiral, O., Heras-Saizarbitoria, I., & Brotherton, M.-C. (2019). Professionalizing the assurance of sustainability reports: The auditors' perspective. *Accounting, Auditing & Accountability Journal*, 33 (2), 309–334. https://doi.org/10.1108/AAAJ-03-2019-3918

Braam, G., & Peeters, R. (2018). Corporate sustainability performance and assurance on sustainability reports: Diffusion of accounting practices in the realm of sustainability development. *Corporate social Responsiveness and Environmental Management*, 25 (2), 164–181. https://doi.org/10.1002/csr.1447

Chen, P.-C., Ballou, B., Grenier, J.H., & Heitger, D.L. (2019). Sustainability assurance's link to reporting quality. *Journal of Accountancy*, online. https://www.journalofaccountancy.com/news/2019/oct/sustainability-assurance-link-to-reporting-quality-201919354.html

Cohen, J.R., & Simnett, R. (2015). CSR and assurance services: A research agenda. *Auditing*, 34 (1), 59–74. https://doi.org/10.2308/ajpt-50876

Emerick, D. (2022). What is sustainability report assurance? *ESG | The Report*. https://www.esgthereport.com/what-is-esg/the-g-in-esg/what-is-sustainability-report assurance/#:~:text=Sustainability%20Report%20Assurance%20might%20seem, what%20they%20say%20is%20true.

Epstein, M. (2008). Implementing corporate sustainability: Measuring and managing social and environmental ımpacts. *Strategic Finance*. January.

Fermin, M.B. (2022). Why ESG sustainability report assurance matters to your business. *SGS News*. https://www.sgs.com/en-id/news/2022/03/why-esg-sustainability-report-assurance-matters-to-your-business

Filosa, M., Alqaseer, F., & McGovern, M. (2021). The state of US sustainability reporting. *Harvard Law School Forum on Corporate Governance*. https://corpgov.law.harvard.edu/2021/11/02/the-state-of-us-sustainability-reporting

Fuhrmann, S., Ott, C., Looks, E., & Guenther, T.W. (2017). The Contents of assurance statements for sustainability reports and information asymmetry. *Accounting and Business Research*, 47 (4), 369–400. https://doi.org/10.1080/00014788.2016.1263550

Global Reporting Initiative – GRI. (2013). The external assurance of sustainability reporting.

Guthrie, J., & Abeysekera, I. (2006). Content analysis of social, environmental reporting: What is new?. *Journal of Human Resource Costing & Accounting*, 10 (2), 114–126.

Hodge, K., Subramaniam, N., & Stewart, J. (2009). Assurance of sustainability reports: Impact on report users' confidence and perceptions of information credibility. *Australian Accounting Review*, 19 (3), 178–194. https://doi.org/10.1111/j.1835-2561.2009.00056.x

IAASB. (2022). Sustainability assurance. Focus area. https://www.iaasb.org/focus-areas/sustainability-assurance

IESBA. (2022). Sustainability reporting and assurance: A focus on ethics and independence. Focus area. https://www.ethicsboard.org/focus-areas/sustainability-reporting-and-assurance

IFAC. (2023). The state of play in sustainability assurance. IFAC Content Series (Contributing to the Global Economy). https://www.ifac.org/knowledge-gateway/contributing-global-economy/discussion/state-play-sustainability-assurance

IFAC, & AICPA & CIMA. (2023). The state of play: Sustainability disclosure & assurance (2019–2021 trends & analysis).

Jindřichovská, I., Kubíčková, D., & Mocanu, M. (2020). Case study analysis of sustainability reporting of an agri-food giant. *Sustainability*, 12 (11), 4491. https://doi.org/10.3390/su12114491

Junior, R.M., Best, P.J., & Cotter, J. (2014). Sustainability reporting and assurance: A history analysis on a world-wide phenomenon. *Journal of Business Ethics*, 120 (1), 1–11. https://doi.org/10.1007/s10551-013-1637-y

KPMG. (2021). Assurance over ESG disclosures. Building corporate trust through in-depth reporting. *Insights*. https://kpmg.com/xx/en/blogs/home/posts/2021/12/esg-assurance-can-underpin-a-sustainable-future.html

Laine, M., Tregidga, H., & Unerman, J. (2022). Sustainability accounting and accountability. https://doi.org/10.4324/9781003185611

Lobo, G., Homroy, S., & Zengin-Karaibrahimoğlu, Y. (2022). What do we know about sustainability reporting assurance quality? *The British Accounting Review papers*.

Manetti, G., & Toccafondi, S. (2012). The role of stakeholders in sustainability reporting assurance. *Journal of Business Ethics*, 107 (3), 363–377. https://doi.org/10.1007/s10551-011-1044-1

Martínez-Ferrero, J., & García-Sánchez, I.-M. (2017). Coercive, normative and mimetic isomorphism as determinants of the voluntary assurance of sustainability reports. *International Business Review*, 26 (1), 102–118. https://doi.org/10.1016/j.ibusrev.2016.05.009

Marx, B., & van Dyk, V. (2011). Sustainability reporting and assurance. *Meditari Accountancy Research*, 19 (1/2), 39–55. https://doi.org/10.1108/10222521111178628

Miralles Quiros, M.M., Miralles Quirós, J.L., & Daza Izquierdo, J. (2021). The assurance of sustainability reports and their impact on stock market prices. *Cuadernos de Gestión*, 21 (1), 47–60. https://doi.org/10.5295/cdg.201262mm

Perego, P. (2009). Causes and consequences of choosing different assurance providers: An international study of sustainability reporting. *International Journal of Management*. 26 (3), 412–425.

Perego, P., & Kolk, A. (2012). Multinationals' accountability on sustainability: The evolution of third-party assurance of sustainability reports. *J Bus Ethics*, 110, 173–190. https://doi.org/10.1007/s10551-012-1420-5

PwC Sustainability Report (2021). https://www.pwc.com/gr/en/PwCGR-SustainabilityReport-2020-2021.pdf

Rao, S.S. (2012). Corporate sustainability reporting: Investigation of assurance process, assurance characteristics and assurance frameworks used. 213.

Reimsbach, D., Hahn, R., & Gürtürk, A. (2018). Integrated reporting and assurance of sustainability information: An experimental study on professional investors' information processing. *European Accounting Review*, 27 (3), 559–581. https://doi.org/10.1080/09638180.2016.1273787

Ruhnke, K., & Gabriel, A. (2013). Determinants of voluntary assurance on sustainability reports: An empirical analysis. *Journal of Business Economics*, 83 (9), 1063–1091. https://doi.org/10.1007/s11573-013-0686-0

Sìmnett, R., Vanstraelen, A., & Chua, W.F. (2009). Assurance on sustainability reports: An international comparison. *Accounting Review*, 84 (3), 937–967. https://doi.org/10.2308/accr.2009.84.3.937

Steenkamp, N., & Northcott, D. (2007). Content analysis in accounting research: The practical challenges. *Australian Accounting Review*, 17 (43), 12–25. https://doi.org/10.1111/j.1835-2561.2007.tb00332.x.

Threlfall, R., King, A., Shulman, J., & Bartels, W. (2020). The KPMG survey of sustainability reporting 2020. December, 0–62.

Unerman, J. (2000). Methodological issues – Reflections on quantification in corporate social reporting content analysis. *Accounting, Auditing & Accountability Journal*, 13(5), 667–681. https://doi.org/10.1108/09513570010353756

Yuthas K.J., & Epstein, M.J. (2012). Analyzing sustainability impacts. Strategic finance, January 2012. Business Faculty Publications and Presentations, Poland State University.